Teachers College • Columbia University
Comparative Education Studies
General Editor • George Z. F. Bereday

JOHN DEWEY'S IMPRESSIONS OF SOVIET
RUSSIA AND THE REVOLUTIONARY WORLD
MEXICO—CHINA—TURKEY

Introduction and Notes by WILLIAM W. BRICKMAN

JULLIEN'S PLAN FOR COMPARATIVE
EDUCATION 1816–1817

By STEWART FRASER

SOCIETY AND EDUCATION IN JAPAN

By HERBERT PASSIN

CULTURE AND THE STATE
MATTHEW ARNOLD AND CONTINENTAL
EDUCATION

Introduction and Notes by PAUL NASH

FINANCING SOVIET SCHOOLS

By HAROLD J. NOAH

CHARLES E. MERRIAM'S
THE MAKING OF CITIZENS

Introduction and Notes by GEORGE Z. F. BEREDAY

ABRAHAM FLEXNER'S UNIVERSITIES
AMERICAN, ENGLISH, GERMAN

Introduction by ROBERT ULICH

EDUCATION AND DEVELOPMENT IN WESTERN
EUROPE, THE UNITED STATES, AND
THE U.S.S.R.: A COMPARATIVE STUDY

By RAYMOND POIGNANT

EDUCATION AND DEVELOPMENT IN WESTERN EUROPE, THE UNITED STATES AND THE U.S.S.R.

EDUCATION AND DEVELOPMENT

in Western Europe, the United States, and the U.S.S.R.

A COMPARATIVE STUDY

RAYMOND POIGNANT

Teachers College Press

TEACHERS COLLEGE · COLUMBIA UNIVERSITY

Originally published in 1965 by the Institut Pédagogique National under the title L'Enseignement dans les Pays du Marché Commun: Etude comparative sur l'organisation et l'état de développement de l'enseignement dans les pays du Marché Commun, aux Etats-Unis, en Grande-Bretagne et en U.R.S.S. (*Brochure No. 25 in the series* Mémoires et Documents Scolaires).

Foreword

In the old days the study of Comparative Education consisted of descriptive presentations of the school systems of various countries. To get away from this *Auslandspädagogik,* comparative educators, inspired by Michael Sadler, attempted to concentrate instead on analyses of educational problems in cross-cultural perspective. I. L. Kandel's *Comparative Education* was the first to rotate countries in order to illustrate themes such as administration or teacher training. Today Harold Noah and Max Eckstein, in their new book *Toward a Science of Comparative Education,* concern themselves with the application of cross-national data to the testing of specific hypotheses relating education to aspects of society, such as economic growth and religious ideology. Between these two books lies the story of the movement of Comparative Education away from simply presenting information on schools in individual countries.

It is a distinct merit of Raymond Poignant's volume, which appeared in French in 1965 and is now being offered in an English edition, that it attempts to use the descriptive school materials from several countries in an analytical and simultaneously comparative treatment, thus integrating the old tradition and the new. Poignant's approach is that of a student of development; his concern is to assess the output of educational institutions and the correspondence or lack of it with the needs of modernization. His primary concern is with Western Europe, but for comparative purposes materials from the United States and the U.S.S.R. have been continuously interwoven. It is a pity that materials from Japan were not available to the author at the time of writing. For information on that most important country the reader is referred to Herbert Passin's *Society and Education in Japan,* published earlier in this series.

Poignant's work is being offered at this somewhat late date to the English reading audience because the book is rapidly acquiring the stature of a classic. It is salutary to remember amidst the vastly expanding reaches of Comparative Education that the school, its pedagogical content, its administrative arrangements, and its statistics are at the center of our concerns and should not be lost from view. Such materials can be greatly highlighted and placed in focus if they are arranged simultaneously in a comparative manner.

G.Z.F.B.

Preface

In February 1960, the problems involved in education and in scientific and applied research were the subject of discussion at a meeting of the Action Committee for the United States of Europe.[1] The members of the committee considered these to be of vital importance for the future of Europe and were anxious to determine whether the training facilities available to young people and the human and material resources devoted to scientific research were in line with the demands of our time. They requested their chairman, Jean Monnet, to examine the feasibility of drawing up as complete a report as possible on the subject. The European Community Institute for University Studies[2] agreed to undertake

[1] This committee, under the chairmanship of Jean Monnet, comprises most of the political parties and trade unions of the six member countries of the European Community.

[2] The European Community Institute for University Studies was established in 1958 for the purpose of encouraging—especially at university level—studies of economic, social, and political problems involved in the gradual integration of those countries which make up the European Community. The Institute's Board of Directors consisted of Louis Armand, Dino Del Bo, Pietro Campilli, André Donner, Paride Formentini, Walter Hallstein, Étienne Hirsch, Max Kohnstamm, and Jean Monnet.

this task and set up a Study Committee. Gaston Berger was profoundly interested in both educational and European problems, and agreed to organize this committee and to act as its chairman. For educational problems, the Rapporteur was Raymond Poignant.

The tragic death of Gaston Berger in the autumn of 1960 was a great loss to the committee which he inspired and which owed much to his guidance in its early activities. The present report is dedicated to his memory in recognition of the contribution he made. The committee suffered another loss with the death of Dean Aymard who, after the death of Gaston Berger, agreed to become joint chairman of the committee with Gerhard Hess.

The work proved much more difficult and time-consuming than was originally anticipated. The collection of comparative data on the educational systems and the analysis and comparison of this data raised almost insurmountable problems. It was entirely due to the skill of the Rapporteur and his capacity for hard work that the study which is now offered to the public in English was completed at all. This report, therefore, essentially owes much to Raymond Poignant.

Mention must also be made of the experts from various European countries who assisted the Rapporteur in assembling the material essential for the report. Thanks are due to the following: F. Edding and Chr. Führ of the Federal Republic of Germany; V. Geens and J. van Mele of Belgium; L. F. Embling, C. A. Moser, and Simon Pratt of Great Britain; G. Gozzer and Umberto Paniccia of Italy; and F. A. Goudart and R. Z. Swaab of The Netherlands.

Thanks are also due to André Molitor, E. Pelosi, Giovanni Polvani, and Ivo Samkalden who were members of the committee but who, called to other official duties, were unable to continue until the study was completed.

The committee unanimously recognized the vital importance of education for the future of the countries concerned and the necessity of providing all young people with access to educational levels which were previously reserved only to an elite. The fact that, very often, educational reforms begin to bear fruit ten or more years after they have been instituted makes the study and adoption of reforms even more urgent at the present time.

As pointed out in the Introduction, the committee discussed the report as a whole, but were not asked to subscribe to every word of the Rapporteur's conclusions. While some members felt that they would support the reservations expressed in the report itself in regard to the comparability of educational systems and diplomas and the possibility of drawing conclusions from such comparisons, all concurred in the broad lines of the Rapporteur's argument.

The committee and the Rapporteur had not been empowered to draw up an action program and for this reason the report is limited to providing the reader with as accurate a picture as possible of the comparative situation of education in the nine countries included in the study. They feel it necessary, however, to make an exception on one specific point: Aware of the enormous effort which the preparation of this report required and the improvements which could readily be introduced in the light of the knowledge acquired, and also aware of the advantage of continually following the evolution of such a vital problem, they feel compelled to urge the institutions of the European Economic Community and, more especially, the Commission of that Community, to ensure that the work be continued and kept up to date, at any rate in regard to the synthesis of statistics and existing studies.

The statistical bureau of the European Community, in conjunction with the statistical bureaus of member countries, would certainly be able to prepare and publish comparative reports periodically on the situation of education in the countries of the Community and in the other major industrialized countries. It would be a source of great satisfaction to the members of the committee to know that the work will be continued in this form in the future.

It is, in any case, the hope of the committee that the present report and the conclusions which the Rapporteur has drawn will make it possible for European school and university problems to be viewed in a broader context and will lead to an extension and an acceleration of action already undertaken by the respective countries.

THE EUROPEAN STUDY COMMITTEE FOR THE
DEVELOPMENT OF EDUCATION AND RESEARCH

Brussels, November 16, 1965

MEMBERS OF THE EUROPEAN STUDY COMMITTEE FOR THE DEVELOPMENT OF EDUCATION AND RESEARCH

Professor ALPHONSE AREND, Educational Adviser to the Ministry of Education of the Grand Duchy of Luxembourg

Professor FELICE BATTAGLIA, Rector of the University of Bologna

Professor VINCENZO CAGLIOTI, Chairman of the National Research Council of Italy

Dr. H. VON HEPPE, "Senatssyndikus" of the City of Hamburg

Professor Dr. GERHARD HESS, Rector of the University of Konstanz and former President of the "Deutsche Forschungsgemeinschaft"

Mr. ÉTIENNE HIRSCH, former Chairman of Euratom

Professor Dr. PH. J. IDENBURG, Director-General of the Netherlands Central Statistics Bureau

Mr. MAX KOHNSTAMM, President of the European Community Institute for University Studies

Professor E. L. MASSART, Rector of the Antwerp University Centre

Mr. P. PIGANIOL, Scientific Adviser to the Board of the Saint-Gobain Company; former Delegate-General for Scientific and Technical Research (France)

Mr. JACQUES SPAEY, Secretary-General of the Belgian National Scientific Policy Council

Professor Dr. H. WENKE, Professor of Education at the University of Hamburg

Contents

List of Tables

EDUCATION AND DEVELOPMENT IN WESTERN EUROPE, THE UNITED STATES AND THE U.S.S.R.

Introduction

A comparative history of the development of the educational systems in those countries which are now economically the most advanced reveals a long process, closely linked to economic and social development. To a large extent, just as Walter Rostow was able to analyze stages in economic growth which, subject to certain variations, recur in the history of all the industrialized countries, so it is possible to distinguish roughly identical historical phases in the establishment of school and university systems.

In Western Europe, for example, at the beginning of the nineteenth century only 40 to 50 per cent of children attended primary classes, although most children from the "upper" social levels received secondary—and, to some extent, higher—education. They, and they alone, provided a country's political, administrative, and economic leadership. Even though extensive in certain social strata, however, secondary and higher education still affected only a minute fraction of the total number in the corresponding age groups.

During the nineteenth century, primary education gradually spread in the "lower" levels and, at various dates, depending on political circumstances, was made compulsory.

During the same period, and in spite of the impetus from the Industrial Revolution, the development of secondary and higher education was relatively slow because of the social factor involved in schooling at those levels.

After World War I, and more so after World War II,

TABLE 1   RECENT GROWTH IN FULL-TIME SCHOOLING, 14 TO 17 YEARS OF AGE

| | | Percentage of Age Group Enrolled | | | | |
	Age	1950	1952 or 1953	1959	1960 or 1961	Growth
Federal Republic of Germany	15	—	34.5	—	43.9[e]	+ 27
	17	—	12.6	—	16.4[e]	+ 30
Belgium	14	—	63.7	—	81.0[e]	+ 27
	17	—	25.9	—	39.0[e]	+ 51
France	14	50.0	—	—	68.2	+ 36
	17	14.0	—	—	30.4	+117
Italy	14	—	31.0	—	63.4[d]	+101
	17	—	8.9	—	23.5[d]	+160
Netherlands	14	70.4	—	—	83.0	+ 18
	17	21.4	—	—	34.0	+ 58
England and Wales[a]	15	29.8	—	—	42.2	+ 41
	17	6.6	—	—	12.0	+ 82
United States	14 to 17	83.3	—	—	89.2	+ 7
U.S.S.R.[b]	15 to 19	22.8	—	34.8	—	+ 52

[a] Not including full-time "further education" pupils in 1962; if these pupils are included, enrollment figures will be 45 and 14.8 per cent, respectively.

[b] Nicholas DeWitt, *Education and Professional Employment in the U.S.S.R.* (Washington: Government Printing Office, 1961), p. 139.

[e] 1963.

[d] 1962–1963.

TABLE 2 CHANGES IN PERCENTAGE OF ENROLLMENT, BY EDU-
CATIONAL LEVEL—FRANCE

	1800	1900	1945	1960
Primary	30.0 to 40.0	100.0	100.0	100.0
Secondary	1.5	3.0	12.0	40.0
Higher	0.6	1.2	4.0	7.0

all countries in Western Europe, under the influence of a
complex series of factors which will be analyzed in due
course, committed themselves to a broad and rapid expansion
of secondary and higher education. Table 1 illustrates this
trend.

France offers a typical illustration of the changes, and
Table 2 highlights the importance of the time factor in the
historical development of Western educational systems.

At the present time, many of the developing countries are
far from having reached the level of educational development attained by European countries at the end of the eight-
eenth century, and the gap between the degree of development in school systems is no less striking than the well-known
gap in the extent of economic development. A comparison
between the position of the youthful Republic of Chad[1] and
the United States as shown in Table 3 provides an example
of the extent of these disparities.

A whole range of intermediate situations exists between
these two extremes, but the trend is obvious: a regular
growth in enrollment at all levels of the educational system.
In so far as all national economies are moving more or less
inevitably toward industrialization and the development of the
tertiary sector—and the converse is scarcely conceivable—it
would seem that, despite present disparities, all school systems (at any rate, in their modern forms), like all economic
systems, tend in the long run toward a sort of imaginary
"point of maturity" where maximum education will be pro-

[1] This extreme situation is, of course, in no way peculiar to
Chad.

vided for a maximum number of children, perhaps the only limitation being the individual's lack of ability to succeed in secondary or higher education.

No country has yet reached, or is anywhere near reaching, this point of maturity and, accordingly, all countries, whether developed or developing, are affected by the problems of growth. On the other hand, the difficulties to be solved in the various countries are obviously very different, depending on the stage reached.

As far as the developing countries are concerned, and disregarding the need to ensure training of the minimum number of cadres essential to spark economic expansion, the great human, social, and political problem at the present time is the rapid elimination of illiteracy, a problem which, as we have stated above, was only gradually solved in Western Europe throughout the nineteenth century and even, in certain

TABLE 3   DISPARITIES IN ECONOMIC DEVELOPMENT AND IN EX-
TENSION OF SCHOOL ENROLLMENT

	Republic of Chad	United States
ECONOMIC DEVELOPMENT		
	1960	1962
Working population by major economic areas:		
Primary (agriculture, forestry, fisheries)	88.3	7.6
Secondary (industry, mines, building)	6.7	35.2
Tertiary (services, including transport and communications)	5.0	57.1
Gross domestic product per capita (1959)	$56.00	$2,700.00
EXTENSION OF SCHOOL ENROLLMENT		
	1959	1961
Primary	12.8	100.0
Secondary	0.25	90.0
Higher	0.001	20.0

Mediterranean countries, in the first half of the twentieth century.

Addressing the second commission of the United Nations General Assembly, the Director-General of Unesco, René Maheu, recently indicated the extent of illiteracy in the world: Two-fifths of the adult population, i.e., approximately 700 million people, are unable to read or write. Illiteracy among children is no less serious since, in 1963, in 85 African, Asian, and Latin American "developing" countries, only 110 million out of 210 million children attended primary school, and of this 55 per cent of school-going children, many may well relapse into illiteracy. As a result, far from being reduced, the population of illiterate adults increases each year by between 20 and 25 million. Considering the extent of this world problem, Maheu proposed an international campaign to achieve a substantial reduction in illiteracy through coordinated effort, to be made by the countries themselves with outside aid.

The figures highlight one of the main difficulties now confronting these 85 countries: How can illiteracy be reduced more rapidly today than the now industrialized countries were able to do in the past?

It is not the purpose here to deal with this agonizing problem and its possible solutions but, rather, to consider how some of the more developed countries handled the advanced stages in the growth of their educational systems.

What are the cause-and-effect relations between the phases of economic growth and the growth of school systems? Is education a "consumer item" which increases with the rise in living standards or is it an "investment" which precedes economic growth? Both hypotheses are to some extent correct, and the truth is that they mutually affect one another.

Nowadays it is scarcely contended[2] that economic progress, an imperative for both developed and developing coun-

[2] Even though it has not yet been possible to make a serious attempt to measure the effect of the "human investment" in economic growth.

tries, is governed as much by qualitative human factors (inventive genius, technical skill, educational level of the population as a whole, and so on) as by material or quantitative factors (capital, extent of manpower, and so on) which were once regarded by the economists as the only essential factors.

Thanks to the establishment of the European Coal and Steel Community, the European Common Market, and Euratom (European Atomic Energy Community), a vast internal market is gradually taking shape in the Western European countries. It comprised 180 million inhabitants in 1965 and alters the order of magnitude of the possibilities open to each of the member countries for economic expansion and higher living standards. Given the basic importance of the human factors indicated above, however, this European economic construction can produce its full effect only if education is considered as a parallel and fundamental element in the European countries concerned.

The six countries of Western Europe undoubtedly have an exceptionally long and fruitful tradition in culture and education; undeniably, they have the most ancient universities, and their secondary schools, deriving from the colleges of the Renaissance, have long served as examples to the whole world and, in many respects, continue to do so. Conversely, precisely because of these magnificent traditions, they may perhaps have rather more difficulty than other and younger countries in adapting their educational systems to the human, democratic, and economic demands of our age.

At a time when the United States is planning once again to double enrollment in its colleges and universities during the decade which will come to an end in 1970; when the U.S.S.R. has just quintupled the numbers completing their secondary or higher education between 1950 and 1962; and when the United Kingdom, in its 1944 Education Act, stipulates ten years of compulsory education—this question has become a major concern of the leaders, past and present, of the European Communities who are now members of the

Board of Directors of the European Community Institute for University Studies. It has led to a comparative study on the organization and development of educational systems in the six Common Market countries and the three other countries which are particularly interesting in the present comparison because of the presumably advanced state of their educational systems, namely the United States, the United Kingdom, and the U.S.S.R.

It goes without saying that this comparative study might well have been extended to other countries which have also reached similarly high levels of development, including the Scandinavian countries, Canada, Japan, and certain countries in Eastern Europe. Obvious considerations of time and resources limited the scope to the nine countries mentioned above.

This study attempts to assemble and present as clearly as possible a body of descriptive information or statistics, which are mostly in the public domain already, in a relatively short document that can be easily and rapidly consulted.

The objective comparison of this data should reveal the guidelines of the various national educational policies, allow comparisons of all kinds which the general public and those responsible for educational policies should have clearly in mind, and make it possible to answer questions concerning the Common Market countries which we have previously raised.

The main purpose is to inform a wider public about a problem whose importance has already been underlined but whose constituent elements are still appreciated by only a small group of specialists. Although relating comparative data on various educational systems, this is not a study in "comparative education" in the sense understood by some experts in that discipline: Any comparisons regarding the spirit of education, educational methods, and, fundamentally, educational content have been deliberately excluded.

In view of the purpose outlined above, the first question is to what extent is it genuinely possible to compare the organization of education and the state of its development in various countries and, more especially, to express these in numerical terms.

THE VALUE, DIFFICULTIES, AND LIMITATIONS OF A COMPARATIVE STUDY

COMPARISON OF THE STRUCTURES OF EDUCATIONAL SYSTEMS AND CURRICULA

The organization of the various national school systems—and this applies particularly to the older countries of Europe—is the product of a long historical process. It reflects both the social and economic structures within these countries and the cultural and educational concepts which are more or less traditionally accepted, and even the particular concept of democracy which prevails in each.

From this point of view, it is difficult to appreciate the specific quality of national school and university organization from the outside and make value judgments.

Subject to this reservation, which must be continually borne in mind, it is nonetheless obvious that the development of industrial civilization in the nine countries to which the present study is limited has gradually made the economic and social structures more and more alike, as shown in Table 4.

Ways of life have accordingly drawn closer together in these countries and, to a large extent, there has also been a tendency toward uniformity—irrespective of frontiers—in both the attitudes of families toward their children's schooling and the authorities' concepts of educational organization.

Secondary and higher education, restricted until recently to a small group—socially as much as intellectually—will tend, either slowly or more rapidly according to the country concerned, to become available to the broad masses and, in this connection, all the national statistics are revealing.

In these circumstances, and without entering into endless debate on the best ways of reforming education, it is of in-

TABLE 4 WORKING POPULATION, IN PERCENTAGE, BY MAIN AREAS OF ACTIVITY

	Year	Primary Area	Secondary Area	Tertiary Area
Federal Republic of Germany	1955[a]	18.6	46.7	34.7
	1962[d]	13.3	48.2	38.5
Belgium	1955[a]	8.9	45.5	45.6
	1961[b]	7.5	47.7	44.8
France	1954[a]	26.7	36.8	36.5
	1962[b]	20.6	38.6	40.8
Italy	1955[a]	36.6	34.4	29.0
	1962[d]	27.9	40.6	31.5
Luxembourg	1960	16.4	42.2	41.4
Netherlands	1955[a]	11.9	39.8	48.4
	1960[d]	10.8	42.3	46.9
United Kingdom	1956	4.5	50.5	45.0
	1960[d]	4.4	48.6	47.0
United States	1950[c]	12.0	36.0	52.0
	1962[e]	7.6	35.2	57.1
U.S.S.R.	1955[c]	43.0	31.0	26.0
	1959[e]	38.8	34.9	28.3

[a] Statistics of the European Communities.

[b] 1962 census for France; 1961 census for Belgium.

[c] Cahier No. 31 of the *Institut National d'Etudes Démographiques* (Paris).

[d] National yearbooks.

[e] International Labour Office Yearbook.

terest to see how educational organization in the various countries is adapting to inevitable change.

An educational system is not characterized only by the nature of the various branches available to students, but also by the actual programs in these branches (timetables and curricula), and the teaching methods employed.

As already pointed out, there can be no question, in the present study, of attempting detailed investigations in these areas. At most, in certain specific fields—scientific education, for example—an effort may be made to emphasize certain features of the school systems studied and their repercussions on the education of pupils and students.

Some Measures of Development of School Systems, and Difficulties in Using Them

Various criteria could be used simultaneously to analyze the state of development of national school systems within their existing national structures. Some are purely quantitative and reveal, for example, the size of the school-age population receiving a given type of education (enrollment by age and type of education); others are qualitative (ratio of students to teachers); still others reflect simultaneously both quantitative and qualitative factors in extending schooling (educational expenditure). Most criteria do not provide absolutely sure bases for comparing educational development in the various countries; many are affected by factors extraneous to education, and this invalidates comparison.

Again, the statistical data on which comparisons rest are not always reliable. In some countries, they do not even exist. From the outset, therefore, it is essential to emphasize the need for extreme circumspection in using the various criteria for comparison and to realize that, on many points, the available statistics are not always adequately comparable.

1. *Educational expenditure*   The extent of educational expenditure in a given country would of itself seem to be an excellent yardstick for measuring the effort made to ensure the intellectual development and vocational training of the population. In actual fact, it is far from ideal. It should indicate the size of the school-going population and the quality[3] of the education, all things being equal, but does not really do so.

Expenditure is governed not only by the enrollment num-

[3] A more satisfactory student/teacher ratio greatly increases the expenditure.

bers and the student/teacher ratio but by factors which have no direct or clear relationship to the development of education in the school-age population, including (1) the considerable and divergent variations in birth rate over the last twenty years in the countries concerned (see Table 14); these bring concomitant changes—upward or downward—in the school-age population, and these changes, all things being equal,[4] justify relative variations in total educational expenditure from country to country; (2) the average pay of teachers in relation to per capita income varies markedly, directly affecting total expenditure.

Discounting the fact that it is so largely relative, the measure of educational expenditure is also not very useful because of the statistical uncertainty which may exist in many countries regarding its real amount. This matter has never been adequately investigated. State budgetary expenditure is generally more or less established[5] but expenditure by others is less clear in the case of entities such as local communities, private schools, vocational training provided by industry, and individual families. These uncertainties are less in certain countries: in the United States, statistics on private education are good; in the Soviet Union, education is fully nationalized; and in Belgium and The Netherlands, most expenditure on private education is borne by the state. On the other hand, in Germany, France, and Italy, expenditure on private education and by local communities can only be roughly estimated.

It must also be noted that the provision of vocational and technical training by private enterprises[6] for their staffs varies considerably from one country to another, and this may affect public expenditure on vocational and technical schools.

[4] The working population and the national product are not immediately affected.

[5] Provided such expenditure is defined in the same way in all the countries.

[6] In most of the countries, expenditure on training or refresher courses for their staffs by public and private enterprises is simply excluded from the statistics on educational expenditure.

However, the extent to which this yardstick may be used is relative; the only really admissible criterion is educational expenditure as a percentage of the gross national product (GNP), since (1) comparisons involving expenditure, when converted into foreign currency, are distorted by uncertainties regarding the true validity of the rates of exchange; and (2) comparisons involving the percentage of state expenditure from its general budget are pointless because of variations from country to country in the way in which expenditure is borne by the state, the provinces, and the local authorities, respectively.

2. *Enrollment rates*[7]   In appraising a country's effort to educate its youth, the rates of enrollment by age would seem, at first glance, to offer a valid measure. In reality, the use of this measure in international comparisons involves major difficulties. It is possible, for example, to compare the total enrollment rates at fifteen years of age in most European countries, beyond the age for compulsory schooling; but, within this figure, account must be taken of the distribution of pupils between the various types of education.

This is further complicated by part-time education.

In the Federal Republic of Germany, for example, the full-time enrollment rate at fifteen years of age in 1961 was 37 per cent, a relatively low figure in comparison to other European countries, but if the figures for part-time vocational schools *(Berufsschulen)*[8] are included, the rate rises to 97 per cent.

The fact that in certain countries vocational training combines school training and training on the job makes it difficult to carry out comparisons based only on full-time enrollment rates. Conversely, it is virtually pointless to compare rates

---

[7] Ratio between the number of pupils attending school and the corresponding age groups.

[8] Schools providing an additional eight and twelve hours of general education per week for close to 1.8 million (1963) boys and girls from fourteen to eighteen years of age, young workers or employees in industry, commerce, or agriculture.

which cover such different establishments as *lycées* and *Berufsschulen*. Hence, it becomes necessary to analyze the enrollment rates by type of education and, preferably, to make comparisons of the different partial rates.

3. *Percentage of graduates per age group*   A comparison of annual numbers successfully completing their studies at different levels with numbers for the corresponding age groups gives the percentages of those reaching a given level of general or specialized education. This is an excellent yardstick for measuring educational development over a period of time in a given country, and the way in which intelligence is more or less fully developed or "exploited" at school or university level.

It also has the advantage of partly eliminating the question of the comparability of full-time, part-time, and correspondence course education. Regardless of the form of education, the result only is appraised, i.e., the intellectual level reached, based on success in a common examination.

Utilization of this criterion in international comparisons presupposes that the level of examinations in the different countries can be compared and equivalences established.

This difficulty has already been officially solved for certain diplomas, since most countries have been impelled to define equivalences because of the enrollment of foreign students in their schools. These equivalences are basically established at two levels.

SECONDARY SCHOOL LEAVING CERTIFICATES

Examination of the standards applied in the various countries indicates that equivalence is granted to all general secondary school leaving certificates in the seven Western European countries covered by our study[9] and that the same

[9] The European Convention of December 11, 1953, in principle establishes equivalence for secondary school leaving certificates granted in the member countries of the Council of Europe for access to their public universities.

equivalence is recognized in most of these countries for the "qualification certificate" awarded on completion of the eleventh class in Soviet secondary schools.

This therefore constitutes official recognition of a similarity between secondary studies in European countries whose traditions and educational levels are very close to each other. In actual fact, in spite of this legal assimilation, it is certain that the selective nature of the secondary educational process, and hence the real "level" of final secondary examinations, differs to a fairly significant extent from one country to another. No real weighting is possible, and many divergent interpretations could be made.

As for the United States, as a general rule a high school certificate is not accepted as equivalent to the secondary school leaving certificate; only a statement attesting that the candidate is qualified to enroll in a "junior" year of an American university (following two years of study toward a Bachelor of Arts or a Bachelor of Science degree, or two years in junior college) count as the equivalent of the final secondary classes.

FIRST UNIVERSITY DEGREE OR DIPLOMA

With regard to the first diplomas in higher education, equivalences are less systematically established since they only affect the rarer enrollment of the foreign student seeking a doctorate in another country. In France, for example, the list of existing equivalences for purposes of enrollment for doctorates concerns a limited number of countries only; as far as others are concerned, individual decisions are made in each case.

Generally speaking, it can be said that assimilation is systematic between the first diplomas of those European countries in which university education is on a largely comparable level. This assimilation extends to diplomas from Soviet universities and institutes.[10]

[10] The problem of the real equivalence of Soviet diplomas with

The American Bachelor's degree, however, is not generally accepted as an equivalent of the first diploma by European universities, and such equivalence is only granted to the Master's degree.[11]

The United States apart, therefore, comparisons are possible and of undoubted interest as far as the two key points are concerned—secondary school leaving certificates and the first university diploma.

Many other diplomas are awarded, however, especially in technical and vocational establishments. These are, relatively speaking, less standardized from country to country. Even so, valid comparisons may be made for the "skilled worker" or "technician" levels, although more serious difficulties arise in regard to the levels midway between worker and technician (foremen, technical assistants, and the like) or between technician and engineer.[12]

It should further be noted that, in regard to vocational and technical diplomas, national statistics are frequently incomplete. As a general rule, they do not cover all staff trained by institutions or even by the army or by public administrations. As a result, possible comparisons involving diplomas other than final secondary and higher diplomas are undoubtedly much more hazardous and can only be employed with the greatest circumspection.

---

diplomas from Western European countries, more especially in the technical disciplines (engineering diplomas), is sometimes questioned. In actual fact, all recent publications by engineering missions returning from the U.S.S.R., especially in the United States, stress the high quality and level of studies in Soviet engineering schools. Nicholas DeWitt (formerly at the Russian Research Center, Harvard University, and now at the University of Indiana), author of the monumental *Education and Professional Employment in the U.S.S.R.,* emphasizes the absolute qualitative comparability of Soviet scientific and technical diplomas with American diplomas.

[11] This links up with the lack of equivalence for the final high school diploma mentioned above.

[12] Cf. the "higher technicians" in France and the graduates of the *Ingenieurschulen* in the Federal Republic of Germany.

QUALITATIVE EVALUATION OF THE CONDITIONS IN WHICH EDUCATION IS PROVIDED

In a qualitative evaluation of conditions affecting education two criteria, among others, may be used: the level of recruitment for teachers, and the numerical breakdown of classes (pupil/teacher ratio, average number of pupils per class, and so on).

The level of teacher recruitment—evaluated, for example, in years after the secondary school leaving certificate—is an extremely interesting element of comparison in that the value of education is closely tied to that of the teaching body. However, the criterion of years spent in study and preparation does not indicate whether recruitment is selective or not, and hence leaves in doubt an important aspect of the real level of the teaching body.

The criterion of pupil/teacher ratio is extremely difficult to evaluate. On the one hand, statistics concerning secondary and higher teachers, when they exist, do not always clearly distinguish (e.g., in Italy and Belgium) between full-time and part-time teachers, and the inclusion of part-time teachers obviously distorts the ratio. On the other hand, the pupil/teacher ratio is determined both by the weekly timetable of lessons which pupils must observe and by the weekly timetable of activity required from the teachers. These timetables, however, are not identical in all countries, and the differences are far from negligible. This also significantly distorts the comparability of pupil/teacher ratios.

To sum up, all these considerations must be borne in mind to avoid drawing unduly cut-and-dried conclusions from the comparisons set out in the present study.

PREPARATION AND CONTENT OF THIS STUDY*

After the purpose of the survey was determined, the committee drew up a detailed questionnaire with a view to as-

* The general statistical sources for each of the countries are

sembling data for each of the nine countries, prepared identically to facilitate comparison. Answers to the questionnaire were obtained with the assistance of various experts from the Common Market countries and Great Britain.[13]

From the replies and, to a large extent, from various other documents, the Rapporteur prepared a detailed survey for each country, following an identical pattern.

1. The general organization of the educational system at all levels;
2. Recent developments in primary, secondary, and higher education;
3. Trends in educational expenditure;
4. Educational reforms under way or planned;
5. Development plans or forecasts (where these exist).

In regard to the U.S.S.R., these data were based primarily on documents and statistics published by the Soviet authorities, and on various surveys of educational organization in the Soviet Union published in the United States, in Europe, or by international bodies.[14]

These nine surveys combine to form a body of documentation[15] on the present situation of education in the nine countries. They do, however, reveal some uncertainties or gaps.

The present synthesis was drawn up by the Rapporteur on the basis of these preliminary surveys. It does not claim to incorporate all the data assembled, but merely those descriptive or quantitative elements which seem most characteristic and most interesting. The administrative aspects of educational

---

given in the Appendix. When the information is taken from a special source, this is mentioned as it occurs.

[13] The names of those who cooperated with the committee are given in the Preface.

[14] Especially Unesco.

[15] These will not be published.

organization are not covered.[16] Neither are certain special forms of education (art, training of retarded children, and the like). Adult education, despite its growing importance, will not be systematically considered.

The problem then arose of determining the most practical form in which to present so ambitious a synthesis, and the following outline was chosen.

Chapter 1. The organization and state of development of general primary and secondary education.

Chapter 2. The organization and state of development of secondary vocational and technical education and higher education.

Chapter 3. Human, material, and financial resources devoted to education.

Finally, the *Conclusion* summarizes general trends and formulates basic criteria which can be extracted from this study and applied pragmatically in the reforms of the future.

Chapters 1, 2, and 3, dealing with questions of fact, were submitted for approval to the committee as a whole. The Introduction and the Conclusion were discussed by the committee but, to maintain unity, responsibility for their final wording was left to the Rapporteur.

[16] It will not be possible to deal separately with private education; the enrollment figures are included in the total figures.

1. The Organization and State of Development of General Primary and Secondary Education

PRESCHOOL EDUCATION, DURATION OF COMPULSORY EDUCATION, AND AGE OF ADMISSION TO SECONDARY STUDIES

OPTIONAL PRESCHOOL EDUCATION

The optional preschool education which precedes compulsory elementary schooling is now systematically organized in all the industrialized countries. As shown in Table 5, attendance at these establishments generally covers the period between three years of age and the beginning of compulsory schooling.

THE DURATION OF COMPULSORY EDUCATION

Education was made compulsory in all the countries covered by this survey either in the second half of the nineteenth or, at the latest, in the early years of the twentieth century. Since then, further legislation has gradually extended the compulsory period.

TABLE 5   DURATION OF PRESCHOOL EDUCATION

	Duration	Age	Name of Institutions
Federal Republic of Germany	3 years	3 to 6 years[a]	Kindergärten
Belgium	3 years	3 to 6 years[b]	Ecoles gardiennes
France	4 years	2 to 6 years[c]	Ecoles maternelles—Jardins d'enfants and classes enfantines
Italy	3 years	3 to 6 years	Infant schools
Luxembourg	2 years	4 to 6 years	Ecoles gardiennes or jardins d'enfants
Netherlands	2 years	4 to 6 years	Infant schools
United States	3 years 1 or 2 years	2 to 5 years 5 to 6 or 7 years	Nursery schools Kindergartens
U.S.S.R.	4 years	3 to 7 years	Kindergartens
England and Wales	3 years	2 to 5 years	Kindergartens

[a] One year only (from six to seven) for kindergartens attached to primary schools; the other preschools are not administratively integrated in the public education system.

[b] There are sometimes *pré-gardiennes* classes for children between two and three.

[c] Attendance at the *écoles maternelles* begins at three years of age in most of the communes.

Table 6 gives for each country the duration of the present compulsory period, the age limits, the dates of the last laws applicable, and improvements decided upon or planned.

Until World War II, the duration of compulsory education was generally eight years in Europe, except for the U.S.S.R., where it had been established in 1930 at four years in rural areas and seven years in urban areas, and changed to seven years in all areas in 1949.

At the end of World War II, the United Kingdom raised the period to ten years (from five to fifteen years of age) under the Education Acts of 1944 and 1945, and plans to extend it to eleven years as soon as circumstances permit.

The other European countries tend to follow suit: Luxembourg and seven German *Länder* have raised the period to nine years (from six to fifteen years of age) and recently decided to make this generally applicable. France has decided (Decree of January 5, 1959) to extend it to ten years (from six to sixteen years of age) beginning in 1967 and 1968. Belgium and The Netherlands have similar plans. Italy, which has not yet been able to provide schooling for all children between six and fourteen, although this was decided as early as 1923, is not at present planning to extend compulsory education.

In the U.S.S.R., the 19th Congress of the Communist Party (1952) planned to raise the period gradually to ten years but the law of December 24, 1958, limited it to only eight (from seven to fifteen years of age). Extension of the ten-year school (from seven to seventeen years of age) to all young people by 1970 was stipulated in the program of the 22nd Congress of the Communist Party in 1961.

Most of the states in the United States have fixed compulsory education at nine or ten years (from six[1] to fifteen or sixteen years of age). Three states have fixed the upper limit at seventeen years of age, and four others at eighteen years of age, i.e., the full period of elementary and secondary schooling.

In certain European countries (the Federal Republic of Germany, France, Luxembourg), full-time compulsory schooling is supplemented by compulsory part-time education up to seventeen or eighteen years of age. This supplements the general or theoretical training of youths and girls who have left school at the end of the compulsory period and gone directly into industry, commerce, or agriculture where they receive on-the-job vocational training.

[1] Sometimes seven years of age.

TABLE 6 DURATION OF COMPULSORY FULL-TIME EDUCATION

	Duration	Age Limits	Date of Last Law Applicable	Planned or Proposed Developments
Federal Republic of Germany	8 to 9 years[a]	6 to 14 years 6 to 15 years[a]	1962, 1963, or 1964	The general application of a 9-year compulsory period was decided by the Hamburg Convention of October 28, 1964[b]
Belgium	8 years	6 to 14 years		Extension proposed by the 1958 Pacte scolaire: 9 years (6–15) in 1965; 10 years (6–16) in 1968
France	8 years	6 to 14 years	1936	Extension decided by the Decree of January 5, 1959: 10 years (6–16) as from 1967[c]
United Kingdom	10 years	5 to 15 years	1944 or 1945	Extension to 16 years of age to be introduced as soon as circumstances permit
Italy	8 years	6 to 14 years	1923	
Netherlands	8 years	7 to 15 years[d]	1950	
Luxembourg	9 years	6 to 15 years	1963	

22

U.S.S.R.	8 years	7 to 15 years	1958	Extension to 10 years about 1970
United States	9, 10, 11, or 12 years	6–7 years to 15–18 years	Dates vary according to states	

[a] In seven of eleven states.

[b] The Hamburg Convention, concluded on October 28, 1964, between representatives of the *Länder* of the Federal Republic of Germany, stipulates that the duration of compulsory schooling "may be raised to ten years."

[c] Because of the delay in instituting new educational structures, it would seem unlikely that this extension can become effective before approximately 1972, after completion of the school building program provided for under the fifth plan (1966–1970).

[d] Most pupils begin school at six years of age.

23

The Age of Admission to General
Secondary Education

At the level of the first compulsory classes, frequently known as "elementary classes," children in the nine countries concerned all receive virtually identical education[2]—rudiments of the mother tongue, arithmetic, and so on—and the content differs very little from one country to another. This is the period when education is common to all the school-age population, i.e., the period of the "single school."

Within the period of compulsory schooling, which covers a minimum of eight years, education cannot be limited solely to the programs of the elementary cycle. The question therefore arises of determining at what point pupils should transfer to the first general secondary classes where the programs involve new subjects (mathematics, foreign languages, ancient languages, and the like) which were either not studied at all in the final primary classes or only to a limited extent.

Examination of the organization of studies in the nine countries reveals (see Table 7) that the normal duration of study in the elementary classes of the primary schools is far from being identical: four years in Germany and the U.S.S.R.; five years in France and Italy; six years in the Benelux[3] countries; and six years[4] in the United States.

The result is that, in the Federal Republic of Germany, children of ten years of age can normally go on to secondary school, whereas in the Benelux countries they are still in the elementary classes at the same age and their general secondary studies are reduced to a period of six years (see Table 7) without it being possible to claim that on reaching eighteen years of age, at the end of their secondary schooling, they have received a less satisfactory education. In other words,

[2] Except that certain private institutions, such as the preparatory schools in the United Kingdom, have special programs of their own.

[3] Belgium, The Netherlands, and Luxembourg.

[4] Eight years in those states which have retained the old form of organization.

TABLE 7 DURATION OF ELEMENTARY PRIMARY AND "LONG" SECONDARY EDUCATION

	Age at Which Compulsory Schooling Begins	Duration of Elementary Primary Education Preceding Secondary Education	Normal Age of Transfer to Secondary Education	Duration of Complete Secondary Education	Total Duration of General Pre-university Study
Federal Republic of Germany	6 years	4 or 6 years	10 or 12 years	9 or 7 years	13 years (6–19)
Belgium	6 years	6 years	12 years	6 years	12 years (6–18)
France	6 years	5 years	11 years	7 years	12 years (6–18)
Italy	6 years	5 years	11 years	8 years	13 years (6–19)
Luxembourg	6 years	6 years	12 years	7 years	13 years (6–19)
Netherlands	7 years[a]	6 years	12 years	6 years	12 years (6–18)
Great Britain	5 years	6 years	11 years	7 years	13 years (5–18)
U.S.S.R.	7 years	4 years	11 years	7 years (6 years)[b]	11 years (7–18) (10 years)[b]
United States	6 or 7 years	6 or 8 years	12 to 14 years	6 or 4 years	12 years (6–18)

[a] From six to seven years of age.
[b] The new reform, decided in August 1964, reduced the duration of the secondary course to six years and the total duration of general education to ten years, i.e., to the total duration in force prior to the 1958 reform.

25

the distinction between primary and secondary at this period of the child's education is relative only.

COMPARATIVE ORGANIZATION OF GENERAL SECONDARY EDUCATION: EXTENDED SINGLE-TRACK SCHOOL OR TWO-TRACK EDUCATION?

Depending on the country, pupils move from the elementary to the secondary school at ten, eleven, or twelve years of age, but the basic distinction lies elsewhere. The most pronounced differentiations occur in the structure of general education following the elementary classes, and these reflect not only varying educational concepts, but also a difference in the concept of the school's obligations to society and democracy.

Broadly speaking, there are two major types:

1. *The single-track school,* extended through general secondary education, at the very least until the end of the period of compulsory education as found in the United States and U.S.S.R. In both countries, it is recognized that secondary education is not a special form of education reserved for a more or less high proportion of the relevant age groups but a normal stage in education open to all within the limits of compulsory schooling. Accordingly, following on the elementary classes, all young people follow the same general courses at least through the first cycle of the secondary school.[5]

2. *The more or less diversified two-track education,* corresponding (subject to reforms which are under way[6]) to structures still in force in most of the European countries covered by this study.

Depending on the traditional organization, which goes back to the nineteenth century, education in these countries undergoes a marked change for children of ten, eleven, or twelve years of age when, on the basis of their capacity and

[5] Except, in the United States, for those states which have retained the eight-year elementary school.

[6] These will be found in the Conclusions.

their parents' wishes, they may remain until the end of the compulsory period in the extended primary classes[7] which last for two years in Belgium, three in France, and four in Germany;[8] proceed to general secondary education of various kinds—"long" courses leading to higher education, "short" or "upper primary" courses, special courses for girls, and so on; or, on occasion, proceed immediately to the lower level of technical and vocational education as in Belgium and The Netherlands.

As will be mentioned later, the British and Italian school systems represent an intermediate formula: the terminal primary classes in these countries, in principle, have been discontinued.[9]

Within the deliberately limited scope of this study, it is impossible to examine all details of the organization of education in each country. However, some of the essential features will be singled out for discussion.

THE RANGE OF GENERAL SECONDARY EDUCATION IN EUROPEAN COUNTRIES

The general secondary educational structure in the countries of Western and Southern Europe is as a rule a complex one, with the levels and outlets more or less graded and with each system having its own features and purposes.

[7] These classes are generally an integral part of primary school.

[8] In France and Belgium these classes are gradually tending to disappear as a result of the development of secondary education. In the Federal Republic of Germany they still occupy an important place. The Hamburg Convention of October 28, 1964, stipulated that the higher cycle of the primary school should be known as a "principal school" *(Hauptschule)* in which study of a foreign language would be optional.

[9] In the United Kingdom, the terminal primary classes were eliminated under the 1944–45 reform and replaced by "modern schools." In Italy, subsequent to the 1923 reform, children between eleven and fourteen years of age were in principle accepted in two types of secondary school: the middle school and the vocational orientation school. These two types were merged under new legislation in 1962 (see Conclusion).

For the sake of clarity, these institutions may be classified roughly into four categories: "long" or pre-university, "short" or upper primary, reserved for girls, and teacher training.

"LONG" OR PRE-UNIVERSITY EDUCATIONAL INSTITUTIONS: ORGANIZATION OF STUDIES AND FINAL EXAMINATION

In the seven countries concerned, these institutions provide courses of from six to nine years,[10] leading to a general secondary school leaving certificate which is usually required for entrance to universities or advanced studies.

The traditional task of these institutions, therefore, is to provide a general basic culture, literary and scientific, that will enable students, if they wish, to take full advantage of higher specialized courses. In actual fact, in all the European countries, most of those holding a "long" certificate at present go on to higher education, even though this certificate is to an increasing extent used as a requirement in recruiting personnel for certain public or private jobs.

The various "long" courses are sometimes given within a single institution and sometimes in separate institutions representing various specializations: classical, modern, scientific. They may include several successive cycles leading to intermediate examinations. In Italy, the first cycle is given in independent institutions, namely the middle schools.

Table 8 gives the organization for each country.

To prepare for subsequent specializations at university level, "long" secondary education, while retaining a substantial common cultural basis, is tending to become diversified and to specialize through separate sections for the classical, modern, scientific, or economic and even artistic disciplines.

In Western European countries, these fall into several groups: Latin and Greek (classical literary), Latin-languages (classical and modern literary), Latin-science (mixed literary

---

[10] As noted in Table 7, the duration of secondary schooling takes account of the length of the elementary cycle.

and scientific), modern (social science and economics), and modern (science).

France also has a "technical" *baccalauréat* with courses in technology and industrial design, and practical manual training on the job, being provided in the modern scientific section.

In Great Britain, grammar school pupils are not divided into sections with programs laid down by educational regulation; as their studies progress, they enjoy increasing freedom in the choice of courses. In the two successive examinations[11] of the General Certificate of Education (G.C.E.), they are free to choose from a very broad range of subjects—in London, forty subjects are offered at Ordinary Level and twenty-nine at Advanced Level.[12] This system leads to a much greater specialization during the final years of the grammar schools than is the case in other European countries.

All in all, this diversification of "long" secondary education in the seven countries concerned leads to relatively dissimilar types of education which in fact—and sometimes in law[13]—make for partial preorientation in the selection of higher studies.

The certificates awarded on completion of "long" secondary schooling are shown in Table 8. They are granted either after an examination taken at the end of the terminal year or, in Great Britain,[14] after two successive examinations. The extent to which these examinations are selective varies to a

[11] The first examination (Ordinary Level) is taken at the end of the fifth secondary class; so far, very few secondary "modern" pupils sit for this examination. The second examination (Advanced Level) is taken two years later (two years of study in a sixth form).

[12] Pupils take between one and eight subjects at Ordinary Level and between one and five at Advanced Level; at Ordinary Level, certain basic subjects (English, mathematics) are compulsory.

[13] Conditions governing access to higher education are discussed later in this study.

[14] France had two successive annual examinations up to 1965, when the preliminary *baccalauréat* examination was abolished.

TABLE 8   DIFFERENT TYPES OF "LONG" SECONDARY SCHOOLS

	Institutions[a]	Duration of Studies	Terminal Certificate
Federal Republic of Germany	Gymnasium[b] (classical, modern, or scientific)	9 (or 7) years	Reifeprüfung Abitur
Belgium	Athénées (boys), Lycées (girls)	6 years	Certificat d'études moyennes supérieures[c] Examen de maturité
France	Lycées classiques et modernes and lycées techniques	7 years	Baccalauréat
Italy	1st cycle: middle schools	3 years	Matriculation
	2nd cycle: classic or scientific lycées	5 years	
	Total	8 years	
Luxembourg	Classical course	7 years	Final secondary certificate
	Modern course[d]	6 years	
	Course for girls	7 years	
Netherlands	Gymnasia (classical)	6 years	State diploma
	Modern colleges (h.b.s.)[e]	5 or 6 years	
	Lycées[f]	—	
	Secondary schools for girls[g]	5 years	
United Kingdom[h]	Grammar schools[i]	7 years	General certificate of education (Advanced Level)

[a] Private institutions may have different names.

[b] In most of the *Länder* there are also secondary schools leading to a certificate which gives access to higher studies, and institutions which enable young adults, from eighteen to twenty-five years of age, who have completed their vocational training, to prepare for the *Abitur* through two or three years of full-time courses in institutions known as *Kolleg*.

[c] The Law of June 8, 1964, draws a distinction between the *certificat d'études moyennes supérieures*, awarded on the basis of school marks, and the *examen de maturité*, which alone provides access to university studies.

[d] The modern course does not provide access to higher technical and commercial studies.

[e] *Hogereburgershool.*

[f] The *lycées* group all the sections of other institutions.

[g] *Middelbare School voor meisjes.*

[h] Mainly England and Wales.

[i] In Great Britain independent private schools known as Public Schools play an important part in school organization. Their courses last five years, following eight years of special elementary education in preparatory schools.

fairly marked degree from country to country (cf. details for certain European countries given below).

General secondary education of a more limited duration (three, four, or five years) exists in all European countries. The schools providing these courses are tending to increase in importance in schooling at this level, as may be seen in the Appendix.

Table 9 lists the various types of schools in this category. Unlike the schools offering "long" courses, these have not the same aim in all countries. The basic difference lies in the possibility of access to pre-university education which is afforded to those having completed their courses in these schools.

In Belgium, courses in the middle schools are exactly the same as those in the first cycle of the *athénées* and *lycées;* pupils who have begun their studies in the latter may normally continue them in the second cycle and, in fact, 60 per cent of pupils from the third class of the middle schools proceed to the second cycle.

In France, the curricula of the *collèges d'enseignement général* correspond[15] to those of the first modern cycle in the *lycées;* after passing the examination for the *brevet d'études du premier cycle, C.E.G.* pupils may enter the modern sections of the second *lycée* cycle[16] or the technical sections, and nearly 50 per cent take advantage of this opportunity.

In other words, in Belgium, and to a large extent in France, general "short" education is merely a variant[17] of the

[15] The educational reform of January 1959 combined the two first classes of the *lycées* and the *C.E.G.* in a *cycle d'observation* with common curricula. The new reform, decided on in 1963, and which will be discussed in the Conclusion, extends the system of two-track curricula to all institutions of the first cycle.

[16] Because of lack of space, however, certain *lycées* administer an entrance examination.

[17] Education in the French *C.E.G.*'s and the Belgian middle schools, however, is given by teachers with differing qualifications.

first cycle of "long" education and gives access to the second cycle. The French reform of 1963, moreover, is aimed at the widespread introduction of first-cycle institutions known as *collèges d'enseignement secondaire.* The same does not apply in other countries.

In Germany, admission of *Realschulen* pupils to the terminal *Gymnasium* classes is still more limited because of the differentiation of the programs. Several *Länder,* however, have organized a special transition examination which gives access to special sections of the *Gymnasia (Gymnasiale Aufbauklassen).* Little advantage has been taken of this so far, but provisions in the Hamburg Convention aim at developing it systematically.[18]

In The Netherlands, possession of the certificate awarded by the upper primary school *(u.l.o.)* only gives access to technical schools and teacher training colleges.

In Italy, holders of the *avviamento professionale* certificate must pass another examination in order to be admitted to professional schools or, on the basis of a test, to technical institutes. In Great Britain, pupils who have completed secondary modern or technical schools cannot, in most cases, normally continue their studies in grammar schools. As pointed out below, however, some may subsequently sit for the G.C.E. examinations by attending courses in "further education" schools.

INSTITUTIONS SPECIFICALLY FOR GIRLS

Two countries, Germany and The Netherlands, provide secondary courses specifically for girls, midway between "long" and "short" courses.

1. *In The Netherlands,* courses in the secondary schools for girls last five years; the programs are similar to those of the modern colleges, with the addition of certain subjects

---

[18] After the tenth year in a *Realschule,* the duration of studies in a *Gymnasium* covers a minimum of three years; a second modern language is not a requirement.

TABLE 9 DIFFERENT TYPES OF "SHORT" GENERAL EDUCATION SCHOOLS

	Institution	Duration of Studies	Terminal Certificate
Federal Republic of Germany	*Realschule*	6 (or 4) years[a] (10–16 or 12–16)	Leaving certificate
Belgium	*Ecole moyenne*	3 years (12–15)	Leaving certificate
France	*Collège d'enseignement général*	4 years (11–15)	*Brevet d'études du premier cycle*
Italy	Vocational orientation schools[b]	3 years (11–14)	Leaving certificate
Luxembourg	*Ecole primaires supérieures*[c]	3 years (12–15)	*Diplôme de fin d'études primaires supérieures*
Netherlands	Upper primary schools (*u.l.o.*)[d]	4 years (12–16)	Leaving certificate
United Kingdom	Secondary modern school	4 years (11–15)	Possibly the G.C.E. (O Level)
	Technical school	5 years (11–16)	

[a] Depending on the *Länder*, these studies follow the fourth or sixth primary class.
[b] The *avviamento professionale* school—to be abandoned under the December 1962 reform at the end of the 1965–66 school year.
[c] Final primary courses at a somewhat higher level—will be converted into middle schools.
[d] *Uitgebreid lager onderwijs.*

(dressmaking, music, domestic economy). The leaving certificate does not give access to universities.

2. *In the Federal Republic of Germany,* certain *Länder* have secondary schools for girls *(Frauenoberschulen)* which go through to the thirteenth school year; pupils enter after five or ten years' schooling. The syllabus includes the compulsory study of two foreign languages and places special emphasis on domestic economy and the social sciences. The leaving certificate gives access to higher schools of pedagogy *(Pädagogische Hochschulen)* and, after a supplementary examination, to all university faculties.

TEACHER TRAINING INSTITUTIONS

Several Common Market countries (Belgium, France, Italy, The Netherlands) continue to train primary school teachers, both men and women, in teacher training colleges[19] which provide general secondary education and teacher training courses. Enrollment[20] is open to pupils who have completed the first "long" cycle or to those holding the "short" certificate (other than certificates from the vocational orientation school, in the case of Italy). In France, admission to the public teacher training colleges is subject to an examination based on requirements; in the other three countries, access is more or less free, and the program, especially for girls, represents a specific branch of general secondary education.

In France since World War II, and in Belgium since 1957, the curricula of the teacher training colleges have been similar to those in certain sections of the secondary schools and the future teacher, before receiving any vocational training,

[19] In Belgium, Italy, and The Netherlands, there are special colleges for the preparation of women teachers for preschools.

[20] In France and The Netherlands teacher training colleges provide another program for those holding the secondary school leaving certificate. These students receive vocational training only at the colleges.

sits for the ordinary secondary school leaving examination (*baccalauréat* or *examen de maturité*).

In Italy and The Netherlands, general studies in the teacher training colleges lead to a specific certificate; in Italy, the certificate gives access to the *magistero* faculties (see below) and to the social service schools.[21]

In the other countries (the Federal Republic of Germany, Luxembourg,[22] the United Kingdom), training of teachers for primary schools is provided for candidates who have previously completed the full secondary course.

ACCESS TO GENERAL SECONDARY SCHOOLS

Access to general secondary education following on elementary studies varies from country to country and from one type of institution to another.

1. *Access to "long" education*   The educational tradition in Western Europe tends to restrict "long" education to an elite group which is more or less carefully chosen at the end of the elementary classes. Recently, however, there has been a growing tendency to allow the enrollment of all pupils who have completed their elementary studies in the normal way. At the present time, more or less selective methods are still applied. Subject to the number of candidates, these largely determine the rate of admission in relation to the age groups. There are three main types:

A special secondary school entrance examination[23] This examination generally covers subjects in the last elementary class. It may be accompanied, as in Great Britain, by psychological tests (eleven-plus examinations). Apart from new and more or less experimental techniques, this method of recruitment has been adopted, with different formulas, in the *Länder* of the Federal Republic of Germany, The Netherlands, Luxembourg, and the United Kingdom.

[21] These are private schools which train welfare workers.

[22] Since the Law of July 7, 1958.

[23] When the number of available places is limited, this examination is really competitive.

Direct access for pupils who have passed the final elementary school examination[24] This is the system used in Belgium and, since 1961, in Italy.

Direct access for pupils who have "acquired the normal elementary background" These admissions are determined by an official commission on the basis of the complete school file.[25] This system has been used in France since 1957.

It will be observed that in France and Belgium, because of the close connection between "long" and "short" education, the method of recruitment is the same, as is confirmed by the nature of the first cycle in the Belgian middle schools and the French *C.E.G.'s.*

In Great Britain, the eleven-plus examination is taken by the great majority of pupils in the sixth elementary class. The results determine the distribution of pupils to grammar schools and other secondary schools, those who have obtained the best marks choosing the grammar schools. This examination therefore corresponds, in fact, to a selective test for grammar school recruitment.[26]

2. *Access to "short" education* Recruitment for "short" education in Belgium, France, and Great Britain has already been described.

In The Netherlands and Germany, in view of the existence of relatively developed terminal primary classes, access to the *u.l.o.* schools or the *Realschulen* is still more selective and involves a special examination.

PART-TIME GENERAL SECONDARY EDUCATION BY
CORRESPONDENCE, RADIO, AND TELEVISION

New forms of general secondary education have developed in the various European countries over recent years. Evening classes leading to secondary examinations are organized in

[24] Or, alternatively, through a special examination.

[25] Should the commission give an unfavorable decision, pupils may sit for an examination designed to establish their capacities.

[26] The Public Schools have their own entrance examination which is known as the "common entrance examination."

certain German *Länder* (evening middle schools or *Abendrealschulen,* evening *lycées* or *Abendgymnasium*[27]), and in The Netherlands.

In Great Britain, part-time evening or day classes are organized in connection with the "further education" institutions and courses. The importance of these forms of education is attested to by the fact that 13 per cent of candidates for the G.C.E. (Ordinary Level) and 16 per cent of candidates for the G.C.E. (Advanced Level) are drawn from "further education" courses.

No preparation for secondary certificates is available in part-time schools in France; on the other hand, official correspondence, radio, and television courses have developed to a marked extent over the last ten years through the Centre national de Télé-Enseignment (C.N.T.E.).[28] In 1965, 29,000 pupils studied for the *brevet du premier cycle* or *baccalauréat* in this way. Since 1961, Belgium has organized similar courses which culminate in examinations taken before a central jury.

AMERICAN AND SOVIET SYSTEMS

The structure of general secondary education in the United States and in the Soviet Union is to a large extent the outcome of extending the single-school organization to the secondary level.

The fact that the whole age group has access to the first secondary cycle makes the organization of "short" general education pointless. In addition, at the second-cycle level, neither the United States nor the U.S.S.R. has adopted the system of different sections or separate institutions as has been done in most of the Western European countries. The

[27] There are thirty-six evening *lycées* (with 7,000 pupils in 1964) which organize a three-year course leading to the secondary school leaving examination and requiring seventeen hours per week; there are also twenty-two *Kollegs* (with 2,600 pupils in 1964).

[28] Certain courses are full time.

basic reason lies in the virtually complete absence of any teaching of the ancient Greek-Latin languages at this level.[29] This situation makes the "classical section/modern section" duality of the old European countries purposeless.

The analogy between the organization in the United States and that in the Soviet Union is, however, far from complete.

THE GENERAL SECONDARY SCHOOL IN THE UNITED STATES

This high school is the normal prolongation of elementary school studies. Most students from the elementary schools enter high school without taking an examination and, in principle, advance from year to year with the rest of their class. The high schools are of two types: the four-year high school (classes 9, 10, 11, and 12) which, in a minority of states, follows on the eight-year elementary school; and the six-year high school (classes 7, 8, 9, 10, 11, and 12) which follows on the six-year elementary school and consists of two three-year cycles (junior high school and senior high school).

The programs[30] include common basic subjects (which become of less importance in the higher classes) and optional subjects (electives) which are either more advanced complements in the basic disciplines or new disciplines (foreign languages, drawing, music, domestic economy, commercial courses). This extremely flexible system enables students to vary their studies in accordance with their tastes and capacities[31] and, at the end of the course, may lead to literary or scientific specialization.

On completing the twelfth year, students who have followed

[29] Except in the United States, where they are optional.

[30] Classroom work is supplemented in the urban high schools by extracurricular activities.

[31] This explains why, by and large, students are grouped by age. Several high schools, however, have recently experimented with a system of "sections" to group students according to their intellectual capacity. This would seem to run counter to the American concept of democracy and is not widespread.

the minimum number of courses required and obtained the necessary number of "credits"[32] receive the high school certificate without any further examination, although some states, including the State of New York, have leaving examinations.

Because of this flexibility in educational organization, 70.7 per cent of age groups in 1964 successfully completed their high school studies. The considerable provision of full-time general education does not leave any place at this level for part-time education.

THE SOVIET GENERAL POLYTECHNIC SECONDARY SCHOOL

1. *General organization*   The Soviet Union offers no general secondary education aimed essentially at preparing for higher education as this is understood in Western European countries. According to the program of the Soviet Communist Party, complete secondary education should become the basis of education for all young people, and a large proportion already benefit from it to the full (see below).

General secondary education may be broken down as follows: the last four years of the compulsory eight-year school (classes 5, 6, 7, and 8); and the terminal classes (the three terminal years 9, 10, and 11, established by the reform of December 24, 1958, have been reduced to two years—9 and 10—beginning with the school year 1965–66 by virtue of new decisions taken in August 1964).

According to the programs introduced immediately after the 1958 reform and with a view to eliminating the duality between manual work and intellectual work, education in the three terminal classes tended to combine the traditional secondary subjects with a practical vocational training either in school workshops or, preferably, in actual enterprises. This practical training occupied twelve hours a week (two days of six hours) throughout three years.

In accordance with the decisions taken in August 1964 by

[32] A credit is granted when the student obtains at least a "D" in a descending scale of marks: A, B, C, D, E.

the Central Committee of the Communist Party and the Council of Ministers of the U.S.S.R., however, the total duration of studies was reduced to ten years $(4 + 4 + 2)$ and the weekly vocational training timetable in the two terminal years was substantially reduced (four hours a week with practical six-week courses in the ninth class and two-week courses in the tenth class). The solution adopted in August 1964 would not seem to be final, since a general reform of programs for the ten-year school is currently being considered. The trend would seem to be toward abandoning specialized vocational training at this level in favor of strengthening general polytechnic[33] education.

2. *Entrance conditions*   No special examination is required for entrance to the fifth class, but at the end of the eighth class, pupils take a compulsory final examination after which they may proceed to the ninth class; go on to the vocational or technical school; or go directly into an enterprise.

Entrance into the second cycle is the occasion for an initial selection of pupils although, as will be pointed out later, it is a relatively broad selection. Subject to success[34] in the final examination, the family's preference is apparently the determining factor as regards entry to the terminal cycle.

3. *Content of studies and certificates awarded*   The second cycle of general and polytechnic secondary studies leads to a final certificate awarded by the State (qualification certificate) which is granted after examination by the schools themselves. In 1958, 95 per cent of pupils in the terminal class obtained this certificate.

It will be noted that the Soviet high schools are not divided into sections working on different programs. Apart

---

[33] The emphasis would be on certain subjects such as mathematics and science, and on utilization in productive activities of the scientific principles studied.

[34] Apparently an extremely high proportion of pupils pass this examination.

from certain optional courses of lesser importance, all pupils, unlike European pupils and those in the American high schools, receive an identical general education whose characteristics are indicated below.

In actual fact, this uniformity of programs for the mass of pupils has for some years past been accompanied by a growing effort at diversification with a view to developing specific interests and capacities. This is being done (1) in the schools themselves (organization of clubs[35] outside the compulsory timetable where pupils are grouped according to their tastes and capacities and which facilitate additional instruction, especially in certain basic subjects such as mathematics, physics, languages, etc.); (2) in specialized schools for the teaching of science and languages;[36] and (3) in outside organizations (pioneer clubs, young technician centers, groups organized by higher educational establishments or universities, and so on).

This trend, already pronounced in Soviet secondary education, is expected to develop still further in the near future.

4. *Part-time and correspondence courses: schools for young factory and farm workers*   During World War II, evening courses were introduced for young factory and farm workers. This practice has become established and has developed greatly.

The schools for young factory and farm workers are open to students who have completed the eight-year school (compulsory education) and who are actually working. Studies last three years, thirty-six weeks per year and twenty hours per week. Courses are given in rotation, in the daytime[37] or in the evening. Aside from the practical training, the weekly

[35] Club meetings are generally held twice a week and last from one and a half to two hours.

[36] There are over sixty secondary schools specializing in foreign languages in Moscow and, throughout the U.S.S.R., several secondary schools specializing in the teaching of mathematics and science.

[37] The enterprises provide the necessary facilities.

program of basic subjects differs little from that of ordinary schools.

Through these methods it is possible to complete general polytechnic secondary studies. The reformers of 1958 considered that this type of school should eventually become the basic instrument for completing secondary studies "on the basis of the unity between study and productive labor." In fact, since 1958 and, more especially, in recent years, the full-time terminal secondary classes have developed much more rapidly than the part-time classes.

COMPARATIVE FEATURES OF "LONG" SECONDARY CURRICULA

The various types of education outlined above are characterized not only by their reciprocal relations, duration, and manner of recruitment, but above all by content.

It is not intended to attempt an analysis of timetables, curricula, and teaching methods here, but from the breakdown of timetables alone, certain characteristic aspects of the various educational systems can be isolated. In this connection, Table A-11 in the Appendix shows (1) the total hours in elementary classes preceding secondary education, with the time allotted to mathematics and science indicated separately; and (2) the total hours devoted to "long" secondary education (pre-university), and the time allotted respectively to mathematics and science and to literary subjects (mother tongue, ancient languages, modern foreign languages).

Where the distinction exists, this analysis is made for both the literary and the modern sections.

For Great Britain and the United States, the absence of a set program and the extensive options allowed make such analysis impossible.

Considerable caution is required in drawing conclusions from Table A-11 and, given the varying length of the elementary and secondary cycles in different countries, they should never be cut and dried. Certain interesting observations may, however, be made on important points.

WEEKLY TIMETABLES IN THE DIFFERENT COUNTRIES

Elementary cycle (timetable,[38] and variations, if any, from the first to the final elementary class)

Federal Republic of Germany[39]	from 18 to 36 hours
Belgium	23½ hours (or 28 periods of 50 min.)
France	27½ hours
Italy	24 hours
Luxembourg	from 27 to 28 hours
The Netherlands	from 21 to 26¼ hours
U.S.S.R.	from 24 to 29 lessons (generally lasting 45 minutes)

"Long" secondary education (compulsory timetable, and variations, if any, from the first to the final class)

Federal Republic of Germany[40]	from 29 to 38 hours
Belgium	from 34 to 36 hours
France	from 25½ to 28½ or 29½ hours (according to section)
Italy	from 26 to 29 or 30 hours (according to section)
Luxembourg	from 30 to 31 or 33 hours (according to section)
The Netherlands	from 29 to 35 hours (according to section)
U.S.S.R.	from 33 to 36 lessons (generally lasting 45 minutes)

It will be noted that there are variations of some importance in the weekly timetables from one country to another, but comparisons would seem fruitless because of the varying extent of the homework required. For example, the apparently less onerous timetables of the French *lycées* are largely offset by the substantial amount of homework.

[38] Not including recreation time.
[39] Lower Saxony.
[40] Hamburg.

COMPARATIVE IMPORTANCE ALLOCATED TO SCIENTIFIC
EDUCATION IN THE DIFFERENT COUNTRIES

The main point which emerges from this tabulation is
that, in spite of a total duration of secondary studies limited
to seven years,[41] the total timetables[42] devoted to mathematics and science in the U.S.S.R. are equal to or sometimes
even greater than those of the most scientific sections in other
countries.

Given the uniformity of programs in the Soviet secondary
schools, the result is that all pupils in these establishments
receive mathematical and scientific training which generally
lasts longer than that of secondary students in Western Europe (one third or 40 per cent) who choose the scientific
sections. Moreover, Soviet secondary schools, under the
1958 reform, devote a significant amount of time (over 1,800
hours) to theoretical and practical vocational training.[43]

Within the Common Market countries of Europe, the
timetables are relatively homogeneous except in Italy, where
that of the scientific secondary schools is relatively less than
in other countries.

THE TEACHING OF ANCIENT GREEK-LATIN LANGUAGES

This area occupies an important place in the timetables of
the classical sections in Western European countries, more
especially in Germany (27 per cent of the compulsory timetable), Italy (25 per cent), and the Benelux countries. This
is true also in the British grammar schools and Public
Schools. In France, ancient languages are taught for six
years;[44] this is only half the time allotted in the corresponding German sections, where it continues over nine years.

[41] As organized between 1958 and 1965.
[42] However, lessons may not uniformly last one hour.
[43] This time was substantially reduced under the reform of
1964; the time allotted to the other disciplines does not seem to
have been significantly changed.
[44] Subject to the reform of the French *baccalauréat* which is
at present being introduced.

These subjects are not included in the Soviet timetables and occupy a very limited place among the optional subjects available to American high school students.

THE TEACHING OF MODERN FOREIGN LANGUAGES

This area is particularly developed in the Benelux countries (partly for national linguistic reasons) and also occupies an important place in modern German education. In Soviet secondary classes, the time allotted to foreign languages is markedly brief in comparison with the other European countries.

THE RELATIVE PLACE OF VARIOUS DISCIPLINES IN THE "LONG" SECONDARY EDUCATION TIMETABLE

Table 10 shows, in percentages, the timetable of *required* subjects broken down by main disciplines and by country.

Within the weekly timetables, which are relatively homogeneous,[45] the breakdown between disciplines varies hardly at all in the Common Market countries,[46] but the general structure of Soviet timetables is profoundly different. This difference results not only from the fact that Latin is not taught at all; it is equally apparent in relation to the modern scientific sections of the Western European countries. The Soviet timetables (R.S.F.S.R.)[47] reveal a sort of priority for the teaching of mathematics, science, and technology over the literary subjects. However, the time allotted to history and geography is in line with the European average.

COMPARATIVE STAGE OF DEVELOPMENT OF GENERAL PRIMARY AND SECONDARY EDUCATION

Table 11 shows the percentage changes in enrollment for all educational levels over the last ten years as far as these

[45] Except for those of France and Italy, which are below the European average.
[46] Except for the scientific timetables in the Italian high schools.
[47] Timetable introduced after the 1958 reform.

TABLE 10   Breakdown, in Percentage, of Timetable for Required Subjects, by Main Disciplines

Discipline	Federal Republic of Germany		Belgium		France		Italy		Luxembourg		Netherlands		U.S.S.R.
	I[a]	II[a]	I	II	I	II	I	II	I	II	I	II	
Mathematics, science	20.7	28.5	17.8	25.6	19.0	30.7	13.3	19.0	16.7	28.0	15.0	25.3	32.8
Languages[b]	45.7	33.8	54.1	36.5	51.0	40.5	53.4	46.0	54.8	41.3	60.0	52.0	22.5
History and geography	9.2	10.7	9.2	10.0	12.4	12.0	14.0	14.3	9.0	9.0	—	—	12.0
Music and drawing	8.5	11.2	2.9	7.5	5.1	5.0	4.6	7.0	4.2	9.0	—	—	3.0
Physical training	10.0	10.0	8.3	9.0	7.9	7.8	9.2[c]	9.2[c]	4.6	5.3	—	—	6.1
Manual work[d]	—	—	0.9	1.5	2.2	2.1	—[e]	—[e]	—	—	—	—	22.8
Miscellaneous[f]	5.7	5.9	6.8	10.4[g]	2.0	1.9	4.5	4.5	1.5	6.7	—	—	0.8

[a] I—The more literary section; II—the more scientific section.
[b] Literature, philosophy, mother tongue, foreign languages, ancient languages.
[c] Of this group, 6.4 per cent were girls.
[d] Practical training, manual work, domestic economy.
[e] Of this group, 2.8 per cent were girls.
[f] Civics, religious instruction, supervised activities, and so on.
[g] Includes 1.5 for economic education and 2.5 for supervised activities.

are known. It is based on official statistics from each country (see Appendix, Tables A-1–A-9), and indicates both the extent of the quantitative growth in the various national educational systems over this short period and the very marked disparities in the respective rates of growth.

This evaluation of the degree of development in the different levels of general education and, in Chapter 2, of the other levels of education, will make due allowance for this recent expansion.

DEVELOPMENT OF PRESCHOOL EDUCATION

The importance of education at this level still varies significantly from country to country. In order to evaluate it, and in view of the lack of complete statistics on enrollment figures by age, a comparison may be made between the number of those enrolled and the average size of the school-age groups (see Appendix, Tables A-1–A-9, and Table A-10 on the birth rate). The results are given in Table 12.

It will be noted that at this level, the Common Market countries, and more especially Belgium, The Netherlands, and France, are the most advanced. Although compulsory education begins at seven years of age, the U.S.S.R. has so far achieved only a relatively limited development in preschool education, but progress has been extremely rapid over the last ten years. The same applies to England, although there the low attendance at kindergartens may be explained by the fact that compulsory education begins at five years of age.

As for the United States, it is impossible to make the comparison since the numbers attending nursery schools are not known.

Table 13 shows the enrollment at preschool level for the countries in which such figures are published.

TABLE 11 PERCENTAGE OF INCREASE IN NUMBER OF FULL-TIME PUPILS OVER THE LAST DECADE

Period	Pre-school	Pri-mary	General Secondary	Vocational and Technical	Higher	All Levels
Federal Republic of Germany 1950–51/1960–61	—	−21	+ 44	+ 47	+ 98	—10
Belgium 1952–53/1962–63	+ 31	+24	+ 88	+107	+ 74	+34.9
France 1951–52/1961–62	+ 14	+42	+133	+ 68	+ 74	+51
England and Wales 1951–52/1961–62	+ 16	+ 2	+ 62	+110[a]	+ 58	+22
Italy 1952–53/1962–63	+ 16	− 2	+ 72	+160	+ 22	+18
Luxembourg 1951–52/1961–62	+ 27	+12	+ 74	+ 26	+ 84[b]	+18.8
Netherlands 1951–52/1961–62	+ 13	−15	+110	+103	+ 47	+33
U.S.S.R.[c] 1952–53/1962–63	+209	+44	+ 8	+ 35	+ 38 (+104)[d]	+32 (+42)[d]
United States 1951–52/1961–62	+ 63	+40	+65		+ 73	+49

[a] Full-time education or "sandwich courses" provided in "further education" institutions and not considered as higher education.
[b] Higher courses (first university year in Luxembourg).
[c] The 1953–1963 comparisons in the U.S.S.R. are distorted at elementary and secondary levels by variations in the birth rate due to World War II (see Appendix Tables A-8 and A-10).
[d] Includes evening and correspondence courses.

ENROLLMENT AT ELEMENTARY AND TERMINAL PRIMARY LEVEL

ENROLLMENT VIRTUALLY COMPLETE AT THIS LEVEL

Since education is legally compulsory in the nine countries, attendance is virtually complete at this level. Enrollment figures in the elementary classes as published in the various countries are generally in the vicinity of 99 and 100 per cent up to the age at which secondary studies begin.

Beyond that stage, enrollment remains almost complete within the limits of compulsory education, except in Italy.[48]

THE DIVERGENT INFLUENCE OF THE DEMOGRAPHIC FACTOR ON ENROLLMENT

As indicated in Table 11, enrollment over the last ten years in elementary and terminal classes differs significantly

TABLE 12 PERCENTAGE OF ENROLLMENT IN KINDERGARTENS AS RATIO OF NUMBER IN AGE GROUP

	Percentage of Age Group Attending School	*Year*
Federal Republic of Germany	0.9	1960–61
Belgium	2.7	1962–63
France	1.9	1962–63
Italy	1.3	1962–63
Luxembourg	1.02	1961–62
Netherlands	1.8	1963–64
U.S.S.R.[a]	0.96	1963–64
England and Wales	0.32	1962–63
United States	—	—

[a] Independently of the nursery schools, the U.S.S.R. has organized a relatively extensive network of permanent or seasonal *crèches* for children under three years of age. These frequently form a part of housing schemes or places of work.

[48] Because of social and economic underdevelopment in certain

TABLE 13   PERCENTAGE OF PRESCHOOL ENROLLMENT AT VARIOUS AGE LEVELS, 1960 OR 1961

	2 years	3 years	4 years	5 years
Belgium	—	81.0	93.0	95.0[a]
France	10.6	37.7	65.0	91.6
Luxembourg	—	—	50.0	—
Netherlands	—	—	70.0	88.0
England and Wales	—	11.0	—	—[b]
United States	—	—	—	64.0

[a] Including children already enrolled at this age in elementary classes.

[b] One hundred per cent of children aged five are enrolled in elementary classes.

from country to country: France, 42 per cent; United States, 40 per cent; U.S.S.R., 40 per cent; The Netherlands, 20 per cent; England and Wales, 20 per cent; Italy, 2 per cent; and Federal Republic of Germany, 21 per cent.

The population changes shown in Table 14 provide the basic explanation for these variations, including events in the Federal Republic of Germany and the U.S.S.R.[49] during World War II.

RETARDATION IN ELEMENTARY CLASSES AND THE
IMPORTANCE OF FAMILY AND SOCIAL FACTORS

An extremely interesting point at this level is the extent of retardation in elementary classes. Unfortunately, information on this is not available for all countries and, when it does

---

regions, school attendance in Italy declines after the five elementary school classes. In 1959–60, approximately 30 per cent of children between eleven and fourteen years of age did not attend school. This situation is now being rapidly rectified (see Table 48) and the reform decided on in 1962 should soon lead to complete school attendance up to fourteen years of age.

[49] See Appendix, Table A-10.

TABLE 14   CHANGES IN BIRTH RATE BETWEEN 1938 AND 1960

	Births (in thousands)			1960 Index (1938 = 100)	Birth Rate 1935–	
	1938	1950	1960		1939	1961
GROWING BIRTH RATES:						
United States	2,286	3,554	4,257	186	17.2	23.6
United Kingdom	735	818	918	124	15.3	17.5
Belgium	133	145	154	115	15.5	16.9
France	612	858	819	133	15.1	18.3
Luxembourg	4.4	4.4	5	113	15.0	16.0
Netherlands	178	229	238	133	20.3	20.8
DECLINING BIRTH RATES:						
Federal Republic of Germany	828	772.6	947	115	19.4	17.7
Italy	1,037	908	910	87	23.2	18.5
U.S.S.R.	6,690	4,805	5,341	79	35.0	23.8

exist, is not always presented in the same way, so that comparisons are necessarily only approximate.

1. *In Belgium,* it would seem that, despite the *gardien* system, a high percentage of pupils are one or two years behind as early as the first year of primary school, and this percentage tends to increase progressively up to the sixth year. As seen in Table 15, this condition is more prevalent among boys than among girls. This phenomenon is slightly more pronounced in Italy.

2. *In France,* observations over recent years[50] reveal that, at the level of the fifth elementary class (second year intermediate), while 8 per cent of a given age group completes this class between the ages of nine and ten, 34.2 per cent are one year behind, 13.7 per cent are two years behind, and 5.2 per cent are three years behind.

3. *In the U.S.S.R.,* published statistics do not indicate

[50] Statistical Information Service (Numbers 21, 28, and 38) of the Ministry of National Education.

TABLE 15   DISTRIBUTION, IN PERCENTAGE, OF ELEMENTARY
SCHOOL PUPILS IN BELGIUM[a] AND ITALY

	Belgium[b]		*Italy*[c]	
	FIRST YEAR[d]	SIXTH YEAR[e]	FIRST YEAR	FIFTH YEAR
BOYS				
Advanced	3.6	4.5	1.7	6.2
Normal	80.3	61.5	79.5	45.9
Retarded by 1 year	11.9	21.7	12.6	28.9
Retarded by 2 years or more	4.2	12.3	6.2	19.0
GIRLS				
Advanced	2.6	3.4	1.5	6.9
Normal	83.7	69.9	81.7	54.0
Retarded by 1 year	10.3	18.7	11.5	25.8
Retarded by 2 years or more	3.4	8.0	5.3	13.3

[a] No. 21 of *Etudes et Documents,* published by the Ministry of
National Education.

[b] 1959–60.

[c] Normally six to seven years of age.

[d] Normally eleven to twelve years of age.

[e] 1962–63.

the age of children in the various classes and it is therefore
not possible to establish the extent of retardation. According to Nicholas DeWitt's estimates,[51] the rate of "repeating" in the first four classes amounted to between 6 and 12
per cent in 1954–55. The Soviet educational authorities have
meanwhile made systematic attempts to reduce these figures
and now indicate an average repeating rate of between 4 and
5 per cent for all eight classes in the compulsory period.

4.   *In England and the United States,* the situation is different. The pupils are more inclined to move with their age
group and extensive lags (two years or more) at the end of
elementary grades would seem to be distinctly less. How-

[51] Nicholas DeWitt, *Education and Professional Employment in
the U.S.S.R.,* pp. 148–149.

ever, 31 per cent of pupils in primary classes are over eleven years of age (theoretically a one-year lag), only 2.7 per cent are over twelve years (two-year lag), and 2.5 per cent are over thirteen (three-year lag).[52]

It is difficult to draw conclusions by comparing the English-speaking countries with those in continental Europe. The differences in educational retardation between England and the other countries cannot really be explained by the conditions in which education is provided (see Chapter 3) but lies basically in the differences in educational practice: Educators in the English-speaking countries are opposed to dividing children of the same age in courses at different levels, whereas European educators are more conscious of the "educational level" and more inclined to make a child "repeat" a class when he has not reached an adequately high "level" to go on to the following class. Again, the English eleven-plus examination virtually eliminates repeaters in the final elementary class, whereas they are frequent in European countries in the class preceding secondary education.

The extent of educational lag at elementary class level needs analysis from another aspect—the social background of the pupils. The few surveys on this subject—which should be made systematically in all countries—reveal close correlations between educational lags, or advances, and family or social circumstances.

The pupil from an intellectually advanced social stratum brings his own stock of knowledge to the school, including linguistic ability, and may also have other facilities which greatly contribute to smooth progress in his studies. Children from workers' families, or from social environments where the level of education is not high, have greater difficulty in adapting to the requirements of school work, more especially because of linguistic inadequacies. This is particularly true of rural environments.[53]

---

[52] *Statistics of Education 1962*, Part I.
[53] It goes without saying, in all social environments specific

Retardation in the elementary classes plays an important role in family decisions when the time comes to select secondary studies; accordingly decreasing such retardation through improved individual assistance in the classroom (as well as reducing overcrowding in classrooms) [54] represents one of the bases of any policy aiming at equalizing opportunities for access to secondary studies.

CHARACTERISTIC FEATURES OF GENERAL SECONDARY SCHOOL ATTENDANCE

Table 11 shows the rate of growth[55] of enrollment over the last decade in each of the nine countries of the present survey for all educational levels.

In general secondary education, growth is striking in all the Common Market countries, especially in France (133 per cent), The Netherlands (110 per cent), and Belgium (88 per cent), and also in the United States (66 per cent). The low rate of growth in the U.S.S.R. (8 per cent) is basically due to the effect of World War II on the birth rate[56] with its repercussions on the school-age population between 1950 and 1960, and even later. However, as will be shown later, Soviet enrollment rates have increased to an extraordinary extent over the last decade.

For each of the countries, growth results from two factors —birth rate and enrollment rate—which sometimes cumulate, and sometimes cancel each other out. It is important not to confuse the two. As far as any evaluation of the degree of growth is concerned, the essential criterion is the enrollment figures at various levels of secondary education.

---

family situations may contribute to disturbing the rhythm of children's studies to a serious degree.

[54] See Chapter 3.

[55] The variations are indicated in absolute terms for each of the nine countries in the Appendix, Tables A-1–A-9.

[56] Births in the U.S.S.R. fell from over six million in 1938 to three million and 3.5 million in 1943 and 1944; the birth rate has gradually risen since, but has not yet reached pre-war level.

TABLE 16 DISTRIBUTION OF PUPILS COMPLETING THE ELEMENTARY CYCLE, IN PERCENTAGE OF AGE GROUPS

	School Year	Age Group	Primary Classes[a]		General Secondary Education		Vocational and Technical Education or Domestic Economy	Total
			ELEMENTARY	TERMINAL	SHORT	LONG		
Federal Republic of Germany	1962–63	13 years		73.5	12.0	14.5	—	100.0
Belgium	1962–63	13 years	13.3	9.4 {22.7}	40.5		35.2	98.4
France	1962–63	12 years		55.5	22.0	21.7 {43.7}	—	99.2
Great Britain	1961–62	12 years		2.1	68.0	26.8[b]	3.0	99.9
Italy	1962–63	12 years		47.2	50.8[c]		—	98.3
Netherlands	1961–62	13 years		27.9	28.0	13.9	29.7	99.6
U.S.S.R.	1962–63	12 years		—	99.5[d]		—	99.5
United States	1962–63	12 years		—	99.5[d]		—	99.5
Luxembourg	1959–60	12 years		67.5	5.5	25.5[e]	—	99.5

[a] Includes special education.

[b] Includes 19.2 per cent in grammar schools and the remainder in comprehensive and independent schools.

[c] In 1962–63, the total enrollment was classified under the heading "middle school." In 1959–60, prior to the 1962 reform, children were divided between the *avviamento professionnale* school (21.5 per cent) and the middle school (22.0 per cent).

[d] Statistics are not available to determine the proportion who may still remain in the final elementary classes at this age.

[e] Includes 9.5 per cent in the modern sections.

DISPARITIES IN THE TOTAL ENTRANCE RATES

In order to evaluate relative trends toward general second-ary education in the different countries, we have adopted the method[57] of comparing the distribution of children aged twelve or thirteen, that is, the age at which entrance into the first secondary classes is virtually completed, between the various types of education: "long" or "short" secondary edu-cation, terminal primary classes, vocational education, and so on. Table 16 sets forth this comparison. It confirms what has already been said regarding the organization of studies. In the United States and the U.S.S.R., almost all children go on to secondary school after completing the elementary or primary cycle. In the United Kingdom, rather more than a quarter of a given age group goes on to pre-university sec-ondary school after the eleven-plus examination, and virtually all the remainder go on to modern schools.

The total number of pupils enrolled in "long" and "short" secondary education does not vary significantly from one country to another in the Common Market area (from 34 to 44 per cent), except in Germany where it is significantly less (26.5 per cent). These figures, however, conceal relatively different situations.

In France and Belgium, since "short" education corre-sponds to a first cycle of "long" education, the figures (43 and 40 per cent) show the real extent of admission to final secondary examinations.

In the other countries, accepting the distinction which is still very marked as early as ten, eleven, or twelve years of age, between pre-university and "short" education, the trend toward "long" education is much more limited. This is espe-cially so in The Netherlands and the Federal Republic of Germany: Federal Republic of Germany, 14.5 per cent, and

[57] The various enrollment rates could also be calculated by comparing the enrollment in the first secondary class with the average of the two or three corresponding age groups. This second method would generally give slightly higher enrollment figures but is more difficult to apply to all the countries. The method adopted has the advantage of giving genuinely comparable results.

The Netherlands, 12.2 per cent;[58] Italy, 24 per cent (prior to the reform of 1962); and Luxembourg, 25.5 per cent (16 per cent if the modern sections are excluded).

GRADUATION FROM "LONG" SECONDARY EDUCATION

The full secondary course in the nine countries (see Table 8) culminates with the award of a leaving certificate at the end of the final year. The extent to which these certificates might be considered equivalent was examined in the Introduction which also noted the equivalences officially recognized in the eight European countries covered by this study. Whatever reservations may remain as to the real comparability of these certificates, notwithstanding the official equivalences, it is of interest to see what proportion of age groups in each country complete their general secondary studies, and the changes that have taken place in this respect over the last decade (see Table 17).

In the United States, the exceptionally large number of holders of high school diplomas confirms what has already been said; these diplomas, however, are not, on the average, comparable to those awarded in European secondary schools.

In the European countries, the figure in 1950 was roughly 4 to 5 per cent of the age group, but developments over the last decade have greatly accentuated the divergences.

The U.S.S.R. provides an example of exceptionally rapid development; the percentage of full secondary graduates rose from 4 per cent in 1950 to approximately 27 per cent in 1958 and 30 per cent in 1964. This is the result of the decision in 1949 to generalize the first secondary cycle, and of the effort to extend the "ten-year schooling" which preceded the 1958 reform.

In Western Europe, countries such as Belgium and France

[58] In these two countries, the percentages of admission to "long" secondary education, following a marked growth up to 1956 or 1957, have been virtually stable for several years past, and even show a slight decline in the Federal Republic of Germany.

TABLE 17 NUMBER OF CERTIFICATES OF "LONG" SECONDARY EDUCATION AWARDED, IN ABSOLUTE TERMS AND AS A PERCENTAGE OF AGE GROUPS

Country and Type of Certificate	1950–51		1960–61		Rate of Increase in 10 Years	Subsequent Year	
	NUMBER OF CERTIFICATE HOLDERS (in thousands)	AGE GROUPS[a]	NUMBER OF CERTIFICATE HOLDERS (in thousands)	AGE GROUPS[a]		NUMBER (in thousands)	AGE GROUPS[a]
FEDERAL REPUBLIC OF GERMANY[b]	31.5	4.3	61.4	6.7	+ 56	*1962–63* 64.3	8.1
BELGIUM							
Certificat d'humanités	*1954–55* 9.1	6.7	12.7[c]	11.7	—	*1962–63* 15.8	13.0
Enseignement normal primaire	1.9	1.5	1.6[c]	1.5	—	1.9	1.6
	11.0	8.2	14.3	13.2	+ 60	18.0	14.6
FRANCE	33.1	5.1	61.5	10.9	+113	*1963–64* 86.7	12.3
ENGLAND AND WALES Number of passes (G.C.E. "A")[d]	77.0	—	182.0	—	+136	*1962–63*	
School leavers[d]	—	—	56.8	9.1	—	70.3	10.4

					+/−	1962–63	
ITALY							
Matriculation	25.8	3.1	32.6	3.8	—	32.04	4.2
Secondary diploma	17.1	2.1	23.5	2.8	—	23.4	3.0
LUXEMBOURG	0.21	5.2	56.1	6.6	+ 26	55.44	7.2
		5.0	0.32	8.5	+ 70	—	—
NETHERLANDS			*1959*			*1963*	
Secondary school leaving certificate	8.4	4.8	10.0	5.8	—	14.6	7.3
Education for girls	1.2	0.7	2.7	1.5	—	3.6	1.8
Secondary and commercial schools	1.6	0.9	3.7	2.2	—	5.0	2.5
	1950		*1958*			*1963–64*	
U.S.S.R. [e]	11.2	6.4	16.4	9.5	+ 48	23.2	11.6
	242.0 (220.0)	4.0	1600.0 (1340.0)	27.0	+575	1400.0	30.0
						1962–63	
UNITED STATES [f]	1221.0	50.8	1803.0	64.3	+ 28	1960.0	70.7

a These rates are the average for the two sexes; however, in certain countries, the rates are in fact considerably higher for boys than for girls.

b Includes West Berlin; certificates other than the *Abitur*, which give access to higher studies (*Sonstige Hochschulberechtigte*), are included; i.e., 3,309 in 1963.

c After 1961, the primary normal schools began to award the *certificat d'humanités*.

d Have passed at least one examination, and includes recipients of the "Further Education" certificate.

e The number of recipients of certificates from full-time schools is indicated in brackets.

f Includes certain vocational education certificates similar to the high school certificate.

TABLE 18   PERCENTAGES OF "LONG" SECONDARY EDUCATION
CERTIFICATES AWARDED TO BOYS AND GIRLS, RE-
SPECTIVELY, IN 1959 OR 1960

	Boys	Girls
United States	48	52
U.S.S.R.[a]	48	52
France[b]	49	51
Belgium	67	33
Italy	61	39
Great Britain	67	33
Federal Republic of Germany	65	35
Luxembourg	66	34
Netherlands	62	38[c]

[a] Enrollment in classes 8 to 10 in 1955.

[b] This apparent equilibrium conceals very pronounced disparities in the various *baccalauréat* groups, for example, in science
and technology, 85 per cent of certificates are obtained by boys.

[c] Includes special secondary education for girls which, in 1960,
accounted for almost half.

and even Luxembourg, which since the postwar period have
followed a policy of making secondary studies broadly accessible, are beginning to note the consequences at the terminal class level where the enrollment figures have risen very
markedly. Developments in England in terms of "passes" are
virtually identical. The situation in Germany, Italy,[59] and
The Netherlands is relatively more stable, at any rate with
regard to pre-university secondary education.

GRADUATION BY GIRLS FROM "LONG"
SECONDARY EDUCATION

In this area, the nine countries fall into two groups: complete equality of the sexes in France, the United States, and
U.S.S.R. with even a slight advantage for girls; and enroll-

[59] Italy has not as yet benefited, in the *gymnasia* and high
schools, from the extensive increase in enrollment at middle-
school level in recent years nor, of course, from the 1962 reform.

ment of girls in the terminal secondary classes[60] still relatively restricted (see Table 18).

It will be noted that, because of these disparities in the second group of countries, the percentage of certificate holders among boys is higher than the average indicated in Table 17.[61]

THE COMPARATIVE PATTERN OF GENERAL SECONDARY STUDIES, AND THEIR "YIELD"

The various national statistics do not always make it easy to establish the pattern of studies in general secondary schools, either because of the lack of sufficiently precise data or because of the actual complexity of the school systems.

1. *In the United States and the U.S.S.R.,* where the pattern of secondary studies is in principle easiest to analyze because of the structure of the educational system, published statistics allow only very rough estimates regarding the process of selection.

In the United States,[62] of one thousand pupils enrolled in the fifth grade of primary schools in 1952, 904 were received in the ninth grade—the level of admission to secondary school under the old system—and 604 completed their secondary studies in 1960. This data would seem to indicate that a small percentage of pupils (10 per cent) leaves school on completion of the compulsory period without having entered the ninth grade. During the last three grades, the drop in school attendance was relatively large (30 per cent), and this loss may be explained by the completion of the compulsory period. However, it would seem that, since 1960, school attendance up to eighteen years of age has increased, as indicated by the percentage of certificate holders in 1963 (see Table 17).

[60] Enrollment is often more evenly balanced at first-cycle level but subsequently the enrollment of girls declines.

[61] For example, in the Federal Republic of Germany in 1963, the figure was 9.9 per cent for boys and only 6.1 per cent for girls.

[62] *Progress of Public Education in the U.S.A. 1960–1961.*

According to DeWitt's study already mentioned,[63] approximately 98 per cent of children in the U.S.S.R. who had enrolled in the first class entered the fifth class (first secondary class) in 1954–55 but some children had already lagged behind to a substantial extent[64] in the elementary classes. Because of these initial lags, and their extension into the secondary classes, only 65 to 75 per cent could therefore have completed their seventh class studies within the period of compulsory schooling. At this level, as already pointed out, the continuation of studies becomes more selective: between 42 and 50 per cent[65] only moved on to the eighth class and, in 1958, 27 per cent obtained the final certificate.[66] It should be noted that the fall in school attendance after the seventh class does not necessarily represent dropouts or failures since, as will be indicated later, it is at this level that the movement toward the secondary vocational and technical schools begins.

Since 1954–55, however, the situation has significantly changed. The "repeating" rates have been reduced, and access to the full-time terminal classes has increased still further (30 per cent of certificate holders in 1964).

2. *In the Common Market countries of Europe and in the United Kingdom,* the pattern of secondary studies remains relatively selective at all levels, notwithstanding the initial screening which takes place at the first class. However, the decline in numbers when compared with the initial classes does not necessarily mean failure or dropout but often indicates a change-over to another form of education. More particularly, following the first secondary cycle—or after the G.C.E. (Ordinary Level) in the United Kingdom, or the tenth-class examination in the Federal Republic of Germany

[63] Nicholas DeWitt, *Education and Professional Employment in the U.S.S.R.*

[64] *Ibid.,* p. 50.

[65] Including schools for young workers.

[66] The percentage passing the examination is very high—95 per cent.

TABLE 19   PROGRESS OF PUPILS WHO ENTERED THE FIFTH CLASS
IN 1952 OR 1953—FEDERAL REPUBLIC OF GERMANY

	Bavaria		Rhineland-Westphalia	
	BOYS	GIRLS	BOYS	GIRLS
5th class	100	100	100	100
8th class	76	82	93	97
9th class	67	67	83	88
10th class	62	60	75	81
11th class	46	38	61	51
13th class	39	31	49	38

SOURCE: Robert Burger, *Liegt die Höhere Schule richtig* (Freiburg [Breisgau]: K. G. Herder, 1963).

—an extensive and normal change-over to secondary technical or vocational education takes place in many European countries, as in the U.S.S.R.

For this reason, comparisons between the secondary entrance numbers and the proportion of secondary school leaving certificates awarded, and figures for "yield" calculated on this basis, are virtually pointless. The "yield" of the various cycles (or groups of classes) is better calculated separately. Several examples drawn from national statistics in the Federal Republic of Germany, France, Italy, and Great Britain follow.

In the Federal Republic of Germany, the progress of pupils who entered the fifth class (the initial class in the *Gymnasium*) in 1952 or 1953 is shown in Table 19.

The dropouts seem to be relatively few during the first four years (especially in Westphalia) but become pronounced at the ninth year (end of compulsory schooling), and still further, at the eleventh year when pupils have obtained the *Mittlere Reife* which gives them access to the social, commercial, and technical schools.[67]

[67] As pointed out earlier, the number of entrants at this level from the *Realschulen* is still insignificant.

In the thirteenth year, the rate of failures in the final examination, *Mittlere Reife*, is less than 10 per cent.

In France, while a small number of *C.E.G.* pupils (from the terminal primary classes) also enter the modern fourth class, an equivalent number of *lycée* pupils at this level go on to the *C.E.G.'s.* The record of pupils who entered classical and modern sixth classes in public *lycées* in 1953–54 is shown in Table 20.

The total "yield" of the first *lycée* cycle is 82 per cent but there is considerable change-over from classical to modern. Some more of the "loss" is accounted for by a change to the *C.E.G.'s.* Very few dropouts or changes occur among pupils in the classical section at the beginning of the second cycle, or in the modern section which, indeed, acquires substantial numbers from the *C.E.G.'s.*

The decline in numbers in the terminal classes, notwithstanding repeaters, is due to the very selective nature of the *baccalauréat* probatory examination taken by pupils in the first class[68] (the average rate of passes in this examination was 58 per cent). In the following year, the *baccalauréat* examination also represents a second and rather severe screening (rate of passes, 65 per cent).

In Italy, the record of a middle school class (first three-year cycle) showed, for the first year, 100 per cent; for the second year, 87 per cent; and for the third year, 77 per cent. The rate of passes in the final examination was between 81 and 83 per cent.

In 1958, 18 per cent of an age group (129,000 certificate holders) obtained the middle school certificate and some 16.5 per cent continued their studies thus: 7.4 per cent in high schools and normal establishments; 6.2 per cent in technical

---

[68] Until the discontinuation of the probatory examination in 1964. Following on this decision, it would seem that the number proceeding from first class to terminal class has increased (approximately 80 per cent); however, the rate of passes in the 1965 *baccalauréat* remained virtually unchanged.

schools; and 2.5 per cent in vocational schools. Dropouts on completion of middle school are relatively insignificant.

The record of the classes which entered the second secondary cycle and the technical institutes in 1953 and 1954 is shown in Table 21.

The increase in enrollment in the fifth class is explained by the number of repeaters who had failed in the terminal examination. The rate of passes in the matriculation or terminal certificate examination varies from 60 to 75 per cent.

In Great Britain, in 1962, the enrollment rate at fifteen years of age in the grammar schools was still 18.5 per cent but dropped to 8.5 per cent at seventeen years of age. This indicates that a large number of pupils left school at about sixteen years of age after having obtained the G.C.E. (Ordinary Level). This is confirmed by the decline over a two-year interval in the number of candidates for the G.C.E. O-Level and A-Level. The number of candidates for the G.C.E. O-Level in 1959 was 314,000, and the number of candidates for the G.C.E. A-Level in 1961 was 94,000. The rate of passes is 58 per cent on an average at the Ordinary Level examinations, and 68 per cent at the Advanced Level.

In conclusion, the dropout pattern in "long" secondary education (as indicated by data which is no doubt unduly fragmentary) would not seem to vary very significantly in the Western European countries. However, the terminal ex-

TABLE 20   PROGRESS OF PUPILS WHO ENTERED THE CLASSICAL AND MODERN SIXTH CLASSES IN PUBLIC LYCÉES IN 1953–54—FRANCE

	Classical Section	Modern Section	Total
6th class	100	100	100
3rd class	61	104	82
2nd class	56	123	90
1st class	61	121	91
Terminal classes	—	—	75

amination is much more selective in England and France, and even in Italy, than in the other countries.[69]

It may also be noted that the fall in general secondary enrollment at the beginning of the second *lycée* cycle is more marked in Germany, England, and even Italy, than in France.

This disparity may be explained by the fact that recruitment for commercial and industrial courses in the technical *lycées* draws to a greater extent on the general *collèges* than on the first cycle of the classic and modern *lycées*.

REGIONAL AND SOCIAL VARIATIONS IN ATTENDANCE AT SECONDARY SCHOOLS

The enrollment figures presented above for each of the nine countries in this survey represent national averages. They also reveal the differences which may exist in secondary school attendance by girls and boys. Still more marked dis-

TABLE 21　PROGRESS OF CLASSES WHICH ENTERED THE SECOND SECONDARY CYCLE AND TECHNICAL INSTITUTES IN 1953 AND 1954—ITALY

	Gymnasia and Classical High Schools	Scientific High Schools	Normal Institutes	Technical Institutes (Industrial)
1st class	100	100	100	100
2nd class	86	92	94	91
3rd class	83	89	83	76
4th class	72	77	90	—
5th class	75[a]	85	—	74

[a] Increase in this class is due to repeating caused by failures in final examination.

[69] Enrollment is much higher than the number who obtain the school leaving certificate in any particular year. In France, for example, in 1954, nearly 120,000 pupils were enrolled in the public and private secondary terminal classes (17 per cent of the seventeen- and eighteen-year age groups); only 86,000, including outside candidates, passed the *baccalauréat* (12.3 per cent of the age groups).

parities are revealed if school attendance is examined in reference to regional variations and to variations in social background.

These are major practical problems in determining educational policy and have been the subject of increasingly detailed study in all Western European countries. It will not be possible here to deal with all the results, but certain examples may be used to indicate the extent of these variations and to analyze briefly the causes.

REGIONAL DIFFERENCES IN EXTENSION OF SECONDARY EDUCATION: THEIR IMPORTANCE AND CAUSES

Regional variations in enrollment rates may be examined either in the context of various administrative districts (departments, districts, provinces, federated states, and the like) or on the basis of different types of residential centers (urban, rural). Published studies have used either one or the other.

No effort will be made here to compare the results from country to country. The size of the administrative districts involved varies according to these studies, and the more limited the framework the greater the likelihood of disparities. Conversely, statistics relating to large administrative units already constitute averages between the extreme divergences which are no longer evident. A cautious approach must also be adopted in regard to the comparability of statistics covering urban and rural zones, since their definition is rarely homogeneous.

THE IMPORTANCE OF REGIONAL VARIATIONS

1. *In Federal Germany,* the percentage of enrollment of pupils at thirteen years of age in general secondary establishments (*Realschulen* and *Gymnasien*) may vary almost 100 per cent (from 18.6 to 34.8 per cent). However, in 1963 these regional variations related essentially to the *Realschulen* (from 4.3 to 23 per cent), the figures for the *Gym-*

nasien being more homogeneous (from 12.2 to 16.6 per cent),[70] as shown in Table 22.

2. *In Belgium,* in 1961, secondary education was generally more developed in the French-speaking provinces and Brabant than in the Flemish provinces. The extremes were Brabant with an enrollment of 20.6 per cent for the age group from ten to twenty years, and Luxembourg with an enrollment of 9.7 per cent for the same age group.

3. *In France,* regional variations are analyzed on the basis of the more limited *départements,* and so are very much more pronounced. The transition rates to the sixth class[71] vary by as high a proportion as one to three (1961–62): Seine, 72.6 per cent; Var, 62.2 per cent; Corsica, 60.7 per cent; Loir-et-Cher, 23 per cent; and Mayenne, 22 per cent.

4. *In The Netherlands,* the divergences from province to province are of the same order of magnitude[72] as in Belgium.

TABLE 22   REGIONAL VARIATIONS IN ENROLLMENT OF THIRTEEN-YEAR-OLDS IN SECONDARY SCHOOLS, 1963—FEDERAL REPUBLIC OF GERMANY

	Type of Secondary School		
States	REALSCHULEN	GYMNASIEN	TOTAL
Schleswig-Holstein	22.6	12.2	34.8
Bremen	18.2	16.6	34.8
Bavaria	11.7	14.0	25.7
Rhineland Palatinate	4.3	15.4	19.7
Saar	5.1	13.5	18.6

[70] These percentages apply to very large administrative units and already represent averages.

[71] Ratio between the enrollment in the second-year intermediate and in the sixth class of the following year.

[72] In 1950, the average enrollment in "long" secondary education for the age group from twelve to seventeen years varied for boys from 9.5 per cent in Drenthe to 18.2 per cent in Utrecht, and for girls from 5.8 per cent in Drenthe to 13.7 per cent in North Holland.

Within the provinces, enrollment varies to a very marked extent, depending on the location. The distribution of one hundred pupils (boys and girls) leaving primary school in 1962 is shown in Table 23 by type of residential location.

The movement to upper primary schools *(U.L.O.)* varies relatively little, while entrance to secondary studies varies greatly with the type of commune: 2.3 for boys and from 1 to 3.6 for girls.

5. *In the U.S.S.R.,* the problem of regional variations in secondary school enrollment arises in different terms since admission to the first secondary cycle (classes 5 to 8 since the 1958 reform) comes within the framework of compulsory education. Variations can therefore arise only in the three terminal classes.

In the absence of details for enrollment rates by class and by region, these variations may be evaluated by a comparison, in the fifteen republics of the Soviet Union, between the proportion of pupils enrolled in the last three classes and the total enrollment in primary and secondary classes;[73] and by a

TABLE 23 DISTRIBUTION OF ONE HUNDRED PUPILS LEAVING PRIMARY SCHOOL IN 1962, BY TYPE OF RESIDENTIAL AREA—THE NETHERLANDS

Type of Residential Area	*Upper Primary Schools*		*Secondary Schools*	
	BOYS	GIRLS	BOYS	GIRLS
Commercial and administrative towns	33.2	36.7	22.5	19.2
Industrial towns	30.7	33.5	19.6	15.0
Slightly industrialized communes	30.4	32.9	13.4	9.1
Rural communes	28.5	31.6	9.7	5.9

[73] This comparison gives a reasonably valid picture of development for the terminal cycle if the reasonable assumption is made that variations in birth rate for the age groups concerned are roughly similar from one republic to another.

comparison between the proportion of children in rural zones enrolled in terminal classes and the proportion of rural population in the total population of the U.S.S.R.

According to DeWitt's study already quoted,[74] the average proportion in 1955 of pupils in classes 8, 9, and 10, as compared to the total enrollment in classes 1 to 10, was 18.7 per cent for the U.S.S.R. as a whole. In nine republics, this proportion was within 1 or 2 per cent of the general average, while in four others it was significantly lower (12 or 14 per cent) and in one (Georgia) it was substantially higher (27 per cent).

With regard to the divergence between urban and rural, it should be noted that 43 per cent of those enrolled in the terminal secondary classes are in rural zones, and that the rural population accounts for 48 per cent of the total U.S.S.R. population. The divergence is therefore very limited and would seem to indicate a reasonably homogeneous development of complete secondary education in town and in country. Given the higher birth rate in the country,[75] the real divergence is certainly much more marked than would appear from the above comparison. This is all the more certain since, at that time, priority had been given to the development of the complete ten-year school in the towns (Resolution of the XIXth Congress of the Communist Party, 1952).

All in all, it is difficult on the basis of the above information to obtain a very accurate picture of the situation in the U.S.S.R. There would, however, seem to be a tendency toward a homogeneity of terminal secondary education throughout the Soviet Union to a much greater extent than in Western Europe.

6. *In the United States,* variations in school attendance between urban and rural populations at the level of the secondary terminal classes would seem to be extremely limited. The enrollment rate at sixteen and seventeen years of age is

[74] DeWitt, *op. cit.,* p. 145.
[75] This seems to be established by the fact that 57 per cent of those enrolled in the four elementary classes attend rural schools.

78 per cent for the urban population, 78 per cent for the rural nonagricultural population, and 73 per cent for the agricultural population.

THE CAUSES OF REGIONAL VARIATIONS

Regional divergences in secondary enrollment derive from a complex set of factors which affect the educational supply and demand alike. In other words, the enrollment is higher when the school network is more developed and, where noncompulsory education is concerned, when families are more anxious to send their children to school.

1. *Variations in the supply: the obstacle arising from the dispersal of populations*   The extent of secondary education is obviously related to the facilities available. In the nine countries covered by this survey, the authorities responsible for deciding on the location of secondary schools are politically and morally obliged to observe a certain equality between the administrative districts.

However, this concern with equality encounters a material obstacle which varies in importance from region to region: the dispersal of the population. In the underpopulated rural zones it is difficult to place secondary schools[76] within immediate reach of all the families concerned. Accordingly, in all the countries, the rural populations enjoy fewer facilities than the urban populations, and attendance at secondary school implies that the children must make a more or less long journey each day or become boarders. This difficulty, added to the other factors referred to below, is undoubtedly one cause of the disparities between town and country. To overcome this, the educational service in the strict sense of the term must be supplemented by a series of ancillary services (school canteens, boarding facilities, special transport, and so on) which are already extensively developed in certain countries, especially in the United States.

[76] Unlike primary schools, these cannot be organized in very small units.

Apart from the limitations imposed by this inevitable "geographic" factor, however, it may be asked whether the secondary educational supply is genuinely an independent variant under the free control of the public authorities or whether, on the contrary, it is not tending in all countries to reflect, more or less rapidly and automatically,[77] the educational demand of the populations themselves. If so, the primary cause of regional variations must lie in the different attitudes of populations toward secondary education.

2. *Variations in the demand: the special importance of the social background factor*   The conclusions of surveys in the various European countries are in full agreement: Within a given locality or even within a given region, that is, in identical conditions as far as the proximity of the secondary school is concerned, the attitude of families in the different social groups varies fundamentally; some systematically send their children to secondary school and others only occasionally.

What factors determine these variations in family attitudes? All research done in this area suggests *socioeconomic and psychological explanations*. The degree of secondary school attendance is directly related to a series of factors, the most important of which would seem to be occupations of the parents or their social background; family income; size of the family; religion and race;[78] language;[79] regional cultural traditions, and so on.

The dominant factor, which partly overlaps the income factor, is the child's social background. A study of the facts reveals that the geographic factor itself (distance from school) varies greatly in importance according to whether the parents do or do not have a strong wish, and the means,

---

[77] This would depend on the political systems and also on the more or less restrictive educational traditions.

[78] Within a given occupational environment statistics reveal significant differences in secondary school attendance depending on the religion and race of the parents.

[79] As in the case of Belgium.

to enroll their children in a secondary school; as far as the peasant populations are concerned, it is frequently no more than an additional difficulty along with other reasons for nonenrollment.

The importance of the consequences of social background in secondary education, and possible explanations, will now be considered.

SECONDARY EDUCATION AND SOCIAL BACKGROUND

THE RANGE OF DISPARITIES IN OPPORTUNITIES FOR ACCESS TO SECONDARY STUDIES ACCORDING TO SOCIAL CATEGORY

National statistics on opportunities for admission to general secondary education according to social background are not presented in all countries on the basis of the same occupational classifications. This gives rise to difficulties in establishing accurate comparisons between countries, but nonetheless these remain highly significant.

TABLE 24   DISTRIBUTION, IN PERCENTAGE, OF CHILDREN ADMITTED TO GRAMMAR SCHOOLS, BY SOCIAL BACKGROUND—ENGLAND

Occupation of Father	County	
	S.W. HERTFORDSHIRE	MIDDLESBROUGH
Professional workers, business owners, managers	59	68
Clerical workers	44	37
Foremen, small shopkeepers, etc.	30	24
Skilled manual workers	18	14
Unskilled manual workers	9	9
Average	22	17

SOURCE: Floud, Halsey, and Martin, *Social Class and Educational Opportunity* (London, 1957).

In Western Europe

The conclusions of surveys carried out in certain countries are embodied in Tables 24, 25, and 26.

The information embodied in Table 25 is supplemented by that in Table 50, which gives the percentage breakdown for 1961–62 of pupils attending various secondary institutions on the basis of parents' occupations, together with an indication of the proportion of the total working population in 1962 represented by each occupational group.

Several key points are revealed by these tables:

In all three countries, the percentage of admission to "long" secondary education is very high (65 to 85 per cent) in the "upper" social categories (liberal professions, senior office staff, industrialists, and the like); they gradually decrease in the "medium" categories, and reach the lowest level with farmers, industrial workers, and, especially, agricultural workers (2.5 to 11 per cent).

The divergence in the opportunities for admission to secondary schooling therefore varies, within the limits of the comparability of the occupational classifications employed, from 1 to 7 for England and France[80] and from 1 to 21 (boys) and 1 to 80 (girls) in The Netherlands.[81]

These pronounced disparities between the occupational groups imply that to a very large extent it is the structure of the working population which primarily governs the average rate of school attendance in a given geographical area.

In spite of the relatively low entrance rate for children of the working class, it will be noted that, in the secondary schools, these children, because of the numerical importance

---

[80] In France, this is solely on the basis of *lycées;* the divergence would be less marked (1 to 3) if allowance were made for access to the *C.E.G.'s* which, as already noted, offer extensive access to the second secondary cycle.

[81] Recruitment for the *U.L.O.* schools (upper primary schools) draws on the "lower" social strata to a much greater extent. This is confirmed in France by the percentages given in Table 25, and in Table 50 for the *C.E.G.'s.*

TABLE 25   Distribution, in Percentage, of Children Admitted (1962) to the Sixth Class,[a] by Social Background—France

Profession of Parents	C.E.G.	Lycées	Total
Senior cadres	19	75	94
Liberal professions	18	75	93
Industrialists, wholesalers	28	57	85
Medium-grade cadres	29	55	84
Office employees	34	33	67
Craftsmen and small shopkeepers	34	32	66
Industrial workers	29	16	45
Farm owners	24	16	40
Agricultural workers	21	11	32
Average	28	27	55

SOURCE: A. Girard, *Revue Population,* Nos. 1 and 3, 1963.

[a] Public and private education. The rates are calculated on the basis of a comparison between enrollment in the preceding primary class and number of entrants in the following sixth school year.

of the social groups involved, nevertheless account for a substantial proportion of secondary school enrollment.

The question nonetheless arises of determining whether the attitude of the various occupational categories is the same in all regions. Table 24 shows the rates of access to grammar schools in two counties which differ greatly in social structure, and offers a partial answer to this question: the rates of school attendance among the middle and working classes in Middlesbrough (a typically industrial county) are distinctly lower (20 to 15 per cent) than those in southwest Hertfordshire (complex economic structure).

In France, a comparative study of sixth-class entrance rates (*C.E.G.'s* and *lycées*) among children of workers and farmers in several *départements* revealed broad similarities in the attitude of these social groups but at the same time showed significant regional variations amounting to between

TABLE 26   Distribution, in Percentage, of Twelve-year-olds Admitted in 1960 to First Year of "Long" Secondary Education, by Father's Occupation—The Netherlands

Occupation of Father	Rate of Admission		
	BOYS	GIRLS	GIRLS COMPARED WITH BOYS[a]
Liberal professions	85	80	94
Senior office staff	85	79	93
Medium office staff	68	56	82
Junior office staff	20	12	60
School teachers	59	52	88
Heads of firms employing staff	23	20	87
Heads of firms without staff	9	5	56
Farmers with workers	15	10	67
Farmers without workers	4	2	50
Nonagricultural workers	5	2	40
Agricultural workers	4	1	25

SOURCE: OECD, Document D.A.S.-E.I.P., 63–22.

[a] It will be noted that the inequality in enrollment between girls and boys in The Netherlands tends to diminish in the upper social strata.

20 and 30 per cent on either side of the average. The influence of these variations on regional enrollment rates is certainly far from insignificant because of the numerical importance of the social groups involved.

These divergences can be explained by a whole complex of specific factors,[82] among which are the size or inadequacy of the supply in certain regions; regional variations in the living standards of the various social groups; and specific motivations among the populations of certain regions.[83]

[82] For England, see Floud, Halsey, and Martin, *op. cit.*

[83] The absence of industrial outlets in certain regions encourages "long" secondary education in preparation for careers in public administration; this is especially the case in the *départements* in southern France.

The percentage of enrollment among children of agricultural workers and industrial workers is much lower in The Netherlands (or in the Federal Republic of Germany) than in England or France.

This is obviously related to the low percentage of admissions to "long" secondary studies which may be observed in The Netherlands (see Table 16). The result is that the very selective requirements for admission do not reduce the opportunities of children from the higher social strata, nor even those from the middle classes, but do reduce the opportunities of children from the working class.[84]

The very different rates observed in The Netherlands for farmers with workers or farmers without workers, even though these families are living in the same geographical environment, confirm what has already been said about the relative influence of the distance factor.

In the United States and the Soviet Union

The situation takes a very different form because of the structure of the educational system and the fact that there is a much higher proportion than in Europe of young people between seventeen and eighteen years of age who complete the full secondary course (70 per cent in the United States, 30 per cent in the U.S.S.R.). The result is that the divergences in the enrollment figures for different occupational categories are certainly much less than in Europe, although by no means nonexistent.

In the United States, the data given later in this study concerning opportunities for access to higher education reflect a more egalitarian system (as compared to Europe) and marked disparities which still distinguish social groups.

As for the U.S.S.R., no study has apparently been published on the social variations in enrollment for the terminal

---

[84] This same observation may be made in the light of statistics for the county of Middlesbrough and the Federal Republic of Germany (not given here).

secondary classes. This will be discussed later when opportunities for access to higher education are examined.

THE CAUSES OF SOCIAL DIFFERENTIATIONS IN SECONDARY EDUCATION, AND RECENT TRENDS

1. *The historical link between the structure of general secondary education and the social hierarchy*   Access to "long" secondary studies in all the Western European countries has really been restricted since the beginning of the nineteenth century to children of the upper or middle classes. These children entered secondary colleges as paying pupils without any special preliminary intellectual selection and, through the classical education derived from the Renaissance colleges, received the type of culture which was characteristic of the bourgeois social strata. Only a handful of brilliant working-class children, intended for teaching or ecclesiastical careers, entered these institutions.

Under the pressure of economic and social developments, "short" secondary education (*Realschulen,* upper primary schools, and the like),[85] designed to turn out office workers and medium-grade executives, gradually developed during the nineteenth century. This was basically for the benefit of the lower middle classes (small shopkeepers, craftsmen, medium-grade officials, and so on) or even for the more advanced working-class or peasant sectors.

At the same time, special secondary schools (known as normal schools) were organized for training primary school teachers and drew their students from the same circles.

The aspirations of the bulk of peasant and working-class children scarcely went beyond primary school which, in Western Europe, was not even compulsory everywhere at the end of the century.

Following World War I, however, and as a result of the progress of democracy, these *de facto* inequalities were gradually denounced in all countries. The adaptation of second-

[85] Secondary schools for girls which did not prepare for the universities were also provided in most countries.

ary education to economic and social developments and its democratization became one of the major themes of government social policy, and recent European constitutions assert the necessity for giving real guarantees of "equal access for all children to education and culture" whatever "their social origin" or "their place of residence."

In all countries, these principles led to a body of measures whose origin frequently goes back to the period between the two world wars.

2. *Efforts to democratize secondary education, and recent results in Europe* The efforts made by the national authorities had several aims: provision of a broader pattern for pre-university secondary school curricula by organizing modern courses[86] along with the classical Greek-Latin courses; a campaign against economic obstacles to secondary education (free education, additional scholarships, and so on); adjustment of the transition from primary to secondary school, replacing the social (or wealth) selection by as rational and objective an intellectual selection as possible;[87] facilities for transitions between general "short" education and pre-university education; and assimilation of special education for girls and normal school education[88] with general secondary education.

As already stated, the United States (followed by the U.S.S.R. since 1949), adopted a system which makes access to the early secondary classes general within the limits of compulsory education and, at any rate at the level of these classes, does away with social distinctions providing opportunities for admission.

These measures have been speeded up by continued economic progress in the meantime. The results themselves have been amplified by the growing rise in standards of living; they

[86] The syllabuses in the first classes were more or less closely interrelated with those of the "short" courses.

[87] The ways in which this selection is made, however, are still diverse—a fact which indicates the difficulty of the problem.

[88] For the additional general education study years.

are seen, on a total basis, in the percentage of increase by educational level shown in Table 11 and in the rise in the proportion of secondary certificate holders (Table 17).

From the point of view which is of concern here, it is important to make a more precise analysis in order to establish how the attitude of different social groups toward general secondary schooling has been modified. The studies published in the different countries frequently provide only partial answers to this question, although these are nonetheless extremely significant. Data for Great Britain, The Netherlands, and France are given below.

These three tables reveal that in the upper social categories, the growth of enrollment has been relatively limited due to the fact that very high rates, bordering on the maximum, were already established at the beginning of the period; enrollment rates have developed rapidly in the middle classes, whose attitude, as far as certain groups are concerned, is coming to resemble very closely that of the upper-level categories; and the extension of secondary education has been even more marked among manual workers (workers and peasants); however, in these sectors, progress was made easier by the fact that the numbers were so low at the beginning. By and large, these different rates of growth reveal a long-term trend toward equality, but it may be asked whether they will necessarily continue.

In actual fact, in certain countries (Britain, France, Bel-

TABLE 27   PERCENTAGE OF ELEVEN-YEAR-OLDS ADMITTED TO GRAMMAR SCHOOLS AND PRIVATE SECONDARY SCHOOLS, BY SOCIAL BACKGROUND—ENGLAND AND WALES

	1931–1940	1946–1951	Variations
Nonmanual workers	38.9	48.5	+24
Manual workers	9.8	14.5	+49

SOURCE: OECD, *Aptitude Intellectuelle et Education*, p. 103.

gium, Italy), the growth in enrollment rates would seem to be continuous, although at different "rhythms"; conversely, recent statistics for the Federal Republic of Germany and The Netherlands show a stabilization of the rate of entrance into "long" secondary schools which can only indicate a halt in the expansion of school attendance among the middle and working classes.

In any event, notwithstanding the very significant changes in enrollment rates since the end of World War II, the characteristics of secondary education still remain substantially different according to the social background of the children concerned. The causes underlying these differences, or at any rate some of them, come immediately to mind. It is desirable to note these and, especially so in order to state the problem in the right terms, to try to establish their respective importance.

3. *The complexity of the problem of democratizing education* The causes underlying the social differences in

TABLE 28   PERCENTAGE OF TWELVE-YEAR-OLDS ENROLLED IN "LONG" SECONDARY SCHOOLS, BY SOCIAL BACKGROUND —THE NETHERLANDS

| | *Social Category* | | | |
	UPPER	MIDDLE	WORKERS	*Average*
BOYS				
1942	45	14	4	10
1949	50	15	4	11
1960	67	25	7	17
Variations, 1949–1960	+35	+66	+ 75	+54
GIRLS				
1942	36	7	2	6
1949	45	9	2	7
1960	63	10	4	13
Variations, 1949–1960	+40	+43	+100	+85

SOURCE: OECD, Document D.A.S.-E.I.P., 63–22.

TABLE 29   Distribution, in Percentage, of Enrollment in Sixth Class,[a] 1954 and 1962, by Social Background—France

Occupation of Parents	1954[b] Total	1962[c] Total	Variations
Senior executives	84	94	+ 11
Liberal professions	87	93	+ 7
Industrialists and wholesalers	68	85	+ 26
Medium-grade executives	47	84	+ 78
Office workers	43	67	+ 55
Craftsmen and small shopkeepers	39	66	+ 69
Industrial workers	21	45	+114
Farm owners	16	40	+150
Agricultural workers	13	32	+146
Average	29	55	+ 89

[a] Public institutions and equivalent private institutions.

[b] The whole of France, less the Département of the Seine, whose omission reduces the percentages for the senior executives and liberal professions in 1954.

[c] All France.

opportunities for access to and success in pre-university secondary studies may be roughly classified in three main groups: economic causes (family income); psychosociological causes (different cultural and occupational motivations); and educational reasons (influence of the family from the point of view of developing children's aptitudes and adaptability to secondary education). This classification, while of value to our study, must not be allowed to conceal the close interrelations between the three groups of factors.

The standard-of-living factor   All the statistics reveal a close correlation between the extent of family income and secondary enrollment rates. The handicap of inadequate income, even allowing for the fact that schools are free and scholarships are available, weighs heavily on working-class families. This handicap, moreover, is frequently aggravated within the same social environments by the size of the family.[89] In addition to the cost of schooling in the strict sense of the term (never nonexistent, in spite of social assistance), there is the prospect of an absence of earnings, and working-class families frequently count on contributions from the earnings of the older children.

This problem of income level ties in with all the problems of material facilities which play an important part in school work, particularly in the home.

It would appear, however, that, once a certain "threshold" of income has been reached, the economic situation ceases to be an absolute barrier to "long" secondary education and, because of the rise in living standards, this threshold is reached in all countries by a growing number of working-class families.

In any case, such families are all the more reluctant to enroll their children in secondary schools because the possible results are remote and uncertain.[90] After seven, eight, or nine years of schooling, the certificate awarded does not necessarily give access to employment and often implies still further study. For this reason, working-class families prefer types of secondary study[91] which guarantee a quicker, even if a more modest, result and a salaried position. They will only take the risk of enrolling in "long" secondary schools those children whose excellent marks in primary school seem to ensure success (see Table 31).

The range of cultural and occupational motivations Traditionally, middle-class families enroll virtually all their children in "long" secondary education. This is a well-established cultural tradition, but is equally related to career pros-

[89] Working-class and peasant families frequently have more than the average number of children.

[90] For the same reason, primary school teachers hesitate to advise them to undertake the long general courses.

[91] The French *C.E.G.'s,* which serve as a "turntable" between the second secondary cycle and the vocational and technical schools, are favored by working-class families for this reason.

pects. It is through secondary studies that children from families representing the liberal professions and the upper levels of the civil service, trade, industry, the university, can prepare to take up these careers in their turn.

The same cultural traditions do not exist—understandably —in the working classes. In this environment, in fact, this type of culture is not necessarily desired: for the upper classes, secondary studies tend to make children more like their parents; for workers and peasants, such education tends to make children different from their parents.[92]

Similarly, the ambitions of working-class families regarding the occupational future of their children differ. Most of them are very eager that their children should enjoy social advancement but this is sought in the environment with which they are familiar through vocational and technical training (industrial, commercial, agricultural) or in sectors which are outside their own but which are nonetheless accessible and familiar (positions as office workers, junior- and medium-grade officials). It is obviously very difficult for the mass of peasants and workers to want their children to have careers with which the parents are ill-acquanted. To a certain extent, it may be said that such limited ambitions merely reflect a realistic appraisal of the family's economic possibilities and that everything seems to come back to the standard-of-living factor.

Without underestimating the interdependence of family ambitions and their economic possibilities, it may be noted that, with the same income, motivations may be fundamentally different and that, to a certain extent, family ambitions are psychologically based and independent of income.

In social categories of the office worker and junior official types whose standard of living is not really higher than that of the workers and peasants but who are better informed and more familiar with intellectual activities—and better equipped

---

[92] The importance of this should not be overestimated in modern societies, where it is increasingly tending to diminish.

to give their children within the family that educational assistance whose importance is stressed later in this study—ambitions are higher and the children are already enrolling on a very large scale in the secondary schools (see Tables 24, 25 and 26).

This explains the inevitable phenomenon of the "stage" with which all sociologists are familiar: a peasant's or worker's son may become a school teacher and the son of a school teacher may become a doctor, a lawyer, an engineer.[93] It merely confirms the importance of lack of information and lack of social accessibility in limiting the ambitions of working-class families.

However, these psychosociological limiting factors are no more final than the economic factors. On the contrary, they seem to be steadily declining in importance with the extension of information media which break through a certain isolation hitherto surrounding the lower classes, with the lessened rigidity of former social stratification, and, especially, with the increasing awareness of the working classes that their children are entitled to have the same opportunities in the future as any others.

This social and psychological evolution is, of course, not taking place at the same rate in all European countries (see Tables 27, 28 and 29).

Educational success and the anti-educational influence of the family and social environment It has already been noted that, even at the elementary school level, children from the working classes on the average achieve less satisfactory results than others and reveal more retardation. This naturally raises the question of whether, by way of correlation, the better results obtained by children from intellectually more evolved social strata do not, on the average, reflect differences in the level of intelligence.

---

[93] When considered in relation to the occupation of grandparents, the democratization of education is seen to be much more satisfactory.

None of the studies undertaken in the various countries suggests that there are any significant differences in the natural or innate intelligence level of children from different social groups. It would therefore not seem that the social variations in educational success represent genetic differences.

On the other hand, it is certain that children's innate aptitudes find considerable opportunities for development in the family and social environment, independently of the school. In the more intellectually advanced environments, this educational influence exercised by the family operates particularly along the lines desired or required by the school itself; in other environments, it is much less marked, nonexistent, or differently oriented. The facts indicate that the teacher's influence is more effective if the child's aptitudes have already received a certain development in the family environment before he reaches school or if he continues permanently to receive such assistance.

These differences in the family's educational influence, and hence in the possibilities for developing children's aptitudes, thus have a direct effect on success at school. Girard's study, referred to earlier, tends to indicate that the percentage of

TABLE 30   RESULTS, IN PERCENTAGE, IN SECOND-YEAR INTERMEDIATE,[a] BY FAMILY ENVIRONMENT—FRANCE

Occupation of Parents	Excellent	Good	Average	Poor	Bad
Senior cadres	19	36	29	13	3
Liberal professions	15	35	34	13	3
Medium cadres	17	39	27	12	5
Farmers	8	28	33	21	10
Workers	5	23	34	25	13
Average	8	27	33	22	10

SOURCE: Girard, *op. cit., Revue Population,* No. 3, 1963, p. 438.
[a] Evaluated solely on the basis of marks awarded by teachers in this class.

TABLE 31   Enrollment in Sixth Class (Lycée and C.E.G.), by Social Background and School Results[a]—France

Occupation of Parents	Excellent	Good	Average	Poor	Bad
Liberal professions	97	97	90	59	10
Senior cadres	100	98	92	72	50
Farmers	76	64	32	9	5
Workers	91	79	42	10	3

SOURCE: Girard, *op. cit., Revue Population,* No. 3, 1963. This table clearly reveals that the "intellectual" selection in France for entrance to the sixth class is much more severe among the working class than in the higher social strata.

[a] Results attested by marks in second-year intermediate.

passes at the end of elementary school is significantly higher among the upper or middle classes than in the working class but, in actual fact, the extreme social variations in the percentages of good or very good pupils, however significant, are only in the order of 1 to 2.

The social disparities in school success are much more pronounced (rate of success varying from 1 to 5) in results of the eleven-plus examination recorded in the work by Floud, Halsey, and Martin, already referred to, but the yardstick is not the same. At most it may be concluded in the light of these two studies that the more selective the examination—especially at eleven or twelve years of age—the heavier the social handicap seems to be.

It will be noted that the social differences in school success are aggravated by the particular circumspection shown by lower-class families in enrolling their children in secondary schools. Girard's study clearly demonstrates that in working-class circles, it is virtually only those children with excellent or good marks who enter the sixth class, whereas children from the upper classes enter the sixth class even if their results at primary school are poor or even bad.

TABLE 32 PROGRESS, IN PERCENTAGE, OF A GROUP ENTERING SIXTH CLASS IN CLASSICAL AND MODERN LYCÉES, BY SOCIAL BACKGROUND—FRANCE

	Farmers	Industrial Workers	Medium Cadres	Liberal Professions and Senior Cadres
6th class	100	100	100	100
3rd class	72	59	85	92
1st class	35	21	55	86[a]

SOURCE: Based on information supplied by the statistical information service of the Ministry of National Education.

[a] These percentages are corroborated by a study carried out under the direction of Professor Jean Fourastié (Conservatoire des Arts et Métiers, Laboratoire d'Économétrie, Paris, 1965) covering two groups from the Ecole Polytechnique and the Ecole Centrale de Paris: 80 per cent of the boys and 60 per cent of the girls from these families obtained the *baccalauréat*.

But the family influence on school success is not restricted to the elementary level and, indeed, is more marked throughout secondary education.

Table 32 confirms this for France; all the other European studies lead to the same conclusion.[94]

Whatever prudence may be exercised in interpreting Table 32,[95] it clearly reveals that the dropouts are limited in the upper social categories and reach a maximum among the children of workers and farmers. The same may be observed in the statistics of all the European countries.

This difference in the rate of success during secondary studies cannot be explained by differences in the children's

[94] For England, see the work, already mentioned, by Floud, Halsey, and Martin.

[95] A proportion of the apparent "loss" represents, more especially among children of workers and farmers, a change-over to technical education which cannot be regarded as necessarily equivalent to failure.

level of intelligence. On the contrary, it is in those social groups where the rate of enrollment in *lycées* is highest (65 to 85 per cent), that is, where the school-going population seems to be subject to the least effective intellectual selection (see Table 31), that the failures are rarest.[96] Conversely, working-class children, in spite of a lower enrollment rate—which implies a more severe selection (see Table 31)—have a high rate of dropout.

These observations illustrate the decisive influence of the family on school success at this level. Some pupils are continually encouraged and supported by their families along the exact lines which the teachers wish to be followed; others—and this applies to the overwhelming majority of children from the lower strata—do not benefit from the same family assistance and, indeed, are frequently disoriented by the nature of educational demands and by the gap between the culture which is proposed and that of their social environment.

Although it should not be overdramatized—after all, thousands of working-class children in all countries complete their secondary schooling in the normal way and go on to higher education—the problem is one of undeniable gravity. How is the secondary school to adapt to its new influx of pupils? How can it offset or limit the influence of family and social factors?

[96] The fact that the children of these social groups, a high proportion of whom (65 to 85 per cent) take "long" secondary courses without any real intellectual selection, can subsequently obtain such a high rate of success scarcely allows us to conclude, as is sometimes attempted, that there is a natural limitation on the possibilities of success in secondary education.

2. The Organization and Stage of Development of Secondary Vocational and Technical Education and Higher Education

THE GROWING IMPORTANCE OF VOCATIONAL AND TECHNICAL TRAINING SCHOOLS AT ALL LEVELS

Traditionally, the training provided in all Western European countries by general secondary institutions is not aimed at specific occupations. The object is to develop one's general culture and produce the "educated man," that is, one who has acquired as complete a mastery as possible of his mother tongue, a more or less complete mastery of one or more foreign languages, a more or less limited knowledge of "mathematical tools," a sufficiently broad receptivity in regard to human societies past and present and the physical world, and who has thereby learned to reason.

This culture, which incidentally is an end in itself, will in most cases—especially in the case of boys—provide the basis for more specialized studies in preparation for a given occupation.

At the other extreme, the primary task of higher education today is to train senior cadres and highly skilled specialists of all kinds. Originally, no doubt, the universities were more concerned with speculation and, in certain countries, are inclined to prefer that their courses remain purely scientific. In fact, however, present-day university curricula, established as a preparation for official degrees, always combine higher intellectual training—a more complete degree of pure knowledge in certain sciences—with a direct or indirect preparation for employment in a more or less clearly defined occupational area.

At other employment levels, industrial, agricultural, commercial, and trade enterprises have long provided specialized on-the-job training for their staffs based on the general training provided by the schools. In this connection, it should be noted that the certificates awarded on completion of "short" or "long" secondary education are not without value as regards direct access to employment. To an increasing extent, they represent an adequate qualification for many jobs in the tertiary sector (public services, banks, insurance, commercial enterprises, and the like) where vocational training is gradually acquired by the actual practice of the work concerned. Independently of this trend, however, the evolution of trades and production techniques since the end of the nineteenth century has increasingly led to the training of skilled workers and of office employees and medium-grade cadres being entrusted to the schools. A rapid advance is being made in the educational systems of all countries by vocational schools (training workers and office staff) and technical schools (training medium-level cadres). This has been intensified since the end of World War II (see Table 11 and Appendix, Tables A-1–A-9).

The structure and educational organization of these establishments is much more complex than in general educational institutions. This complexity results from various factors: the purpose of the courses, which must be adapted to a wide range of economic activities; in most countries, the range of ministries involved as organizers: Education, Agriculture, Health, Industry, Transport, Labour, Defence, and so on; and the sharing of responsibility between the enterprise and the school for certain types of training (as in part-time school courses). The role now assumed by enterprises, especially in worker training, still varies greatly from one country to another.

At all levels of vocational training, the intensified development of science and technology, the necessity for occupational mobility, the new demands of democracy, raise new problems of vocational upgrading, refresher courses, and labor advancement for staff already employed. To a large extent, these problems can only be solved by providing training in existing schools and universities or establishing specialized institutions.

For these reasons it is impossible to deal here with the detailed organization of such education in the nine countries. The major principles and features will be discussed.

In considering all the educational establishments which play a role in vocational and technical training, it is customary to draw a distinction between secondary vocational and technical education and higher education.

LACK OF ANY CLEAR DISTINCTION BETWEEN SECONDARY VOCATIONAL AND TECHNICAL EDUCATION AND HIGHER EDUCATION

The boundary between higher education and vocational or technical education is not clearly and decisively marked in any country, and varies from one country to another.

If the Unesco classification is adopted, higher education consists of all those courses which, after the age of eighteen or nineteen, follow complete secondary education, that is, depending on the country concerned, which follow on eleven, twelve, or thirteen years of elementary and secondary education. Indeed, the organization of education and the administrative classifications make it very difficult to apply this rule. Two main examples[1] are:

TRAINING FOR INDUSTRIAL LABOR

The secondary vocational and technical schools organize a whole range of training for specialized and skilled workers, technical assistants and technicians, and higher technicians (or technical engineers). The first levels of training are generally intended for pupils who have not completed full secondary courses; education comes to an end at eighteen or nineteen years of age, that is, at the terminal secondary classes.

On the other hand, the training of senior technicians (or technical engineers) continues for one, two, or three years beyond that age, and is given more and more frequently to pupils who hold secondary school leaving certificates.

Accepting the Unesco classification, this level of technical study corresponds to higher education and in certain countries (United States, Belgium) courses of this kind are organized in institutions which are administratively classified (from the point of statistics also) as higher educational institutions. In the other countries, they are organized in secondary institutions of the technical *lycée* type and are so shown in the statistics.

TEACHER TRAINING

In most of the Common Market countries (Belgium, France, Italy, Luxembourg, The Netherlands) and in the U.S.S.R., the training of primary school teachers is provided in normal schools which are not to be identified with higher educational establishments, although they generally provide training beyond the level of the secondary leaving certificate.

In the United States, Britain, and the Federal Republic of Germany, teachers for elementary schools are trained in in-

[1] Other examples could be given, especially in preparing for community, agricultural, medical, and social careers.

stitutions which may or may not be integrated with universities but are always regarded as higher educational establishments.

These two examples illustrate the difficulty of comparing the degree of development of higher education in the different countries on the basis of national statistics. In order to apply the Unesco criterion, it would be necessary to add to the figures for higher education a part[2] of the figures for certain establishments which are administratively classified as secondary.

SECONDARY VOCATIONAL AND TECHNICAL EDUCATION

In most of the nine countries secondary vocational and technical education may be divided between two main training levels corresponding to two types of institution: vocational schools, designed for the training of workers and office staff; and technical schools, which provide for the training of various medium-grade cadres.

In actual fact, the distinction between the two is not always so clear-cut. The level of study in the vocational schools tends to go as high as the lower medium-grade cadres, and the lower level in certain technical schools (cf. Belgium) corresponds to worker training.

These forms of training in all their aspects may be provided entirely by the school (general education, theoretical technical education, practical education). The school may also be limited to providing a supplementary general training or theoretical technical education through part-time courses (day, evening, or correspondence courses) and leave practical training to the enterprises themselves. Depending on the

[2] This is the great difficulty: the statistics cannot easily be adapted to the purpose and, in any case, the establishment of correlations of "level" between technical studies and the secondary school leaving certificate is necessarily somewhat arbitrary.

country, or even within a given country, both methods may be used for the same type of training.

It is impossible to establish general criteria for the age at which vocational and technical studies begin. In some countries (Belgium, The Netherlands, Italy[3]), some degree of vocational or technical specialization follows immediately after completion of the elementary classes, at eleven or twelve years of age. Generally speaking, these studies begin at the end of the terminal classes in the compulsory school period or after three or four years of the general secondary school.

This complexity in the organization of vocational and technical education rules out the possibility of studying such education by the nature of the questions involved and impels us to utilize a country-by-country presentation. The key data on the state of development will be given for each of these countries in figures, and the secondary-level enrollment will be summed up in a general table.

A comparative synthesis will show how the age groups in each country are divided between general secondary, vocational, and technical education, and direct entry into jobs.

UNITED STATES OF AMERICA

ORGANIZATION OF VOCATIONAL EDUCATION

Secondary vocational and technical education in the United States tends to train workers, specialized and skilled office staff, and medium-grade cadres. It has four distinct branches: agricultural education, business education, home economics, and trade and industrial education—not only industrial trades but special preparation for nurses, medical assistants, and the like.

This instruction is organized (1) in specialized sections of the high schools, or simply by the choice of subjects— usually the case in business education, home economics, and agricultural education; (2) in specialized institutions (techni-

[3] The *avviamento professionale* school was abolished under the reform of December 1962.

cal high schools, vocational high schools) which admit pupils at the end of the junior high school or after the eight-year primary school followed by a preparatory year; (3) for pupils in these different institutions, either full time or alternating school work and work in a firm (cooperative program); and (4) for young people and adults already employed, through part-time courses, generally evening courses, in the same schools.[4]

The certificates awarded on completion of agricultural education and business education have the same value as the certificate of the academic sections for enrollment in an institution of higher education.[5] Studies in the industrial sections lead to a trade certificate (vocational high school) or a secondary certificate (technical high school). In fact, pupils holding these industrial certificates subsequently receive either (and this is the commonest case) training within firms which leads to an apprenticeship certificate, or more advanced specialization in certain disciplines (engineering, chemistry, and so on) provided in establishment at post– high school level (junior or community colleges, technical institutes) which rank as higher educational establishments. The development of this instruction by the school, however, is fairly recent and, by and large, relatively limited in comparison to requirements, but the enterprises, more especially the industrial enterprises, play an important role in the training of their staffs at different levels.

DEVELOPMENT OF VOCATIONAL EDUCATION

Considerable progress has been made in these various types of vocational education since the end of World War I: 168,000 pupils in 1918, 3,768,000 in 1960, and 4,072,000 in 1962. Of this total, 46 per cent in 1960 were attending full-

---

[4] There are numerous correspondence courses, generally run by private organizations.

[5] Pupils studying home economics receive the normal high school certificates.

TABLE 33   DEVELOPMENT OF VOCATIONAL EDUCATION, 1953 TO 1962—UNITED STATES *(in thousands)*

Courses	Evening Classes	Part-time Classes	Full-time Classes	Total
Agriculture				
1953	275.1	47.8	429.3	752.2
1960	266.7	65.5	463.9	796.1
1962	—	—	—	822.6
Distributive occupations				
1953	127.7	81.2	—	208.9
1960	267.7	39.6	—	307.3
1962	—	—	—	321.0
Home economics				
1953	486.1	58.6	782.4	1,327.1
1960	586.1	54.9	946.8	1,587.8
1962	—	—	—	1,725.6
Industry				
1953	328.6	181.1	223.4	733.1
1960	485.0	256.5	272.3	1,013.8
1962	—	—	—	1,005.3
Practical nursing				
1960	15.5	—	24.6	40.1
1962	—	—	—	48.9
Area programs[a]				
1960	68.3	—	32.9	101.2
1962	—	—	—	148.9
Totals: 1953	1,217.5	368.7	1,435.1	3,021.3
1960	1,689.3	416.5	1,740.5	3,846.3
1962	—	—	—	4,072.3

SOURCE: Annual reports of the State Board for Vocational Education.

[a] Training of "technicians" under the National Defense Education Act of 1958.

time courses, 10 per cent part-time day courses, and 44 per cent evening courses.

Table 33 shows enrollment figures for 1953, 1960, and 1962 for each type of training and for each category.

In 1960, the 1,740,000 pupils enrolled for full-time vocational education accounted for approximately 19 per cent of the enrollment (8,490,000) in classes 9, 10, 11, and 12 of the high schools and vocational schools.

A substantial proportion (41 per cent) of those enrolled in vocational education choose home economics. Agricultural education also occupies a large place (25 per cent) and is apparently taken by between 4 and 5 per cent of the fourteen-to-seventeen age group.[6] By comparison, the proportion taking industrial education is apparently relatively low (16 per cent of those enrolled full time), which confirms that industrial training for skilled workers and foremen is mainly provided by the enterprises themselves, possibly in conjunction with part-time school education.

The rate of enrollment by age and by type of course is not included in the American statistics. On the basis of the average rate of enrollment (89 per cent) between fourteen and seventeen years of age and the above figures, the breakdown of school enrollment may be estimated as shown in Table 34.

TABLE 34   BREAKDOWN OF ENROLLMENT AT THE TERMINAL CLASS LEVEL OF THE HIGH SCHOOL, 1961—UNITED STATES

| Age | Full-time Courses | | | Part-time Courses |
	GENERAL	VOCATIONAL	TOTAL	
14 years	92	5	97	3
15 years	75	20	95	5
16 years	65	20	85	8
17 years	55	15	70	15

[6] This continues at the level of higher education.

SOVIET UNION

TWO LEVELS OF TRAINING

1. The training of skilled manpower is mainly organized in the vocational and technical schools[7] of the State Committee for Vocational and Technical Training attached to the Council of Ministers of the U.S.S.R.

These schools admit pupils either on completion of the compulsory education period or during or even after completion of secondary education.[8] There is no entrance examination, students being accepted within the limits of the places available. Apart from this, admission is based on previous school results. Courses last between one and three years and provide training for workers in industry, railways, mines, agricultural machinery, and agriculture. The level of qualification reached in these schools varies in accordance with the level of recruitment and the duration of studies (specialized or skilled workers, or even technical assistants).

Specialized workers and even some skilled workers are trained in the enterprises themselves. As already noted in Chapter 1, moreover, students from the terminal classes of the general and polytechnical secondary schools receive a practical vocational training.

2. Medium-grade cadres are trained in the specialized secondary schools or *tekhnikums* which come under the Federal Ministry of Higher Education and Specialized Secondary Education.

This type of school trains medium-grade cadres for all sectors: industry, transport (technical assistants, technicians); commerce (accountants, and so on); agriculture (assistant agronomists, zootechnicians); public health (nurses, midwives, medical assistants); and education (primary school

---

[7] Urban vocational and technical schools providing day and evening courses, and rural vocational and technical schools.

[8] This practice is becoming more generalized because of the considerable increase in the number of full secondary certificates awarded and the continued rise in the level of training.

teachers, vocational school monitors, physical training teachers, and so on).

Recruitment is, in principle, based on an examination which takes place either after the eighth secondary class or after the complete secondary cycle. Studies continue for four years in the first case, and for two or three in the second. The certificate awarded by the *tekhnikums* entitles the holder to go on to higher education. This certificate may also be obtained through evening classes and correspondence courses. These tend to develop on a large scale, in accordance with the wishes of the 1958 reformers, as is shown in the following statistics.

DEVELOPMENT OF VOCATIONAL AND
TECHNICAL TRAINING IN THE U.S.S.R.

1. The vocational and technical schools underwent steady expansion up to 1957–58. Thereafter enrollment dropped, probably because of the demographic variations mentioned earlier, but has risen again since 1961. In 1940–41, there were 717,000 students; in 1957–58, 1,352,000; in 1959–60, 996,000; in 1961–62, 1,266,000; in 1962–63, 1,390,000; and in 1963–64, 1,491,000, of whom a mere 20 per cent are girls.

The number of graduates from the vocational schools each year has followed the same pattern and has been rising markedly over the last three years. From 1941 to 1949, the average was 495,000 (8 to 9 per cent of an age group); from 1946 to 1950, the average was 678,000 (11.5 per cent of an age group); in 1956, there were 665,000; in 1959, 583,000 (12 to 13 per cent of an age group); in 1961, 739,000 (about 18 per cent of an age group); in 1962, 888,000 (about 20 per cent of an age group); and in 1963, 915,000 (about 22 per cent of an age group).

In addition to the young men and women trained in these schools, there are millions of workers who receive their initial vocational or technical training in the actual enterprises or who attend refresher courses,[9] plus holders of the polytechnic secondary school certificate when these have had specialized vocational training.

2. The special secondary schools *(tekhnikums)* developed very rapidly between the two wars and enrollment has very greatly increased since 1945. In 1914, there were 450 institutions with 54,300 students enrolled; in 1940, 3,773 with 974,000 students; in 1955, 3,757 with 1,961,000 students; in 1959, 3,346 with 1,907,000 students; in 1961, 3,416 with 2,370,000 students; in 1962, 3,530 with 2,668,000 students; and in 1963, 3,625 with 2,983,000 students. Enrollment in evening and correspondence courses is included.

The drop in enrollment resulting from the decline in the

TABLE 35   ADMISSIONS AND GRADUATES IN THE TEKHNIKUMS, BY TYPE OF COURSE, 1940 TO 1963—U.S.S.R.

(in thousands)

		Ordinary Course	Evening Course	Corre- spondence Course	Total
1940:	Admissions	318.0	12.5	51.0	383.0
	Graduates	205.0	2.5	29.0	236.0
1956:	Admissions	386.0	78.0	130.0	594.0
	Graduates	449.0	25.0	36.0	510.0
1959:	Admissions	378.0	99.0	179.0	656.0
	Graduates	396.0	67.0	64.0	527.0
1961:	Admissions	451.3	139.0	280.7	871.0
	Graduates	285.0	54.0	90.0	429.0
1963:[a]	Admissions	500.0	146.0	307.0	954.0
	Graduates	289.0	91.0	131.0	511.0

[a] In 1964–65, the number of enrollments rose to one million and the number of graduates to 550,000 (*Pravda,* January 30, 1965).

[9] In 1963, nearly 3.5 million people had been trained in enterprises as specialized workers and nearly 7 million had attended technical refresher courses for medium-cadres and skilled workers outside their working hours.

birth rate did not affect the *tekhnikums,* a fact which indicates the attraction of this type of training for young people and the importance which the Soviet authorities attach to it.

Table 35 shows admissions and graduations by type of course.

The total number of graduates in 1959 represented 10 to 11 per cent of the corresponding age groups; in 1963, it was 14 to 15 per cent.

Pursuant to the Law of December 24, 1958, which provided that evening classes and correspondence courses should become "the main form of training for specialists," there has been an increase in the relative proportion of these types of education over recent years: 39 per cent of the total in 1959–60, 48 per cent in 1961–62, and 50.6 per cent in 1963–64.

Table 36 shows admissions and graduates by specialty, and the percentage of women graduates.

These statistics reveal several key trends: (1) the considerably increased rate of training over twenty years of technicians in industry and building (tenfold), transport (fivefold), and agriculture (fourfold); (2) the efforts made since before the war to ensure the training of primary school teachers (this slackened after 1950, but has tended to develop again since 1961); (3) the very high proportion of women graduates in education, health, and so on; and (4) the relatively excellent "yield" of part-time education.

In the absence of official statistics for enrollment by age, only a fairly rough estimate of the breakdown of school enrollment after compulsory education is possible (see Table 37).

Great Britain

Secondary vocational and technical education in Great Britain is organized mainly in "further education" institutions under the Ministry of Education.[10]

---

[10] There are some also under the Ministry of Agriculture.

TABLE 36 ADMISSIONS AND GRADUATES IN THE TEKHNIKUMS, BY SPECIALTY, 1940 TO 1963—U.S.S.R.
(in thousands)

	Industry and Building	Transport and Communications	Agriculture	Economics and Law	Health, Physical Education, and Sport	Education	Art and Cinema	Total
1940: Admissions	80	23	40	18	85	117	10	382
Graduates	21	8	21	7	90	85	2	236
1959: Admissions	271	51	111	77	70	62	12	656
Graduates	224	40	89	50	71	45	7	527
Women	33%		36%		83%	77%		46%
1961: Admissions	347	68	135	117	92	91	19.5	871
Graduates	170	37	77	56	31	48.6	7.7	429
Women	33%		38%		85%	77%		48%
1963: Admissions	385	77.6	151	124	102	94.4	20.5	954
Graduates	202	35	65	68	72	58	10.7	511

PURPOSE AND ORGANIZATION OF FURTHER EDUCATION

Courses are provided for pupils leaving secondary school —mainly those from modern and technical schools but also from grammar schools—and for youths and adults. In other words, these institutions provide training courses for adolescents and advancement courses for adults.[11]

These courses supplement general education through pre-

TABLE 37   ENROLLMENT, IN PERCENTAGE, IN SECONDARY EDUCATION AFTER COMPULSORY PERIOD, 1963–64 (ESTIMATED)[a]—U.S.S.R.

	Age					
	15	16	17	18	19	20
General and polytechnic secondary[b]						
Full time	32	27	23	2	1	—
Part time	12	15	10	8	5	—
Specialized secondary *tekhnikums*						
Full time	5	5	6	9	6	3
Part time	2	5	6	8	8	6
Vocational						
Full time	10	13	7	3	1	—
Total						
Full time	47	45	36	14	8	3
Part time	14	20	16	16	13	6
Full time and part time	61	65	52	30	21	9

[a] On the basis of the estimate of the U.S.S.R. birth rate made by Dr. Biraben (*Revue Population,* I.N.E.D., Paris, 1958).

[b] *Classes 9 to 11 only.* It should be noted that at fifteen years (and possibly sixteen years) a small proportion of Soviet children may still be attending school in the secondary classes of the first cycle. Accordingly, the rate of full-time school attendance at fifteen years of age is higher than indicated here.

[11] Independently of further education courses, adult education courses are organized by the universities (extramural departments) and by private groups.

liminary courses and courses in preparation for general secondary examinations (G.C.E. O-Level and A-Level; see Chapter 1),[12] or provide vocational and technical training in virtually all areas (industry, business, health, agriculture,[13] and so on) and, in certain fields, at all levels of qualification from skilled worker to engineer. Especially in the teaching of industrial techniques, courses to a large extent overlap higher education.

Further education is provided through full-time or "sandwich" courses,[14] especially at the higher level, or, for most pupils, through part-time day or evening courses.

Courses are given in institutions that have an appropriate teaching staff. England and Wales have 17 national colleges (including 10 colleges of advanced technology), 22 regional colleges, 500 ordinary technical colleges, 165 art schools, 38 agricultural institutes, and over 7,500 evening institutes[15] which use the premises of all kinds of day schools. Scotland has 15 central institutions and 80 further education centers.

As noted, these courses train workers at all levels. A distinction is made between preliminary courses which last from one to two years and provide supplementary general education (mathematics, English) for pupils who left school at fifteen years of age, together with vocational guidance, and courses which train skilled workers, foremen, or technical assistants, leading to examinations held by the City and Guilds of London Institute or by similar bodies. These examinations are at three levels, corresponding to three, five, or six years of part-time study.

The preparatory courses leading to National Certificates provide training at the ordinary level (O.N.C.) for technical

[12] Participation in general secondary education is growing; in 1960, 46,000 and 15,000 further education pupils sat for the G.C.E. O- and A-Level examinations respectively.

[13] Some of these schools are under the Ministry of Agriculture.

[14] Alternating full-time periods in the factory and the school.

[15] These evening institutes do not generally provide vocational training, although they participate in preliminary courses.

assistants or technicians, and at the higher level (H.N.C.) for technicians or senior technicians.

Full-time courses lead to national diplomas, either ordinary level (ordinary N.D.) or higher level (higher N.D.). The latter is at the engineer-technician level and may give access to professional engineering associations after a period of practical experience.

Courses (generally "sandwich" courses) leading to the diploma in technology, which was established in 1956, are open to students holding the G.C.E. at A-Level. These require a minimum of three years, followed by one year of industrial training. This diploma gives access to professional engineering associations.

Finally, there are other high-level courses which lead to University of London external degrees.

This hierarchy of courses provides significant and real possibilities of advancement for all pupils from secondary schools. Students from secondary modern schools, for example, on completing the preliminary or City and Guild courses, may take the National Certificate courses and subsequently study for an engineering degree. Students holding the G.C.E. O-Level may enroll directly in National Certificate courses; those holding the G.C.E. A-Level may enroll directly in the National Diploma courses. Courses for students holding the G.C.E. A-Level or the O.N.C. are regarded as advanced.[16]

DEVELOPMENT OF VARIOUS FORMS OF FURTHER EDUCATION SINCE 1954

In 1953–54, further education courses were attended by 1,766,900 students in England and Wales; in 1963–64, the total was 2,643,300. The number of students is not as significant as the development of the various forms of further education.

[16] The Robbins Commission report classifies at the higher educational level all students who are taking advanced courses.

TABLE 38   NUMBER OF STUDENTS ENROLLED IN FURTHER EDU-
CATION—ENGLAND AND WALES
(in thousands)

	1953–54	1962–63		1963–64	
Full-time	50.7	140.7	(77.5)[a]	156.7	(86.4)[a]
Aged 15 to 20 years	39.9	116.2	(—)	130.3	(—)
Sandwich	1.0	16.0	(15.6)	18.9	(18.0)
Aged 15 to 20 years	0.6	9.4	(—)	11.4	(—)
Part-time day	333.0	601.5	(473.9)	613.3	(486.9)
Aged 15 to 20 years	260.3	464.0	(—)	475.8	(—)
Evening (major establishments)	550.2	817.8	(442.9)	779.1	(411.6)
Aged 15 to 20 years	190.8	464.0	(—)	287.6	(—)
Evening institutes	832.0	1,039.1	(371.7)	1,075.4	(319.2)
Aged 15 to 20 years	314.9	374.3	(—)	376.7	(—)
Totals	1,766.9	2,615.1(1,381.5)		2,643.3(1,382.3)	

[a] Numbers in parentheses indicate the number of boys in each group.

The main features of this development are (1) the tripling of enrollment in full-time or sandwich courses; (2) the expansion of day-time education, especially for the benefit of young workers authorized to attend these courses by their employers (the day release system); this expansion reflects the partiality of the professional organizations for apprenticeship on the job; (3) the first three categories of courses are primarily intended for young people between fifteen and twenty, mostly boys; and (4) most of those attending evening classes are men and women.

Of the total of 2,643,300 in 1963–64, more than 950,000 were studying for an official diploma.[17] Enrollment for the higher courses rose from 89,000 in 1953 to 147,000 in 1963–64.

In Scotland, 127,800 students were enrolled in further edu-

[17] The evening institutes account for a very small proportion of this type of study.

TABLE 39   NUMBER OF STUDENTS ENROLLED IN FURTHER EDU-
CATION COURSES AT ADVANCED LEVEL,[a] 1958 TO 1963
—ENGLAND AND WALES
(in thousands)

Diploma	1958	1962	1963	Subjects
First degrees[b]	9.5	10.0	12.0	Mostly scientific and and technical
Diploma in technology	2.6	7.2	8.4	Technical
Higher National Diploma or Certificate	44.93	54.5	59.1	Science, technology, building, business
National Diploma in Design	4.11	6.1	6.9	Art and miscellaneous
Art Teacher's Diploma	0.34	0.39	0.4	Art and miscellaneous
Other	28.1	60.0	60.4	Architecture, technology, business
Total	89.6	138.5	147.5	

[a] On a full-time basis or on any other basis. In 1962–63, the number of students at the advanced level, working full time, was 43,000 for Great Britain as a whole.

[b] University degrees.

cation institutes in 1961–62, including 11,100 full-time students and 11,800 enrolled in the higher courses.

In 1962–63, the breakdown of diplomas awarded to further education students in England and Wales was as follows: 2,080 London University degrees and 1,070 diplomas in technology; 21,318 O.N.C. and 12,130 H.N.C.; 1,150 O.N.D. and 1,193 H.N.D.; 1,300 National Diplomas in Design; and 106,000 workers' or foremen's certificates.

To the foregoing should be added the numerous further education students who sit for the G.C.E. O- and A-Level examinations (20 per cent of the candidates at the advanced level).

These statistics reveal the importance of the further education courses from the point of view of the training of skilled manpower and medium- and senior-grade cadres.

GENERAL PICTURE OF ENROLLMENT IN SECONDARY
EDUCATION FROM FIFTEEN TO TWENTY YEARS
(ENGLAND AND WALES)

On reaching the age limit for compulsory schooling (fifteen years), young people in England may choose further general studies; enroll in a further education institution; or abandon education.

Table 40 shows the breakdown of choices for the 1962–63 school year.

TABLE 40 NUMBER OF STUDENTS FROM 15 TO 20 YEARS OF AGE[a] ENROLLED AT SECONDARY LEVEL, 1962–63—ENGLAND AND WALES

	Age					
	15	16	17	18	19	20
Full-time education						
General schools	44.3	24.3	12.5	4.3	0.5	—
Further education	3.1	4.2	3.0	1.7	0.9	0.4
Total	47.4	28.5	15.5	6.0	1.4	0.4
Part-time education						
Day	7.1	14.2	16.5	12.5	9.3	6.9
Evening						
Major establishments	5.1	7.5	9.1	8.4	7.2	6.0
Evening institutes	17.0	9.8	8.6	6.2	5.0	4.3
Total	29.2	31.5	34.2	27.1	21.4	17.2
Total	76.6	60.0	49.2	33.1	22.8	17.6

[a] Not including further education courses classified as advanced education.

FEDERAL REPUBLIC OF GERMANY

The structure of vocational and technical education in the Federal Republic of Germany is rather different from that of the other Common Market countries because of the predominance of part-time education *(Berufsschulen)* with practical training on the job, as training for workers and office staff; and the method of recruitment for technical schools which enroll only those students who already have had some technical training.

The vocational schools provide training for specialized and skilled labor in all areas (industry, business, trade, agriculture, crafts, and so on). This training begins immediately after completion of the primary school (at fourteen or fifteen years of age) and is given in two types of institution.

1. The *Berufsschulen* admit apprentices of both sexes up to the age of eighteen, whether employed or not, who attend full-time courses, that is, six to twelve hours per week, given in one or two days. The purpose is to extend general knowledge and to supplement theoretical and practical training given on the job.

Since this type of education comes within the compulsory range, enrollment is high (1,699,000 in 1963–64). There are five categories: agricultural, domestic, business, industrial, and mining.

Schools of a higher level *(Berufsaufbauschulen)* have been provided in recent years for the more promising students from the part-time vocational schools. Studies cover six terms of twenty weeks each and occupy ten or eleven hours per week. The level of general education provided is equivalent to that of the *Realschulen;* the final certificate opens the way to technical, business, or administrative careers. Fifty thousand students were enrolled in 1963–64.

2. The *Berufsfachschulen* are full-time schools (thirty to forty hours per week). Studies last from one to three years, followed by an apprenticeship examination *(Gesel-*

lenprüfung)[18] or by an examination at the same level organized by the school.

The full-time vocational schools have not developed very greatly and there has even been a decline in enrollment over recent years.[19] In 1950–51, there were 81,800 students, of whom 60,000 were girls; in 1955–56, 146,400 (104,000 girls); in 1960–61, 139,200 (86,900 girls); and in 1963–64, 142,300 (91,800 girls).

Two-thirds of the students are in business schools—generally attended by girls and women; the remainder attend industrial, child welfare, or craft schools.

The *Fachschulen* (secondary vocational schools) provide training for medium-grade cadres, technicians, and specialists for a wide variety of areas: industrial technicians *(Technikerschulen),* agronomists *(Höhere Landwirtschaftsschule),* kindergartens, business technicians, workshop foremen, and the like.

Students in the *Fachschulen* are accepted after attending a full-time or part-time vocational school and after a certain period of practical experience; the minimum age of admission is eighteen years. In 1960–61, there were approximately 2,000 public or private schools of this type, including the *Ingenieurschulen,* with 185,000 students (66,200 girls) against 102,500 (34,000 girls) in 1950–51.

Industrial education is provided at three levels: the lower, which leads to the qualification examination after one or two terms; the medium, which prepares technicians in three or four full-time terms as against seven or eight in evening classes; and advanced, which trains nonuniversity engineers in five or six terms. This training comes midway between that of the technician and the university-trained engineer and is given in *Ingenieurschulen.* In 1964–65, the enrollment in these schools was 58,200 (against 34,000 in 1955), virtually all boys.

[18] Held by the professional organizations.
[19] This may be explained by the drop in the birth rate during the war years.

Admission to the *Ingenieurschulen,* within the limit of the places available, is subject to three conditions. Candidates must be at least eighteen years of age, they must possess a middle school diploma or a *Gymnasium* eleventh-class entrance certificate; and they must have had practical training in a supervised course, or hold the final apprenticeship certificate.

Courses are available in seventeen groups; the final examination leads to the degree of engineer. Candidates who pass this examination with credit may enter the *Technische Hochschulen* (technical faculties). Approximately 5 per cent of graduates from the *Ingenieurschulen* proceed to university courses in this way. A supplementary examination provides the equivalent of the *Abitur* and enables them to enroll in other faculties.

This second form of access to higher education, through vocational and technical studies, ensures that those unable to attend a *Gymnasium* are not excluded from higher education. However, it is long and difficult, and in fact relatively little advantage has been taken of it.

There are also higher *Fachschulen* specializing in commercial courses *(Höhere Wirtschaftsfachschulen)* and social courses *(Höhere Fachschule für Sozialarbeit).*

The number of certificates awarded for industrial courses over recent years is as follows: In the *Technikerschulen,* for the year 1960–61, 8,168; and for 1962–63, 11,075. In the *Ingenieurschulen,* for the year 1960–61, 10,620; for 1962–63, 13,553; and for 1963–64, 14,625.

There are no official statistics for the other categories of graduates from the *Fachschulen.*

The general position regarding secondary enrollment between the ages of fifteen and twenty-five is shown in Table 41.

THE BENELUX COUNTRIES

Full-time public and private vocational and technical education has undergone very substantial development in the Benelux countries.

TABLE 41   NUMBER OF STUDENTS FROM 15 TO 25 YEARS OF AGE ENROLLED IN SECONDARY SCHOOLS, 1960—FEDERAL REPUBLIC OF GERMANY
(in thousands)

	Age						
	15	16	17	19	21	23	25
Volksschule[a]	8.5	1.4	0.4	—	—	—	—
Realschule	8.6	6.2	2.2	—	—	—	—
Höhere Schule	13.8	13.0	11.0	5.3	0.5	—	—
Berufsfachschule	6.0	4.4	2.6	0.7	0.2	—	—
Fachschule	—	—	1.4	2.4	1.2	0.7	0.5
Ingenieurschule	—	—	—	0.2	0.7	0.7	0.3
Total	36.9	36.9	17.6	8.6	2.6	1.4	0.8
Berufsschulen	60.2	25.0	47.1	7.9	1.1	—	—

SOURCE: Von Carnap and F. Edding, *Hochschule für Internationale Pädagogische Forschung* (1962).

[a] Includes the *Aufbauzüge* and special courses.

It is primarily distinguished by the fact that it tends to cover not only the training of skilled workers and medium-grade cadres but also the basic training of industrial and agricultural workers and workers in the tertiary sector. A very substantial proportion of these courses is allotted to domestic economy and agricultural domestic economy for girls. However, unlike other countries, this basic training, at any rate in the early stages, takes place within the period of compulsory education and at the level of the terminal primary classes.

ORGANIZATION OF VOCATIONAL AND TECHNICAL TRAINING

1. In *Belgium*, the training of workers and office staff is organized in the vocational schools or, as pointed out later in this study, in the first cycle of the technical schools. The vocational schools take pupils aged twelve who have successfully completed the sixth primary year or, in the second year, those who have reached thirteen years of age.

Training comprises three cycles: the lower (three or four years) trains specialized workers or, in exceptional cases, skilled workers (with vocational education beginning in the third year); *the upper* (three years) trains highly skilled workers or craftsmen on the basis of training received in the first technical or vocational cycle; and *the complementary* (one or two years) offers still more advanced training in certain trades.

2. In *The Netherlands,* the law on technical, vocational, and domestic economy training specifies two levels, the primary level providing training for workers and office staff.

Access to these courses may be possible, as in Belgium, after the sixth year of study, or on termination of the complete cycle of the primary school.

Training is given in a relatively complex network of schools: (1) primary day technical schools which, in three or four years, train industrial and building workers and craftsmen; (2) special schools for ocean fishing and inland navigation; (3) primary agricultural and horticultural schools lasting four years after the sixth primary year; these schools accept pupils five days a week in the first and second years, four in the third year, and three in the fourth year; and (4) schools of domestic economy for girls, with special agricultural domestic economy, if desired; these schools take pupils on completion of the primary school and generally last two years on a full-time basis.

3. In *Luxembourg,* training begins only after the eighth year of primary school and methods vary according to the branch concerned: either full-time initial training (one or two years) in a vocational school followed by practical training (one or two years) in an enterprise; this type of training is given in business, crafts, and small-scale industry; or, in medium-size and large industrial enterprises, practical training in the factory with attendance at vocational schools for twelve to sixteen hours a week. On the completion of this training, the apprentices receive a certificate of final apprenticeship in their special branch.

1. In *Belgium,* the training of medium-grade cadres is provided in full-time technical schools. These differ from vocational schools in the additional time allotted to general training in the programs at secondary level and in the content of the theoretical technical studies; the courses are organized in two cycles.

The lower cycle (twelve to fifteen years of age), extended by a fourth and even a fifth year devoted to specialization, trains skilled workers. To be enrolled in the first year, candidates must have successfully completed the sixth year of primary school (50 per cent grades) or must hold a primary school certificate. Pupils of twelve years of age who do not meet this condition may be accepted on the basis of an entrance examination.

The law of March 12, 1958, equates this study cycle with the lower cycle of middle education.

The higher cycle (fifteen to eighteen years of age) leads to a technical or equivalent certificate. The weekly timetable comprises thirty-six lessons in the first year and forty thereafter; general training is always very important (eighteen to twenty lessons in the first cycle, eighteen to thirty in the second). The special branches of technical education cover all economic activities.

Students holding the technical school certificate may go on to the higher technical schools and the middle technical normal schools.

2. In *The Netherlands,* the training of medium-grade cadres is provided by secondary technical education. These courses are organized in an extremely wide range of institutions: secondary technical schools (four-year training for medium-grade industrial and building cadres); navigation and navigational and aeronautical mechanics schools; schools of art and applied arts; business schools (four years); middle and secondary agricultural and horticultural schools (three years); middle and secondary domestic economy schools (one to three years); welfare assistants' schools; and teacher train-

ing schools (kindergarten teacher training schools, training schools for men and women teachers).

Generally speaking, access to the secondary technical schools is open, with an examination, to pupils from the second and third years of the *u.l.o.'s* and the general secondary schools and to pupils holding the primary vocational school certificate; and without examination, to pupils holding the U.L.O. certificate and the "long" secondary school certificate (a pass with distinction in science is sometimes required).

Those holding the certificate of the secondary technical and agricultural schools may enroll in the corresponding higher educational establishments; teachers certificated by the teacher training schools may proceed to higher studies in psychology and education.

3. In *Luxembourg,* the training of technicians and technical engineers is provided by the Luxembourg Technical Training Institute, which admits students at approximately sixteen years of age on the basis of an examination and provides three-year courses leading to the technical certificate or four-year courses leading to the technical engineering certificate.

In Belgium and The Netherlands,[20] the training of workers and office employees may be given, after compulsory schooling, under the apprenticeship system operating in enterprises; in this case, a complementary general and theoretical education is provided through evening courses or even, in The Netherlands, through day schools on the basis of one day a week. Primary part-time agricultural education is also provided (postschool courses in Belgium, primary agricultural and horticultural courses in The Netherlands).

Apart from the apprenticeship system, Belgium organizes vocational courses, on the basis of a reduced timetable, which correspond to the levels of the lower and higher full-time cy-

---

[20] This form of education has been included with full-time education in the case of Luxembourg.

cles. Technical courses involving a reduced timetable are also organized at two levels: the lower (three to six years, 240 to 450 hours a year), and the higher (three to four years, 300 to 400 hours a year). These courses lead to certificates and diplomas.

With regard to the training of medium-grade cadres in The Netherlands, certain forms of industrial, business, and art training are given through evening classes.

In Luxembourg, part-time up-grading courses are provided in evening classes in various schools with the cooperation of the enterprises concerned and are aimed basically at training supervisory staff.

In Belgium, the Centre National d'Enseignement par Correspondance, set up in 1961, will extend its activities to vocational and technical training.

DEVELOPMENT OF VOCATIONAL AND TECHNICAL TRAINING[21]

Belgian statistics draw no distinction between vocational and technical training but merely show the distribution of pupils between the lower and higher levels.

Enrollment in full-time education has undergone a considerable expansion (partly for demographic reasons) over recent years: 128,800 pupils in 1952–53; 214,000 in 1960–61; 80 per cent of these, however, are in the lower cycle. In 1952–53, in the lower cycle there were 103,000 students (49,000 boys and 54,000 girls), and in the higher cycle there were 25,000 students (10,000 boys and 15,000 girls). In 1960–61, in the lower cycle there were 177,000 students, and in the higher cycle, 37,200 students. Of the total number reported for the two cycles in 1960–61, 63 per cent were in private schools.

The enrollment in both cycles is shown in Table 42, together with the enrollment in general education. The maximum enrollment in the lower cycle is reached at fourteen

[21] Accurate and complete statistics for Luxembourg are not available.

years of age and in the higher cycle at seventeen years of age. A very definite decline in enrollment will be noted between the lower and higher cycles.

However, the courses in the reduced timetable occupy an important place: 112,000 enrolled in 1959; 123,000 in 1961,[22] that is, between 12 and 15 per cent of the fifteen-to-eighteen age groups and 4 to 5 per cent of the nineteen-to-twenty-four age groups; 12,000 pupils were enrolled in 1961 in the postschool agricultural courses, and 20,000 young people were apprenticed under contract.

The number of vocational and technical certificates awarded in 1952 may be broken down as shown in Table 43.

TABLE 42   ENROLLMENT IN GENERAL AND VOCATIONAL AND TECHNICAL SECONDARY EDUCATION, 1962–63—BELGIUM
(in thousands)

	Age						
	11	12	14	15	17	19	21
Vocational and technical education Lower cycle							
Boys	0.3	18.9	36.9	30.5	10.8	1.1	0.1
Girls	0.5	23.8	37.5	23.9	5.9	0.4	0.2
Higher cycle							
Boys	—	—	—	3.6	10.3	5.8	2.2
Girls	—	—	—	8.4	11.1	2.5	1.1
General education Lower cycle							
Boys	3.1	34.8	36.5	18.9	1.3	1.0	—
Girls	2.8	35.0	34.9	15.0	1.1	0.3	—
Higher cycle and teacher training							
Boys	—	—	1.6	14.0	20.1	5.8	0.9
Girls	—	—	1.5	15.2	15.5	3.2	1.0

[22] Including 63 per cent in private schools.

In The Netherlands, enrollment in full-time vocational and technical courses at primary and secondary levels over the period 1950 to 1964 is shown in Table 44. However, figures for part-time education in 1964–65 should be added: 117,300 in primary technical schools or courses, and 64,900 in secondary courses.

In 1963–64, the number of certificates awarded on completion of secondary-level courses were distributed as follows:[23] secondary technical, 2,562 certificates or 1.2 per cent of the age groups; agricultural and horticultural, 283 certificates or 0.15 per cent of the age groups; social welfare, 1,037 certificates or 0.5 per cent of the age groups; middle domestic economy, 1,750 certificates or 1.5 per cent of the age groups, and secondary domestic economy, 879 certificates or 0.45 per cent of the age groups.

The total number of certificates involved approximately 3.8 per cent of the age groups. As explained later, some of these certificates (industrial and agricultural education) provide access to corresponding branches of higher education.

TABLE 43   NUMBER OF VOCATIONAL AND TECHNICAL EDUCATION CERTIFICATES AWARDED, 1962—BELGIUM
(in thousands)

	Boys	*Girls*	*Total*	*Percentage of Age Group*
Lower cycle				
Full-time courses	12.8	8.1	20.9	
Part-time courses	10.0	5.5	15.5	
			36.4	25.6
Higher cycle				
Full-time courses	5.5	6.2	11.7	
Part-time courses	1.8	0.2	2.0	

[23] In the same year, 5,257 teachers (men and women) were trained (2.5 per cent of the age groups).

TABLE 44   ENROLLMENT IN FULL-TIME VOCATIONAL AND TECHNICAL EDUCATION—THE NETHERLANDS
(in thousands)

	1950–51	1964–65
PRIMARY		
Technical[a]	71.5	203.5[b]
Domestic economy[b]	57.5	103.6
Agricultural	—	17.3
SECONDARY		
Technical schools	14.4	34.7
Agricultural and horticultural schools	4.1	6.1
Middle and secondary domestic economy	5.3	21.5
Business training	1.7	2.6
Schools of art and applied art	1.2	2.7
Social welfare schools	0.9	2.0

[a] More than nine-tenths in private schools.
[b] Including 129,300 in the primary technical schools, 3,200 in the vocational schools of enterprises, and 71,000 in the apprenticeship system (evening courses).

FRANCE

The organization of secondary vocational and technical education is relatively complex and comes under several ministerial departments.

INDUSTRIAL, BUSINESS, AND TRADE

Training for industrial, business, and trade positions, in public and private institutions, is under the Ministry of Education and, in the case of accelerated vocational training for adults, under the Ministry of Labor.

1. For the public technical *collèges*[24] (or the corre-

[24] In 1962–63, 935 public technical *collèges* and 306 specialized sections in general *collèges* were operating; training for the *C.A.P.* is likewise organized in the technical *lycées*.

The Strasbourg *Académie* includes part-time (one day a week) apprenticeship centers (20,000 enrolled in 1961–62).

TABLE 45 NUMBER OF STUDENTS FROM 11 TO 20 YEARS OF AGE ENROLLED IN FULL-TIME GENERAL AND VOCATIONAL AND TECHNICAL EDUCATION, 1959–60—THE NETHERLANDS

	Age									
	11	12	13	14	15	16	17	18	19	20
GENERAL EDUCATION										
Elementary	99.4	60.2	27.9	9.8	2.0	0.5	0.4	—	—	—
Middle	0.1	17.6	28.1	27.6	23.1	13.1	5.1	1.1	0.2	—
Secondary	0.2	9.1	13.9	14.0	13.1	11.4	9.7	5.8	2.4	0.7
VOCATIONAL AND TECHNICAL EDUCATION										
Technical elementary	—	4.5	12.7	16.1	15.0	13.4	9.7	5.6	2.0	0.7
Technical middle and higher	—	0.0	0.0	0.0	0.3	1.3	2.6	3.2	3.2	2.3
Domestic economy	—	7.5	15.3	13.7	6.3	3.4	2.2	1.2	0.8	0.5
Agricultural	—	0.8	1.7	1.9	1.5	1.3	0.9	0.7	0.5	0.2
Teacher training	—	—	—	—	0.3	1.5	2.9	3.7	3.5	2.7

sponding private institutions) train skilled workers and office staff, pupils are recruited mainly from among young people over fourteen years of age who have completed the terminal cycle of primary school (84 per cent of first-year enrollment) or from pupils leaving the fifth class of the general *collèges* (14 per cent). An entrance examination is frequently held when the number of candidates exceeds the places available.

Programs include substantial supplementary general culture, theoretical technical training (drawing, technology), and practical training in workshops. Training in principle lasts three years (from fourteen to seventeen years of age). It culminates in examinations for the *certificat d'aptitude professionnelle (C.A.P.),* a public examination which is open to students attending public and private vocational schools and to apprentices in enterprises. Following on a training period in industry, holders of the *C.A.P.* may sit for an examination leading to the *brevet professionnel,* a public examination on a higher level than the *C.A.P.,* which represents a qualification for supervisory work.

The development of such full-time education has been relatively rapid: 218,000 in 1951–52; 389,000 in 1961–62, including 157,000 girls; and 395,000 in 1963–64.[25]

In accordance with the Decree of August 4, 1963, on educational reform, the conditions governing access and duration of training will be altered; recruitment will take place after four years in a section of the first general secondary cycle and the duration of courses will be reduced to two years.

2. The technical *lycées*[26] and the technical sections of the classical and modern *lycees* (and the equivalent private institutions) provide for the training of medium cadres and specialists: for technical officers (two years' training, from

[25] Including 217,000 in the public technical *collèges* and 178,000 in private establishments; to these figures should be added the training at a similar level provided in the technical *lycées* (61,000) and the specialized sections of the general *collèges* (56,000).

[26] Public technical *lycées* numbered 289.

fifteen to seventeen years of age), training which is to be transferred hereafter to the technical *collèges;* for technicians (three years' training, from fifteen to eighteen years of age); and for senior technicians (one or two years' training after the technician's certificate has been obtained, or the *baccalauréats* of the technical *lycées*).

The range of training is extremely broad: industrial, commercial, social, hotel managers, crafts, and so on. Each course leads to a certificate after public examination which may give access, in certain circumstances, to higher education.

Since the 1959 reform, recruitment for the sections of the technical *lycées* take place after the first two years of general secondary education (observation cycle) through an entrance examination made necessary by the lack of places. There is a growing trend, however, to recruit pupils after the first cycle of general education, and the new reform adopted in August 1963 has generalized this solution.

A special effort has been made to develop such training over the last decade in public *lycées* and equivalent private institutions. In 1951–52 there were 136,000 pupils; in 1961–62, 260,000, including 90,000 girls, generally in the business sections; and in 1963–64, 251,000.[27]

3. Adult vocational training centers, under the Ministry of Labor, are designed to provide accelerated training (full-time courses lasting from six to twelve months): at the primary level, for specialized or skilled workers in fifty basic specialities; and at the secondary level, for technical officers or technicians in such special branches as industrial design, chemistry, electronics and the like.

The adult vocational training centers also offer part-time

[27] Including the vocational education organized in the public technical *lycées* (61,600); the decline in 1963–64 may be explained by the elimination of the fourth and third classes. The breakdown between public and private education is given in the Appendix, Table A-3.

courses or short courses for the up-grading of actively employed staff.

The number of certificates awarded by the adult vocational training centers in 1962 exceeded 20,000. Under the Fifth Plan (1966–1970) enrollment in these centers is to be increased to 75,000.

4.   Part-time and correspondence courses are designed to meet a relatively wide range of objectives:

Compulsory vocational courses from fourteen to seventeen years of age provide supplementary general and theoretical training for apprentices and young employees in industry, business, and trades, generally through evening classes (150 to 200 hours a year). Enrollment in 1961–62 was high: 160,200 (112,000 boys and 28,200 girls), with 64,000 in the first year (11 per cent of the corresponding age groups).

Trade apprenticeship in 1961–62 comprised: 163,000 (141,000 boys and 22,000 girls),[28] including 65,000 in the first year (11 per cent of the corresponding age groups).

Correspondence courses provided by the Centre National d'Enseignement par Correspondance, Radio et Télévision represent growing numbers (over 27,000 in 1963–64) training for official examinations in various occupational and technical branches. In addition to those provided by the *Centre National* there are numerous private correspondence courses (accountancy, secretarial, and so on).

The up-grading courses organized under a Law of July 31, 1959, are designed to ensure the advancement of actively employed workers. The up-grading courses comprise two levels: vocational, for skilled workers (first level) and supervisory staff,[29] technical officers, and technicians (second level); and senior (level of higher technical education).

Training at first and second levels is organized through evening courses in the technical *lycées* and public technical *collèges* or is made available by private bodies or through

---

[28] A proportion of these are included in the figures for vocational courses.

[29] Courses leading to the *C.A.P.* or vocational certificates.

correspondence courses.[30] Evening courses in 1961–62 were attended by more than 162,000 students of all ages.

AGRICULTURAL VOCATIONAL AND TECHNICAL EDUCATION

Agricultural vocational and technical training is organized in two types of full-time institution: for skilled agricultural workers, training is given over two or three years in agricultural colleges operated by the Ministry of Agriculture or in equivalent private institutions;[31] and for technical officers, technicians, and senior technicians, training is given in the agricultural *lycées*;[32] studies are organized on the model of those in the technical *lycées* operated by the Ministry of Education. Enrollment in full-time public education still amounted to only some 15,000 in 1964–65.

Most young farmers are trained, part-time, either in post-school agricultural and agricultural domestic economy courses, compulsory from fourteen to seventeen years of age (minimum 120 hours a year), organized jointly by the Ministry of Education and the Ministry of Agriculture (80,000 boys and girls in 1961); or in seasonal or periodical courses (first and second levels) and correspondence courses organized by the Ministry of Agriculture or by private bodies (60,000 boys and girls in 1960). All in all, approximately 7 per cent of the fourteen-to-seventeen age group took the different courses at that time.

OTHER FORMS OF VOCATIONAL TRAINING

Various forms of vocational training are organized by other ministerial departments, including maritime schools,

[30] The Centre National de Télé-Enseignement and its branches in Lyons and Lille had an enrollment of more than 56,000 in 1964–65 for courses leading to the *C.A.P.*, the vocational certificates, and certain technical and higher technical certificates.

[31] As of October 1, 1964, in public institutions there were 22 agricultural colleges for men, 45 agricultural colleges for women, and 58 agricultural domestic economy schools.

[32] There were 38 agricultural *lycées* as of October 2, 1964.

TABLE 46   Number of Students from 14 to 20 Years Enrolled in Secondary Education, 1961–62—France
(in thousands)

	Age						
	14	15	16	17	18	19	20
Full-time Education							
Primary classes	13.2	1.5	0.4	0.1	—	—	—
General collèges[a]	20.0	13.8	7.2	2.6	0.7	—	—
Classical and modern lycées[b]	19.7	19.0	18.5	16.5	11.9	6.7	2.7
Technical collèges	10.5	13.0	12.7	5.8	2.0	0.7	0.4
Technical lycées	5.4	6.0	6.6	6.5	4.3	2.4	1.1
	68.8	*53.3*	*46.4*	*31.5*	*19.0*	*10.1*	*4.2*
Part-time education (estimates)							
Industry, commerce, and trades	10.0	12.0	12.0	5.0	1.0	—	—
Agriculture	5.0	6.0	6.0	2.0	1.0	—	—
Total	*83.8*	*71.3*	*64.4*	*38.5*	*21.0*	*10.1*	*4.2*

[a] Includes the vocational sections.
[b] Includes the teacher training schools.

which provide training for specialized workers, medium grade and higher cadres in the Merchant Navy; art education, organized in institutions under the Ministry for Cultural Affairs; and schools under the Ministry of Health which train nurses and welfare assistants, where the students must have passed the first part of the *baccalauréat* or, failing this, a special examination.

VOCATIONAL AND TECHNICAL EDUCATION

Public vocational and technical education certificates awarded in the school year 1961–62 at the various levels of vocational and technical training were as follows: (1) Skilled workers, not including certificates awarded by the

Adult Vocational Education Centers and the agricultural C.A.P.'s, but including 70 per cent of industrial C.A.P.'s and 30 per cent of commercial C.A.P.'s, 128,109 (21 per cent of the age group). (2) Supervisors (vocational certificates), 5,297 (1 per cent of the age group). (3) Technical officers and technicians, 25,464 (4.3 per cent of the age group), which breaks down into three groups: industry, 10,353 (1.8 per cent); business and hotel management, 8,411 (1.4 per cent); and nurses and welfare assistants, 6,700 (1.1 per cent). (4) Senior technicians, 2,211 (0.4 per cent of the age group).

ITALY

Until the 1962 reform, vocational training in Italy began with the eleven-to-fourteen study cycle and was provided by the vocational orientation school *(avviamento professionale)*. Vocational and technical education, properly speaking, takes place in institutions which mostly are under the Ministry of Education.

THE OLD VOCATIONAL ORIENTATION SCHOOL

Education included general modern secondary training and industrial, trade, agricultural, commercial, or maritime pre-occupational training. Pupils entering these schools were required to hold the elementary study certificate, and a certificate was awarded on completion of courses. The study cycle, in fact, was still very similar to general secondary education, and the reform of December 1962 which is now being applied provided for its integration in the first general secondary cycle.

Enrollment in the vocational orientation school has doubled over the last decade: in 1950–51, there were 345,000 students; in 1960–61, 730,000; and in 1962–63 753,000.

FULL-TIME VOCATIONAL EDUCATION AIMED AT TRAINING SKILLED MANPOWER

This type of full-time education is given in the technical schools *(scuole techniche)* and the vocational institutes of the

Ministry of Education. Part-time education is also available.

The technical schools take pupils at about fourteen years of age from among those holding the vocational orientation school certificate. Training lasts two years and culminates in a final examination.

The vocational institutes which since 1950 have tended to replace the technical schools are open to those holding the middle school and orientation school certificates and no entrance examination is required except for candidates over fourteen years of age who do not hold one of these two certificates. Studies last between two and four years, depending on the requirements of the trade concerned, and enable students to obtain a qualification certificate in a given trade.

This type of education is still limited in extent, but the development of the professional institutes has been greatly accelerated since 1960. In 1950–51, there were 28,800 technical schools and 16,700 professional institutes; in 1960–61, there were, respectively, 32,000 and 65,000; and in 1963–64, 12,500 and 170,400.

Part-time education is either compulsory for apprentices, under the Law of January 19, 1955, on the basis of three hours a week, with courses organized by the technical education authorities or by the Ministry of Labor; or optional in the case of training or refresher courses organized by the large public or private enterprises, local communities, trade unions, and associations for the development of technical education.

Since 1959 the Italian radio and television have presented vocational courses *(telescuola)* for children between the ages of eleven and fourteen who are not attending school.

TECHNICAL EDUCATION IN THE TECHNICAL INSTITUTES

Technical education is designed to train medium-grade cadres and specialists in the different economic sectors.

Studies last five years (from fourteen to nineteen years of age).

Holders of the middle school certificate are entitled to enter these establishments (90 per cent of first-year students) while holders of the orientation school certificate may enter after passing an examination (10 per cent of entrants).

There are six types of technical institute: agrarian, industrial (twenty-nine special branches), commercial, for surveyors, nautical, and for girls (domestic economy).

The weekly timetable allots an important place to general education. An examination to determine technical ability *(diploma di perito)* is held at the end of the fifth year (75 to 80 per cent of students pass this examination). This certificate gives access to the corresponding positions and also enables holders to enroll in certain higher institutes in the same speciality: ship-building, agricultural, economic, commercial, statistical. A Law of 1960 extended this channel to higher studies and authorized those holding the certificate of the technical institutes to enroll in engineering schools and science faculties.

The technical institutes have undergone very extensive development. There were 117,000 students in 1950–51; 324,000 in 1958–59; 359,000 in 1960–61; and 432,000 in 1963–64. The number of graduates has followed the same trend. In 1950–51, 17,635 certificates were awarded (2.1 per cent of the age group); in 1954–55, 23,249 (2.9 per cent); in 1957–58, 33,920 (4.1 per cent); in 1960–61, 47,662 (5.6 per cent); and in 1962–63, 49,245 (6.9 per cent).

In 1960–61, graduates were distributed in the various specialties as follows: agriculture, 1,774; industry, 7,970; commercial and surveyor, 33,106; maritime, 1,360; and women, 3,345.

It will be noted that agricultural education and even industrial education account for a relatively small proportion, while commercial education accounts for an extremely large proportion.

SPECIAL VOCATIONAL SCHOOLS

Special vocational schools provide training for midwives (three-year courses available from the age of eighteen to those holding the middle school certificate), nurses, kindergarten teachers (three years after middle school), social welfare staff (this training is available to those who have obtained the *maturità* certificate), and interpreters.

ART EDUCATION AT DIFFERENT LEVELS

Art schools provide introductory courses for children between eleven and fourteen years of age in various crafts (ironwork, woodwork, ceramics, sculpture, drawing, and the like). This training is a particular form of the *avviamento professionale* school.

Art institutes *(istituti di arti)* offer more advanced courses in the various crafts. Admission is restricted to students from art schools and middle schools; studies last from three to four years and lead to a master of art certificate, which entitles the holder to enroll in the Academy of Fine Arts.

The art high schools draw their pupils from the middle schools or, on the basis of an examination, admit other children over fourteen years of age. Studies last four years and include painting, sculpture, decoration, architecture, and so on. They culminate in the art maturity examination.

Table 47 presents a general picture of full-time enrollment in Italy at the secondary level.

COMPARATIVE ENROLLMENT IN GENERAL SECONDARY VOCATIONAL AND TECHNICAL EDUCATION FROM FIFTEEN TO SEVENTEEN YEARS OF AGE

The combination in a single table of the syntheses established for most of the countries in the preceding discussion makes it possible to compare the development of secondary school attendance. The conclusions to be drawn from this table will be examined in the concluding section.

TABLE 47 NUMBER OF STUDENTS ENROLLED, IN PERCENTAGE, BY TYPE OF SECONDARY INSTITUTION, 1962–63—ITALY

	Age											
	11	12	13	14	15	16	17	18	19	20	21	22+
General education												
Elementary school	94.9	47.2	22.4	9.8	1.9	—	—	—	—	—	—	—
Middle school	6.5	50.8	47.6	49.7	18.7	8.1	3.0	1.4	0.9	—	—	—
High school	—	—	0.02	1.8	4.1	4.4	4.9	5.6	3.8	1.5	0.9	0.5
Technical and vocational education												
Vocational schools	—	—	0.2	0.5	2.5	4.1	3.8	3.4	1.8	1.1	0.5	0.6
Technical institutes	—	—	—	0.8	4.2	6.6	8.0	9.5	7.9	6.0	3.5	3.4
Teacher training	—	—	—	0.4	1.8	2.4	3.1	3.5	2.2	1.4	0.7	0.8
Art education	0.06	0.3	0.3	0.3	0.3	0.5	0.4	0.3	0.2	0.1	0.05	0.06
Total: 1962–63	100.0	98.3	80.5	63.4	33.6	26.2	23.5	23.8	16.9	10.3	5.7	5.4
1959–60	81.9	66.1	51.8	33.4	25.0	20.8	17.1	12.8	7.8	4.0	—	—

TABLE 48   COMPARATIVE ENROLLMENT RATES, IN PERCENTAGE, OF

	Federal Republic of Germany (1963)		Belgium (1962–63)		France (1962–63)		Italy (1962–63)	
	15 YEARS	17 YEARS	15 YEARS	17 YEARS	15 YEARS	17 YEARS	15 YEARS	17 YEARS
Primary	14.6	0.3	0.6	—	1.5	—	1.9	—
General secondary								
Short[b]	10.2	2.5	17.0	1.2	14.7	2.5	18.6	3.0
Long	13.3	9.9	14.6[c]	17.9[c]	20.0[c]	16.5[c]	5.9[c]	8.1[c]
Full time								
Vocational	5.8	2.5	} 33.2	19.0	14.3	6.3	2.9[a]	4.3[a]
Technical	—	1.2			6.1	6.8	4.2	8.0
Home economics	—	—			—	—	—	—
Total	43.9	16.4	65.4	38.1	56.6	33.7	33.6	23.4
Part time								
Vocational	} 53.2	54.7	} 9.3	12.7	} 12.0	5.0	} —	—
Technical								
Home economics					} 6.0	2.0		
Agricultural								

[a] Estimated.
[b] Or first cycle.
[c] Includes teacher training.

SOCIAL CHARACTERISTICS OF ENROLLMENT IN SECONDARY VOCATIONAL AND TECHNICAL INSTITUTIONS

Earlier in the study the characteristics of enrollment in general secondary institutions were considered in relation to social background. It was observed that working-class families were reluctant to have their children enroll for long sec-

STUDENTS 15 AND 17 YEARS OF AGE IN THE NINE COUNTRIES

Luxembourg (1959–60)		*Netherlands* (1959–60)		*England and Wales* (1961–62)		*United States* (1961–62)[a]		*U.S.S.R.* (1963–64)[a]	
15 YEARS	17 YEARS	15 YEARS	17 YEARS	15 YEARS	17 YEARS	15 YEARS	17 YEARS	15 YEARS	17–18 YEARS
7.0	—	2.0	0.4	—	—	—	—	—	—
30.0	—	23.1 13.4[e]	5.1 12.6[e]	44.3	12.5	70.0	55.0	44.0[d]	33.0[d]
35.0	—	16.5[f] 0.3	10.6[f] 2.6	— 3.1	— 3.1	— 20.0	— 15.0	10.0 5.0	7.0 6.0
72.0	—	6.3 61.5	2.2 34.0	— 47.4	— 15.6	— 90.0	— 70.0	— 59.0	— 46.0
20.0	—	5.4	10.9	29.2	34.2	5.0	15.0	2.0 — —	6.0 — —

[d] Includes schools for young workers and farmers.
[e] Includes art education.
[f] Elementary technical education and agricultural education.

ondary studies and that, for the economic, psychological, and even educational reasons which were indicated, they preferred to have the children take vocational or technical education which offered speedier access to paid employment.

Statistics on the social background of students in vocational and technical schools clearly confirm these trends. As an example,[33] Table 50 presents the percentage of enrollment in the various types of institution according to social background, and also the percentage which each group represents in the working population. Comparison between the two series of percentages makes it possible[34] to determine an order of magnitude for school attendance in respect of the various social groups.

Children of farmers and farmworkers do not enroll to any greater extent in vocational and technical institutions than in general educational institutions. Allowance, however, has not been made for attendance at the agricultural training institutions of the Ministry of Agriculture and the equivalent private institutions nor, above all, for enrollment in part-time education.

The employers category—the industrial, commercial, and trade sectors—is normally represented, that is, in proportion to the size of the group, in technical *lycées* and, to a slightly lesser extent, in vocational institutions.

The liberal professions and senior cadres, very well represented in long secondary education, show a higher than average attendance at technical *lycées* but a very limited enrollment in vocational schools.

The medium-grade cadres are very well represented in the technical *lycées* and less well in the technical *collèges*.

The office employees category is fairly well represented in the technical *lycées* and to a normal extent in the *collèges*.

Industrial workers (36.7 per cent of the working population) are normally represented in the technical *lycées* (32.5 per cent) and very well represented in the technical *collèges* (49.9 per cent).

Children from the service personnel group account for a very small enrollment in all types of institution.

---

[33] This example is confirmed by the statistics from other countries.

[34] Subject to differences in the birth rate and the duration of active employment between one social group and another.

TABLE 49   ENROLLMENT, IN PERCENTAGE, IN GENERAL, VOCA-
TIONAL, AND TECHNICAL SECONDARY EDUCATION,
1961–62, BY SOCIAL BACKGROUND—FRANCE

Profession of Parents	Percentage of Active Population (1962)	Classical and Modern Lycées	Technical Lycées	General Collèges	Technical Collèges
Farmers	15.7	6.5	6.0	10.0	6.0
Farmworkers	4.3	1.2	1.7	2.7	3.9
Employers in industry and commerce	10.4	—	—	—	—
Industrialists	0.4	2.1	1.7	0.8	0.5
Retailers	6.6	9.2	7.4	7.4	3.8
Craftsmen	3.9	5.3	6.1	6.3	4.6
Liberal professions and senior cadres	4.0	17.1	5.7	2.4	1.4
Medium-grade cadres	7.8	15.9	11.1	10.6	5.6
Office employees	12.6	17.0	17.4	16.7	11.9
Workers	36.7	15.9	32.5	35.0	49.9
Service personnel	5.4	1.2	2.0	1.8	3.1
Private income, not gainfully employed	} 3.1	2.5	3.4	1.8	3.9
Other categories		6.1	5.0	4.5	5.4
Total	100.0	100.0	100.0	100.0	100.0

SOURCE: *Informations statistiques,* Ministry of Education, Nos.
49–50, June 1963.

Apart from farmers and service personnel, enrollment of
the different social groups in the technical *lycées,* as in short
general education (general *collèges*), is relatively better balanced than in long general education. The technical *collèges*
are largely attended by children from working-class backgrounds: 70 per cent of pupils are children of workers,
tradesmen, office employees, and service personnel, and 9.9

per cent are children of small farmers or agricultural workers. This confirms the observations previously made concerning educational trends among children from such backgrounds.

HIGHER EDUCATION

In this section on higher education the following points will be examined:

The general structure of higher education institutions in the nine countries

Comparative methods of recruiting for these institutions

Certain characteristics of the organization of studies

The extent of access to higher studies and the progress of women's enrollment

The number and distribution of higher education certificates by major disciplines

The "yield" of higher education

The social aspects of access to higher education

GENERAL STRUCTURE OF HIGHER EDUCATION INSTITUTIONS

The details set out below are designed solely to provide a general picture of the structure of higher education organization in the nine countries and do not include any details on the administration and financing of these institutions.

In spite of the limited number of countries studied and their relative homogeneity in level of social and economic development, the organization of higher education institutions varies considerably. In some countries, the universities or equivalent institutions (public or private) constitute the basic element in the higher education system. In others, along with the universities, there are a wide variety of public or private institutions organized either within the framework or under the supervision of the Ministry of Education, or under the aegis of other ministerial departments.

UNITED STATES

American higher education institutions numbered 2,080 in 1963–64; nearly two thirds are private, while the others are organized by states[35] or, less frequently, by cities. They offer a wide variety of programs and their structures vary greatly.

The most numerous are the liberal arts colleges, which generally offer four-year programs covering a wide range of disciplines: classical and modern languages, history, philosophy, mathematics, natural science, social science, and so on.

Colleges which group all disciplines, including specialized vocational schools for law, medicine, and education, and which offer the most advanced study programs, are known as universities.

TABLE 50   NUMBER OF INSTITUTIONS OF HIGHER EDUCATION IN THE UNITED STATES AND ENROLLMENT FIGURES, 1959 AND 1963—UNITED STATES

Category	Number of Institutions		Student Enrollment	
	1959	1963	1959	1963
Junior colleges	512 ⎫	577	411,000 ⎫	628,000
Technical institutes	50 ⎭		53,000 ⎭	
Teachers colleges	198	186	351,000	437,000
Technological schools	51	57	104,000	133,000
Theological schools	173	201	41,000	46,000
Schools of arts	46	46	15,000	19,000
Other professional schools	75	79	47,000	68,000
Liberal arts colleges	756	788	965,000	1,292,000
Universities	141	146	1,464,000	1,906,000
Total	2,002	2,080	3,455,000	4,529,000

[35] Certain public institutions have the status of land-grant colleges or land-grant universities when founded on the basis of a concession made by the Federal Government under the Morrill Act of 1862.

Certain specialized institutions may be organized independently of the colleges or universities: teachers colleges or state colleges, institutes of technology, schools of art, theological schools, and the like.

Over the last two decades, independent institutions have developed which offer short programs, generally lasting two or three years: junior and community colleges, and technical institutes. Their programs correspond either to the first two years of the liberal arts colleges or to a very varied special vocational or technical training (technology, commerce, health, agriculture, graphic and applied arts, and so on). The technical institutes are sometimes attached to a junior college or they may be organized independently.

Table 50 shows the number of each of these categories of institution together with their enrollment for the years 1959 and 1963.[36]

UNITED KINGDOM

Higher education in the United Kingdom includes universities and advanced further education courses, plus the primary and secondary teacher training colleges.

At the present time[37] there are twenty-five institutions ranking as universities in Great Britain: nineteen in England, one in Wales (consisting of four colleges situated in different towns), five in Scotland (Aberdeen, Edinburgh, Glasgow, and St. Andrews, and the Glasgow RCST).

There are two universities in Northern Ireland (Belfast and Londonderry) and two theological colleges.

The most ancient and renowned of the universities are Oxford and Cambridge, which traditionally attract the most brilliant students from the grammar schools and the Public Schools. London University, which recruits on a very far-ranging basis, also enjoys an excellent reputation. The provincial (red brick) universities have been established more re-

[36] *Source:* Office of Education.
[37] New universities are being built in York and Norwich and others are planned.

cently by raising the old municipal colleges of arts and technology to the rank of universities. British universities had 118,000 students in 1962–63.

As noted above, certain courses in the principal further education institutions are branches of higher education. The report of the Robbins Committee includes all advanced courses in higher education.[38] In 1962–63 there were 43,000 full-time students in England and Wales and more than 4,500 in Scotland.

The training of primary and secondary school teachers and, in part, the training of teachers for further education are provided in training colleges and in the education departments of the universities.

The 124 general colleges offer a three-year training course for primary and secondary school teachers in general disciplines; the specialized colleges train staff for courses in domestic economy, physical education, and technical, artistic, and other disciplines.

In the universities, the twenty-four departments of education provide one-year courses in teacher training for university graduates who plan to teach.

SOVIET UNION

In 1959–60 there were 719 higher educational institutions in the U.S.S.R.[39] These all come under the general supervision of the U.S.S.R. Ministry of Higher Education; they are administered either by the various Republics of the Union or by certain federal ministries (Ministry of Transport, and so on). They may be divided into two major categories: universities and specialized higher institutes and schools.

[38] The definition of advanced courses has been given in the foregoing section. In actual fact, only a third of those enrolled in this category are studying for the diploma in technology or for university degrees, while the other courses have their counterpart in other countries in courses for technical engineers or technicians.

[39] There were 741 in 1963–64.

The forty Soviet universities[40] are multipurpose institutions comprising a varying number of faculties, usually between five and eight (twelve in the University of Moscow). There are more than thirty types of faculties, but the most common are the following: mathematics, physical science, geology, geography, biology, chemistry, philosophy, philology, history, economics, law. Some universities include medical faculties, technical faculties, and the like.

In 1959, universities enrolled only 12 per cent of all students. The average enrollment is approximately 5,000, and only the universities of Moscow and Leningrad have over 20,000.

The specialized higher institutes and schools, numbering 656 in 1959, provide training for specialized cadres in the economy in six main branches: industrial engineers (176 institutes); agriculture (107 institutes); economics and law (25 institutes); medicine (95 institutes); education (206 institutes); and fine arts (47 institutes).

The average enrollment in 1959 was 3,000, of whom a little more than half were full time. Some of the institutes have an enrollment of between 4,000 and 8,000, and are divided into faculties.

Most higher education institutions have specialized sections for evening courses and correspondence courses. There are also independent institutes providing only evening courses or correspondence courses (23 in 1959, 29 in 1963–64).

THE COMMON MARKET COUNTRIES

The organization of higher education institutions in the Common Market countries[41] is frequently extremely complex. They may be classified into four major categories: universities

---

[40] A certain number of universities organize annexes in neighboring towns for evening classes.

[41] Luxembourg has no higher education institutions. "Higher courses" lasting one year are organized in the Luxembourg Athénée and in the boys' *lycée*.

and equivalent;[42] higher institutions (technical or otherwise), nonuniversity; higher teacher training schools; and higher art schools whose organization will not be dealt with in detail.

The universities and equivalent institutions represent the key element in higher education in all five countries. Some of them, as in Italy, encompass virtually all forms of education at this level. The table below gives the number of these institutions for each country and shows the extent of enrollment. All the universities are made up of a varying number of faculties and institutes.

In France and the Federal Republic of Germany, organization is based on the traditional division into five faculties: law, arts, science, medicine and pharmacy,[43] and theology.[44] In France, the political sciences are the subject of a separate course in seven university institutes. Under the policy of university decentralization, other towns have recently opened faculty institutes or have organized first-year courses in arts and science and the first two years of law or preparation for the *licence*.

University training of engineers in Germany is provided in the *Technische Hochschulen* which are genuine technical universities with at least four faculties (mechanical engineering, electro-technology, civil construction, science) and possibly other specializations (agronomy, mines, economics). In France, special engineering schools are organized within the science faculties (Ecoles Nationales Supérieures d'Ingénieurs, *E.N.S.I.*); however, the structure of the Institut National des Sciences Appliquées, in Lyons (*I.N.S.A.*) set up in 1957,[45] is similar to that of the German *Technische Hochschulen*.

[42] "Equivalent institutions" are those which provide specialized training and have the legal status of universities, or those which have a different status but provide education of the same kind as the universities.

[43] There are independent pharmacy faculties in France in three universities and independent faculties for economics and social science in Germany.

[44] In France, this type of faculty only exists in Strasbourg.

[45] In 1962–63, there were 2,300 students.

TABLE 51   NUMBER OF UNIVERSITIES AND EQUIVALENT INSTITU-

	Number of Institutions	Enrollment
Federal Republic of Germany		
Universities	18	209,300
		(1964–65)
Equivalent institutions		
Technische Hochschulen[a]	8	58,500
Spezial Hochschulen[b]	5	4,800
Theological schools	17	2,600
Belgium		
Universities	4[e]	30,431
		(1962–63)
Equivalent institutions		
Specialized institutions[d]	16	4,830
France		
Universities	19	326,300
		(1963–64)
Equivalent institutions		
Institutes of applied science		
(Lyons, Toulouse)	2	—[*]
Grands établissements and		
grandes écoles[f]	10	
Free faculties or groups of faculties	9	8,000[g]

In Belgium and The Netherlands, universities have the traditional faculties and, in some cases, separate faculties for political science, economics and social sciences, or veterinary science. Institutions similar to the universities are the independent faculties which provide courses in agronomy, veterinary science, technology (the polytechnic faculty of Mons in Belgium, the School for Higher Technical Studies in Delft, Eindhoven, and Enschede in The Netherlands), higher economic and commercial studies, and the like.

The full Italian universities have a still larger number of faculties: law, philosophy and arts, political science, medicine,

TIONS, AND ENROLLMENT, IN THE COMMON MARKET COUNTRIES

	Number of Institutions	Enrollment
Italy		
Universities		
Public	27	180,500 (1962–63)
Private	4	22,000 (1960)
Equivalent institutions		
University institutes	2	7,300
Special institutes	4	7,500
Private *magistero* institutes	6	7,500
Private physical education institutes	4	1,500 (1962–63)
The Netherlands		
Universities	6[h]	47,063 (1962)
Equivalent institutions		
Colleges of higher studies	5	—[e]

[a] Technical universities.

[b] Specialized higher educational schools.

[c] State University of Ghent and Liège, Free University of Brussels, Catholic University of Louvain.

[d] The Belgian law of April 9, 1965, includes the following in this category: the State University centers of Antwerp and Mons; the four university faculties of Brussels, Namur, Antwerp, and Mons; the four specialized higher institutions; and the six schools for advanced commercial studies.

[e] Enrollment included in the total for universities.

[f] Institutions coming under the Directorate of Higher Education, e.g., the Collège de France, the Ecoles Normales Supérieures, the Muséum d'histoire naturelle, the Ecole de Chartres, etc.

[g] Students not enrolled elsewhere in the public faculties (estimated).

[h] Three state universities (Leyden, Groningen, Utrecht), the Municipal University of Amsterdam, and the Free Universities of Amsterdam (Calvinist) and Nimeguen (Catholic).

technology, mathematical science, physics and natural science, veterinary science, agriculture, economics, architecture, *magistero* (teacher training). This structure is explained by the virtually complete coverage of higher education in Italian universities.

Nonuniversity institutions of higher education (technical or otherwise) in each of the countries recruit their students from secondary school graduates and provide specific types of education: seminaries, military schools, legal studies, trade schools, taxation administration schools, and the like. These will not be dealt with here.

In Belgium and France, a series of higher education institutions have gradually been established independently of the universities; incidentally, they are not the same in both countries.

Belgian nonuniversity higher technical education is organized in 125 institutions (approximately 11,000 students) administered by the state, local authorities, or privately.

These institutions provide a wide range of diploma courses: *ingénieur-technicien* (agronomy, chemistry, radio and electronics, building); commercial and accountancy; interpreter and translator; social welfare, nursing, kinesitherapy; specialized educator; and naval officer and pilot. The courses last for two, three, or, in exceptional cases (certain courses for engineering technicians), four years. These are the *short* higher education courses.

The French public and private higher education schools almost all provide long courses (four or five years), mainly in technology, agronomy, and commerce. The so-called *grandes écoles* enjoy very high intellectual and social standing.

Administratively, the following are the main categories:

Fourteen engineering schools which were traditionally placed under the former directorate of technical education, including the renowned Ecole Centrale in Paris and the arts and crafts schools

Engineering schools, under various ministerial departments (the Ecole Polytechnique in Paris, the Mining Engineering School, the Public Works School, the Telecommunications School, the Merchant Marine School)

Public and private higher educational schools, under the Ministry of Agriculture (agronomy, veterinary science, specialized schools)

Private engineering schools (more than thirty institutions, with diplomas recognized by the state)

Higher commerce schools, generally organized by the Chamber of Commerce

Private dentistry schools

In 1963, these various institutions[46] had a combined enrollment of 35,000, including 7,000 who were also enrolled in a faculty in order to take the university examinations.

The Conservatoire National des Arts et Métiers in Paris, and its associated centers in the provinces, have a special position in the French higher educational system. They provide full-time and, more especially, part-time day or evening advanced up-grading courses. The *C.N.A.M.* provides training at several levels—technicians, senior technicians, engineers. In 1961, 33,000 students were enrolled for the courses of the Conservatoire and its associated centers, and 7,500 certificates were awarded annually. Similar courses were organized in the *instituts de promotion supérieure du travail* set up within the universities (3,500 students in 1962–63).

As mentioned earlier in this section, certain countries prepare secondary or even primary teachers in separate higher education institutions which are legally independent of the universities. This applies partly in Belgium and Germany.

In the Federal Republic of Germany, the fifty higher schools *(Pädagogische Hochschulen)* and the corresponding

---

[46] In France, students in the four *ecoles normales supérieures* (secondary teacher training schools) study for university degrees like the other students in arts and science. There are, however, special higher education institutions for the preparation of physical training teachers.

institutes (44,000 students in 1964) prepare teachers for primary and special schools (*Volks-* and *Sonderschulen*), middle schools *(Realschulen),* and vocational schools *(Berufsbildende Schulen).*

In Belgium, teacher training at the higher level is designed to prepare teachers for the first cycle of general secondary education and for technical education.

This is provided in sixty-three *ecoles normales moyennes* and ninety-six *ecoles normales techniques moyennes.* Students are recruited after they have obtained either the humanities certificate or the technical school certificate. Courses last for two years and are organized by speciality (six for the middle schools, five for the technical schools).

CONDITIONS GOVERNING ADMISSION TO HIGHER EDUCATION

Admission to higher education institutions, more especially the universities, is traditionally restricted, with certain exceptions, to those holding the final complete secondary certificate or an equivalent certificate.[47] In all the countries covered by this study, recruitment draws basically on those holding general secondary school certificates. However, there is a gradual tendency to make higher education available to other categories: those holding certain secondary technical school certificates, and those who pass a special entrance examination open to students who have not been able to follow the ordinary secondary course.

TRADITIONAL ACCESS THROUGH GENERAL SECONDARY STUDIES

The way in which those holding general secondary school certificates proceed to higher education varies from country

[47] Some European countries are in principle prepared to permit students who do not have these certificates to enroll for university courses, but they cannot sit for the examinations. In France, students who do not hold the certificates may still enroll in the law faculties with a view to obtaining a certificate known as *capacité en droit.*

to country. In some cases, the secondary school leaving certificate is both a necessary and an adequate precondition for access to university studies; in others, enrollment at the university is subject to additional intellectual tests. Within a single country, moreover, the liberal system (free enrollment of secondary school leavers) may be applied for certain types of institution and a more selective system for others.

1. *The liberal systems*   In most of the countries studied here (the United States, Federal Republic of Germany, Belgium, France, Italy, Luxembourg, The Netherlands), the final secondary school certificate normally gives access to universities and equivalent institutions.

This system, then, excludes any restriction of numbers. To a large extent, the number of secondary school certificate holders, that is, the development of the general secondary schools, therefore determines the number of students. The liberal system is in fact subject to certain variations.

In the United States, only certain state institutions require the high school diploma alone as a precondition for enrollment. The other public and private institutions select their students on the basis of a school record which is frequently supplemented by a conversation test or by the results of a national examination organized by a private body (College Entrance Examination Board) or, even, by an examination which they themselves organize. In actual fact, a student whose request for enrollment in one of the better known institutions has been rejected may find a place in an institution which is not so much sought after.[48]

The public or private specialized vocational schools require that their students possess a more thorough knowledge of certain subjects (a specific number of units in certain high school subjects).

The American recruiting system, having due regard to the

[48] As a general rule, each candidate submits an application to several institutions.

range of educational institutions, is simultaneously selective and liberal.

In Germany and France, the secondary certificate is in principle universally valid and enables holders to enroll in all faculties. Statistical surveys on the history of secondary school leavers in higher education institutions shows, however, that, to some extent, the specialization acquired in the various secondary school sections spontaneously channels students toward certain types of higher study.

In Belgium the Law of June 8, 1964, endows the *examen de maturité* awarded on completion of secondary studies with the same universal validity.

In The Netherlands, the final secondary certificate does not provide access to all types of higher study. Regulations limit enrollment in higher education to the corresponding section of the terminal secondary classes.

In Italy, only those holding the certificate of the classical high schools may enroll where they wish, apart from the *magistero* faculties. Holders of the scientific maturity certificate may not take up legal and literary studies. Admission to the *magistero* faculties is restricted to those holding the certificate of the normal institutes and, in principle, is further governed by the limited number of places.

2. *The selective systems*   This method of selection tends to choose from among candidates holding the final secondary certificate so as to recruit a given number of students (by entrance examination) or, alternatively, so as to admit only those candidates who seem genuinely qualified to make a success of higher education.

In the Common Market countries, selection on the basis of an examination is applied in France for access to the *écoles supérieures* or *grandes écoles,* that is, to most of the engineering schools (university or otherwise) and the commerce schools. Preparation for these examinations, which are of a very high level, is carried on for at least two years after the *baccalauréat* in special classes of the secondary *lycées (classes préparatoires aux grandes écoles)* whose curricula are of higher education level.

In Belgium, access to the faculties and higher schools of applied science is based on an entrance examination.

In Great Britain, the G.C.E. (Advanced Level) does not give the right to enrollment in a university. The university authorities are free to accept or reject applications in the light of the results obtained at the G.C.E. (A-Level) and, in many cases, in the light of an interview with the candidate. A minimum of two and sometimes three passes in the G.C.E. (A) is required for entrance to a university,[49] although other higher education institutions are less demanding.[50]

In the U.S.S.R., admission to the universities and the specialized higher institutes and schools is restricted to those holding the certificate[51] of the general polytechnic or the special secondary schools (tekhnikums). However, possession of these certificates does not give all holders the right to enroll.

Whatever the study system, the students are selected for each institution on the basis of an entrance examination which includes written tests (native language and mathematics) and oral tests selected on the basis of the speciality chosen. The number of places available in each institution and each speciality is determined in relation to general manpower planning.

Priority is given to students who have previously spent two years in an enterprise (38 per cent of admissions in 1958, 57 per cent in 1960). In the higher technical institutes, it is a rule that candidates should have spent a minimum of two years working in an enterprise.[52] The extension of this

[49] The most renowned institutions are the most demanding.

[50] Eighty-three per cent of students entering the university have three or more passes against 34 per cent entering the C.A.T.'s and 14 per cent in the training colleges.

[51] As noted earlier, certificates are obtained either through full-time courses or through part-time or correspondence courses.

[52] In the case of students coming directly from the secondary

insistence on a preliminary period of work has led certain higher education institutions to organize the preparation for the entrance examination themselves. This preparation covers the program of the last secondary class.

THE NEW OR SECOND TYPES OF ACCESS TO
HIGHER EDUCATION

1. *Access to university studies for holders of technical certificates*   As stated earlier, this solution is already established in the United States (vocational education certificates are usually regarded as equivalent to the academic certificates awarded by the high schools) and in the U.S.S.R. (the *tekhnikum* certificate).[53]

In Great Britain, as previously noted, the sequence of further education certificates provides access to higher technical studies even though the cycle of general secondary studies has not been completed. This system is tending to develop in France in the institutions for advanced upgrading studies (Conservatoire des Arts et Métiers and the university *Instituts de la promotion supérieure du travail*).

Other solutions are tending to emerge in the Common Market countries.

In France, the senior technician's certificate, established in 1959, may be equivalent to the *baccalauréat* in certain circumstances, and a recent decree (November 1963) enables holders of this certificate to be exempt from the requirement of the *baccalauréat* as a preliminary to studying for the scientific *licence* by decision of the dean of the faculty.

In Italy, holders of certain technical high school certificates may enter agricultural, commercial, and naval colleges, and this was extended in 1961 to the science faculties and the technical faculties.

---

schools, however, this rule may be applied in the form of a "productive" period *after* the entrance examination has been successfully passed.

[53] In the U.S.S.R. 11 per cent of full-time students come from the *tekhnikums*.

In The Netherlands, holders of certificates from secondary, agricultural, horticultural, or technical schools may enroll for the corresponding higher courses on the basis of an examination.

In Belgium, holders of the secondary technical certificates may ordinarily go on to higher technical studies in nonuniversity institutions.

In Germany, the terminal certificates awarded in certain schools, for example, the business high schools *(Wirtschaftsoberschulen),* the *Ingenieurschulen,* the secondary agricultural schools *(Höhere Landbauschulen),* may, in certain circumstances, entitle holders to study in a single faculty of the corresponding discipline.

Holders of certain technical school certificates, including those of the *Ingenieurschulen,* may obtain complete equivalence of the *Abitur (Hochschulereife)* by passing a supplementary examination.

All these solutions provide an opportunity to those who have been unable to complete their general secondary schooling to proceed, through studies in technical high schools, to higher studies in a certain number of disciplines.

However, higher education in Western Europe except, to a certain extent, Great Britain, has benefited to only a relatively minor degree from this new flow of students from technical institutions.

2. *Special faculty entrance examinations or special secondary school leaving examinations*   Special faculty entrance examinations are held in several European countries for students who have not passed the secondary school leaving examination: in Germany (since 1922), in France (since 1956), and in The Netherlands.

In Belgium (an examination before a central jury) and *in Germany* (the so-called *Schulfremdenprüfung* examination), examinations are held for the benefit of students who have not been able to complete their secondary school education; these correspond to the final secondary school examination. Experience has shown, however, that a relatively small

number of students take advantage of either of these opportunities.

THE ORGANIZATION OF STUDIES

The pattern of studies, the working conditions for students,
and the organization of examinations differ to a significant
degree according to the disciplines and countries concerned.
The observations which follow are necessarily limited to the
broad lines of organization in each country.

UNITED STATES

A distinction must be drawn between general education
and specialized vocational education.

General education[54] is provided at two levels.

Courses for undergraduate students normally last four
years and culminate in the awarding of a Bachelor of Arts
(B.A.) or Bachelor of Science (B.S.) degree. The first two
years are devoted to general education in the lower divisions
of the colleges and universities and also in junior or community colleges. A growing number of institutions award an
associate degree after the first two years of study. The last
two years are devoted to a special area.

Courses for graduate students are organized in distinct
units in graduate schools of the colleges and universities.
They are open to students who have obtained satisfactory
results in their undergraduate studies.

These courses lead: (1) to a Master's degree—Master of
Arts (M.A.) or Master of Sciences (M.S.)—after at least
one supplementary year, culminating in examinations covering the various branches of the program; and (2) to the

---

[54] At the beginning of each half-yearly (or quarterly) term, students, usually with the assistance of a faculty adviser, choose the
lectures and practical classes which they will attend. They are
graded on the basis of their work as a whole and obtain a certain
number of credits. The diploma is awarded when the number of
required credits has been reached and, for certain diplomas, after
an oral examination and the presentation of a thesis.

Doctor's degree—Doctor of Philosophy (Ph.D.) or Doctor of Sciences (D.S.) and so on—after a further two years' study and after defending a thesis involving individual research.

Vocational education is organized in specialized schools of medicine, pharmacy, dentistry, law, pedagogy, veterinary science, technology, agriculture, theology, journalism. Studies in these schools begin either after secondary school or, for law, medicine, and theology, after two, three or four years in a college.

The duration of studies for the first degree varies according to the specialities. Medicine requires three or four years of preliminary university studies and four years in a specialized school; law requires three years of preliminary university studies and three years in a specialized school; engineering recruits its students from among those who have had preliminary university training and requires four or five years in a specialized school; and education requires four years in a specialized school.

Having obtained the first professional degree, generally known as the Bachelor's degree (or sometimes the Master's or Doctor's degree[55]), students may go on to postgraduate studies and obtain the corresponding degrees in their special area (Master of Education, Doctor of Education, Master of Engineering).

It will be recalled that the junior colleges and the technical colleges provide vocational and technical education over a two-year period preparing for careers in business, agriculture, industrial technology, semimedical professions, and the training of certain educators (terminal semivocational education).

In 1960–61, out of 2,028 higher educational institutions, 593 provided courses lasting more than two years but less than four (junior colleges or technical institutes), 739 led only to the Bachelor's degree (or first professional diploma),

---

[55] In medicine, dentistry, etc.

455 led to the Master's degree (or second professional diploma), 210 led to the doctorate or equivalent degree, and 31 prepared for various diplomas.

The range of public and private authorities responsible for the organization of higher education and the freedom of institutions to draw up their curricula and recruit their staffs lead to a considerable diversity in the content and level of studies. Some measure of coordination, however, is ensured by the Office of Education and by the professional associations. The accreditation system (recognition of the value of the course) unifies the level of diplomas to a considerable extent.

SOVIET UNION

Students in Soviet higher education institutions either study full time (42.2 per cent in 1963–64) or, while working in an enterprise, attend evening classes (13.8 per cent) or take correspondence courses (44 per cent). In principle, programs and levels of study are identical, regardless of the type of course chosen; however, on the average, studies last one or two years longer for students who are actively employed at the same time.

Evening and correspondence courses are organized, as already mentioned, either in special sections of the universities or institutes or in specific establishments. Some facilities are granted to workers following these courses—an additional thirty or forty days of annual paid leave is granted to enable them to sit for examinations, four months' leave with a scholarship is allowed in preparation for the final diploma.

Higher university education comprises three levels: qualification, candidature, and doctorate.

First level   The qualification diploma is obtained after a period of study lasting between five and five and a half years;[56] during an initial three-year cycle, students acquire

---

[56] A decree issued by the Council of Ministers of the U.S.S.R. at the end of 1964 reduced university studies to four years.

general scientific knowledge in the area selected and, during the second cycle, specialize in a limited sector of that area. Students sit for two examinations each year, in January and July; at the end of each of the two cycles they must defend a diploma thesis before a jury.

Second level   Students who have obtained the qualification diploma satisfactorily are encouraged to continue their studies through the granting of "thesis fellowships" (postgraduate course or *aspirantura*). They may then follow a three-year course leading to the candidate degree *(Kandidat Nauk)* awarded after special examinations and submission of a thesis.

Third level   Students who have obtained the candidate degree may proceed to original scientific research and, after an average of four additional years, may obtain a doctorate which gives access to careers in higher education and scientific research.

The normal study cycle also lasts between five and five and a half years, extending to six years for medicine.[57] Students sit for an annual examination. The first three years are devoted to general education, which is often the same for the various faculties. Thereafter, students specialize and study for their degrees.

Outstanding students who have obtained their degrees are authorized to continue their studies for three years *(aspirantura)* and subsequently defend a thesis which is equivalent to the candidature.

UNITED KINGDOM

Each university in the United Kingdom organizes its courses and awards its own degrees without state intervention. Students attend lectures, engage in practical work, and participate in small groups (seminars, tutorials). They are regularly in contact with their tutor (a professor or assistant

[57] Decree issued by the Council of Ministers of the U.S.S.R. at the end of 1964 reduced higher technical studies to five years and medical studies to five and a half years.

professor responsible for a group of from twelve to fifteen students) who follows the progress of their work and advises them individually.

As a general rule, university studies are organized in three stages. *The first stage* covers three or four years (five or six for medicine); the student studies for the first degree which is either the ordinary Bachelor of Arts[58] or Bachelor of Science[59] or the Bachelor of Arts or Bachelor of Science with honours. These two categories of degree represent two study programs of different levels.[60] A Bachelor's degree "with honours" is sought by students intending to take up teaching and research.

After the first stage the student may study for higher degrees: *the Master's degree* (M.A. or M.Sc.) which is generally awarded after one or two years of additional studies followed by an examination or a thesis; and *the Doctor's degree,* which is awarded after publication of original research.

FEDERAL REPUBLIC OF GERMANY

Continuation of study in the Federal Republic of Germany is not subject to success in half-yearly or yearly examinations. Depending on the discipline, studies culminate in a diploma, a state examination, a doctorate, or the "Master of Arts" examination or other examinations. These terminal examinations *(Abschlussexamen)* are preceded, in the case of certain disciplines (medicine, dentistry), by a preliminary examination *(Vorexamen).* The student is free to choose at what point he will sit for the terminal examination.

Studies last for a minimum of four or five years (arts, theology, science). In medicine, they cover eleven half-year terms followed by a one-and-a-half-year period of practical

[58] The term "of Arts" covers the literary, economic and social disciplines.

[59] The term "of Science" covers the scientific and technical disciplines.

[60] This should be borne in mind in studying the "yield" from British universities.

work. In law, the first state examination is taken after a minimum of seven half-year terms and is followed by a second state examination after three and a half years' work with the courts and the administration; legal studies also lead to a doctorate.

In the higher technical institutions, studies involve two levels: the diploma is obtained after eight half-terms and a one-year period of practical work *(Diplom-Ingenieur),* and the doctorate is awarded on the basis of a new examination taken after two additional years of study and carries with it the title of *Doktor-Ingenieur.*

Students engaged in advanced research may prepare a second thesis known as the *Habilitation* thesis which opens the way to professorships or teaching posts in higher education.

BELGIUM

University studies are organized at three levels, the first constituting a system for selecting students: the *candidature* calls for two years of studies and two annual examinations in arts, philosophy, and science, and three years of study and three examinations in the natural sciences and medicine; the *licence* is obtained after two additional years of study and two examinations; and the *doctorat* is obtained after at least one additional year in arts and science. The doctorate examination for these disciplines includes the submission of a thesis; the doctorate in law or in medicine does not include a thesis and represents the ordinary terminal degree in these disciplines.

The normal duration of studies is four years for the *licence* in economics and social and political science, psychology and education, philosophy and arts, and science, and five years for the *licence* in pharmacy (pharmaceutical chemist's degree), dentistry, civil engineering, and agronomy. For the *doctorat* in law, economics and social and political science, psychology and education, philosophy and arts, and science the duration of studies is five years, and in medicine, seven years.

The universities also prepare for the diploma of *agrégé de l'enseignement secondaire supérieur* (teaches in the *athénées* and *lycées*) which is obtained with the *licence* or subsequently.

Careers in higher education are open to holders of the doctorate who have in addition obtained the degree of *agrégé de l'enseignement supérieur*. This is obtained by defending a thesis which contributes to the advancement of science, and by conducting a lesson.

FRANCE

Higher studies preceding the first university degree or professional diploma generally culminate in annual examinations. Further studies, the duration and organization of which vary according to the discipline, depend on success in these examinations.

Science and arts[61]   Scientific and literary studies comprise three successive cycles. The first cycle *(propédeutique)* lasts one year and is devoted to the acquisition of basic scientific knowledge, orientation, and an introduction to the methods of higher education. This first year culminates in an examination which is a relatively difficult hurdle. The second cycle lasts two or three years[62] and leads to the first university degree which is known as the *licence*.[63] The organization of the third cycle is discussed later.

[61] The organization of studies in the arts faculties and the science faculties is at present the subject of a draft reform which is to be applied at the beginning of the 1966–67 school year. The details of this reform have not yet been made official and therefore cannot be given here. We will merely outline the present organization.

[62] Sometimes more, depending on the speed with which students obtain the required number of *certificats d'études supérieures (C.E.S.).*

[63] A distinction is drawn between the "educational" *licence,*

Technical   The preparatory cycle of the engineering courses is organized in the *classes préparatoires aux grandes écoles* of the *lycées*. This preparation for the entrance examinations lasts at least two years. The average duration of studies in the schools is three years.

Law and economics   Courses leading to the grade of *licencié en droit* or *licencié en sciences économiques* last four years. The degree of Doctor in these disciplines is obtained after a minimum of two additional years and the defense of a thesis. Short courses (two years) are organized in the law faculties which are open to those not holding the secondary school leaving certificate and which lead to the *diplome d'études juridiques générales*.

Medicine, pharmacy, dentistry   Medical and dental studies begin with a one-year course (corresponding to the *propédeutique* of the science faculties) in preparation for the *certificat préparatoire aux études médicales*. Following this, the medical course lasts five years, plus a six-month period of hospital work, and results in the degree of doctor of medicine; dental studies last four years, and result in a state diploma. The pharmaceutical certificate is normally awarded after five years (a one-year practical course, plus four years in the faculty).

After the basic diploma or *licence,* so-called third-cycle courses are organized in most disciplines for the purpose of providing advanced studies within a given speciality (sometimes in preparation for the *lycée* teacher recruitment examination); and of introducing students to research.

Third-cycle certificates vary from one discipline to an-

---

which is made up of a group of *C.E.S.* established by regulation, and the "free" *licence.*

Since 1961, an effort has been made to organize short courses in the science and arts faculties leading to the *diplôme d'études supérieures techniques (D.E.S.T.) and to literary D.E.S.* These courses have not developed to any great extent and it is planned to reabsorb them into special establishments: the *instituts techniques supérieurs.*

other. In science, they comprise certificates of higher studies and certificates of advanced studies (first year after the *licence*); the *doctorat de spécialité* (or third-cycle doctorate, obtained two years after the *licence* on the basis of a thesis); and the *docteur-ingénieur* certificate.

Success in the *lycée agrégation* examination also, to some extent, marks the culmination of introductory research.

The state doctorate in arts, science, and pharmacy is obtained only after a minimum of five years of research, following the *licence* and the defense of a thesis representing an original contribution to science. It provides access to teaching careers in higher education and in research.

In law, economics, and medicine, admission to the higher levels of the university is through a recruitment examination known as the *concours de l'agrégation*.

ITALY

The first Italian university degree is that of doctor *(dottore)*. Courses leading to this degree normally last four years, but extend to five years in chemistry, the engineering schools, and architecture, and to six years in the medical faculties.

Studies in the technical institutes are divided into two cycles: a common two-year cycle and a three-year cycle devoted to specialization and applied technology.

There are no systematic courses in Italy in preparation for scientific research. Research workers, like the university professors themselves, are largely trained through their work as assistants.

THE NETHERLANDS

Examinations in all Netherlands faculties are at two levels: the *candidature* (after two or three years study), and the doctoral or terminal examination which is known under various names—doctorate, engineering diploma, "arts" diploma in medicine and *apototheker* in pharmacy, diploma of master of laws.

The theological faculty and the higher technical, agronomical, and economic schools also require a preliminary examination after one year's study.

The normal duration of studies to the final examination in the various faculties or schools is as follows: theology, four years; law, five years; medicine, seven to eight years; dentistry, six to seven years; science, six to seven years; letters, five to six years; economics, five to six years; social science, five to six years; veterinary medicine, six years; technology, six years; and agronomy, five to six years.

There is no study cycle beyond the final examination but in most disciplines the period of study is exceptionally long.

In conclusion, it will be noted that one of the differences between higher education systems lies in the fact that, in certain countries (United States, Great Britain, U.S.S.R., France), courses in preparation for scientific research are systematically organized within a third cycle of higher education and lead to specific diplomas.

EXTENT OF ACCESS TO HIGHER STUDIES AND
PROGRESS OF WOMEN'S ENROLLMENT

The extent to which higher education in the nine countries has developed is directly related to the number of those holding the general or specialized secondary certificate who are entitled to enroll in higher education; their desire to enroll; and the relatively selective nature of recruitment, the duration of studies, and so on.

In any comparative study, the definition given in each country to higher education must also be taken into account.

The combination of these factors means that the quantitative recruitment for higher education institutions acquires a specific aspect in each country.[64]

Within the nine countries, the higher education system generally receives a proportion of foreign students, frequently coming from the "third world" countries. We have not sin-

---

[64] Appendix Tables $A = 1-A = 9$ give enrollment Figures in higher education over the last decade for the various countries.

gled out this particular problem which would require a separate study.

UNITED STATES

Figures established in 1959 by the Educational Testing Service on the basis of students from the final high school classes indicate that the transition to higher education is closely linked to the IQ of students although a not insignificant proportion of less-than-average students may also proceed to higher education (17 per cent for boys and 14 per cent for girls).

Most of the high school graduates (see Table 18) are girls who are less anxious than boys to proceed to higher education and who remain for a shorter time in the colleges. Nonetheless, their position in relation to the total figures is steadily rising: in 1950, girls accounted for 30 per cent of the enrollment; in 1956, for 34 per cent; and in 1963, for 38 per cent of which 42 per cent were newly enrolled. The relative proportion of girls varies from one discipline to another.

The percentage of high school graduates in the seventeen-to-eighteen age group rose from 50 per cent in 1950 to 64 per cent in 1960 and to 69 per cent in 1963. Over the same

TABLE 52 ACCESS TO HIGHER EDUCATION, IN PERCENTAGE, AMONG TWELFTH GRADE HIGH SCHOOL STUDENTS, BY I.Q. AND SEX, 1959—UNITED STATES

Intelligence Quotient	Boys		Girls	
	WISH TO ATTEND COLLEGE	ENTER COLLEGE	WISH TO ATTEND COLLEGE	ENTER COLLEGE
Highest (10%)	81	75	67	60
Upper (30%)	68	60	56	46
Middle (30%)	43	36	36	26
Lower (30%)	28	17	26	14
Average	45	36	37	27

period, the number of enrollments in the first year of college rose from 22 to 34 per cent for the same age group (1,046,000 new enrollments in 1963).

SOVIET UNION

Higher education institutions recruit from those who have completed the general secondary school or the special secondary school *(tekhnikums)*. The number of these entrants (full time and part time) has risen considerably. In 1940 there were 285,000 secondary school graduates, 220,000 in 1950, 1,400,000 in 1959, 1,000,000 in 1960, and 1,400,000 again in 1964. *Tekhnikum* graduates numbered 237,000 in 1940, 313,000 in 1950, 528,000 in 1959, 483,000 in 1960, and 555,000 in 1964.

Soviet statistics do not make it possible to determine the respective proportions within these categories which go on to higher education. Table 53 gives the general picture of access to such education: annual number of admissions to universities and institutes; new students according to type of study; number of entrants as a percentage of the seventeen-to-eighteen age group; and proportion of women in the total admissions.

The gradual decline in the proportion of women may be explained by the smaller enrollment in institutes of education and medical disciplines, where women form a substantial majority.

It will also be noted, especially since 1950, that there has been a steady increase in admissions to part-time education; this represents more than 50 per cent of enrollments since 1958 (34.6 per cent in 1950, 49.9 per cent in 1956, 56.5 per cent in 1960, and 58.4 per cent in 1963).

The percentage of admissions in relation to the seventeen-, eighteen-, and nineteen-year classes has risen since 1950 under the dual influence of an increase in the number of students admitted and a reduction in the birth rate in 1942 and the following years.

Comparison of the number of secondary school graduates

TABLE 53   ADMISSION TO HIGHER EDUCATION—U.S.S.R.

	1940		1950		1956		1959		1961		1963	
	Iᵃ	IIᵇ	Iᵃ	IIᵇ	Iᵃ	IIᵇ	Iᵃ	IIᵇ	Iᵃ	IIᵇ	Iᵃ	IIᵇ
Ordinary timetable	154.9 ⎱ 237.5	—			231.2	3.8	227.1	4.6	279.4	5.5	339.0	7.3
Evening courses	6.6 ⎰	—			32.6	—	63.5	—	93.1	—	118.5	—
Correspondence courses	101.9	—	111.6	—	194.9	—	221.1	—	294.4	—	356.8	—
Total	264.4		349.6	7.0	438.2	7.2	511.7	12.0	666.9	20.0ᶜ	814.3	17.0
Percentage of women	58.0		54.0		51.0		45.0		42.0		—	

ᵃ Number of students admitted, in thousands.
ᵇ Percentage of the average of the 17-, 18-, and 19-year age groups. On the basis of the birth rate in the U.S.S.R., as estimated in the special June 1958 issue of *Population* (Institut National d'Études Démographiques). The years 1959 and 1961 correspond to the children born in the period from 1942 to 1945; the year 1963 marks the beginning of the return to the normal postwar birth rate).
ᶜ The method of calculation used raises the percentage since, in fact, a large proportion of the newly enrolled students are older and belong to larger age groups.

166

and the number of those accepted in higher education reveals that up to 1959 there was a steady extension of the selective process at the entrance level: in 1958 and 1959, the enrollment in relation to candidatures varied from 50 to 15 per cent according to the institution and region concerned.[65] Beginning in 1960, the reduction in the number of general secondary school graduates, due to demographic changes, significantly reduced the severity of this selection.

GREAT BRITAIN

According to Ministry of Education statistics, 49,700 students in 1960 and 1961 left the sixth form with the G.C.E. (A),[66] that is, approximately 9 per cent of the average of the seventeen-, eighteen-, and nineteen-year age groups (8.7 per cent in Scotland). A very high proportion of this number (75 per cent) proceeded to higher education (see Table 54).

Table 55 shows that recruitment for the different types of institution differ greatly: (1) the selective nature of recruitment for the universities is shown in the higher percentage (81 per cent) of G.C.E. (A) holders with three passes or more. On the whole, the selection for university entrance depends on results achieved in the G.C.E. (A); (2) recruitment for teacher training colleges is at a much lower level, since 39 per cent of those enrolled do not have the G.C.E. (A) but only the G.C.E. (O); (3) the advanced full-time further education courses are attended by a large percentage of holders of the G.C.E. (A), but holders of the O.N.C. and O.N.D. are also numerous; and (4) the advanced part-time further education courses are mainly followed by holders of the O.N.C. and O.N.D.

Table 56 shows the percentage admission to the various

[65] DeWitt, *op. cit.*, p. 264. The difficulty of effecting a selection at entrance level varies greatly from one institution to another; access to the human sciences is particularly selective.

[66] Of this total, 20 per cent obtained only a single pass and 28 per cent, two passes.

TABLE 54   TREND AMONG G.C.E. (A) CERTIFICATE HOLDERS,
1961—ENGLAND AND WALES

	Total Enrollment (in thousands)	Percentage of Total	Boys	Girls
Universities	22.5	45.0	15.6	6.9
Training colleges	8.2	16.6	1.9	6.3
Full-time further education	6.8	13.7	4.0	2.8
Employment	12.1	24.6	8.3	3.8
Total	46.6	100.0	29.8	19.8

NOTE: In 1961–62, universities received only 45 per cent of the holders of the G.C.E. (A) for that year, and barely one-third of the girls.

As stated earlier, however, access to higher education—at any rate, outside the universities—is not exclusively restricted to holders of the G.C.E. (A). Table 55 shows the proportion of those holding the G.C.E. (O) and the further education technical certificates (O.N.C. and O.N.D.).

types of higher education institutes of boys and girls in relation to age groups.

FEDERAL REPUBLIC OF GERMANY

In spite of the existence of a second line of recruitment through technical education, the essential basis of recruitment to higher education in Germany is still the final secondary school certificate (*Abitur*). The number of these graduates (*Abiturienten*) has risen greatly since 1950. Of these, it would seem that nearly 80 per cent go on to higher institutions of university level (*Wissenschaftliche Hochschulen*), if their numbers are compared to the enrollments in first-year studies.[67] In 1950 there were 31,465 secondary

[67] This number probably includes between 1,000 and 2,000 students who have not graduated from secondary school.

TABLE 55   QUALIFICATION OF ENTRANTS, IN PERCENTAGE, IN THE VARIOUS CATEGORIES OF HIGHER INSTITUTION, 1961—ENGLAND AND WALES

	G.C.E. (A) Levels			O.N.C. or O.N.D.	Other Qualifications (including G.C.E. (O) Level)	Total	Total Number
	3 PASSES OR MORE	2	1				
FULL TIME							
University	83	13	1	—	3	100	25,500
Teacher training	14	24	23	—	39	100	16,300
Further education							
C.A.T.S.	34	27	14	22	3	100	2,700
Others	11	16	21	37	14	100	7,600
PART TIME							
Further education							
Day	2	9	9	78	2	100	17,200
Evening	1	6	6	87		100	11,800

SOURCE: *Robbins Report*, p. 18.

school graduates or the equivalent, or 4.3 per cent of the age group (5.8 per cent of boys, and 2.8 per cent of girls); in 1962 there were 62,320, or 7.3 per cent of the age group (9.1 per cent of boys, and 5.4 per cent of girls); and in 1963 there were 64,326, or 8.1 per cent of the age group (9.9 per cent of boys, and 6.1 per cent of girls). The numbers enrolled include also students who have completed secondary school studies and have certificates admitting them to higher studies *(Sonstige Hochschulberechtigte)*.

The trend in enrollments in the first year of university institutions in relation to age groups is as follows: in 1954, 28,740 (4.3 per cent of the age group); in 1957, 36,819 (4.2 per cent); in 1960, 47,042 (4.6 per cent); and in 1963, 50,812 (5.8 per cent).

Some German secondary school graduates go on to higher institutes of education *(Pädogogische Hochschulen)* whose en-

TABLE 56 PERCENTAGE OF AGE GROUPS ACCEPTED IN HIGHER EDUCATION—GREAT BRITAIN

	Boys	Girls	Total
Full time			
University	5.6	2.5[a]	4.0
Teacher training	1.3	3.8	2.5
Further education	2.9	1.0	2.0
	9.8	7.3	8.5
Part time			
Day	6.1	0.4	3.2
Evening	4.4	0.2	2.3
Private study[b]	2.1	—	1.1
Total	22.4	7.9	15.1

SOURCE: *Robbins Report*, p. 16.

[a] Girls at present represent approximately 25 per cent of total enrollment, as against 23 per cent in 1939.

[b] Membership of professional association.

rollment figures have increased very considerably (11,700 students in 1951, 44,200 in 1963) and represented 0.7 per cent in 1961 and 1.5 per cent in 1963 of the average of the twenty-one- and twenty-two-year age groups.

Although girls account for more than a third of the *Abiturienten,* they represent a relatively small proportion of German university enrollment: 17 per cent in 1950, 22 per cent in 1962, and 24 per cent in 1964. The proportion is naturally higher in institutes which train primary school teachers (62.5 per cent).

BELGIUM

No detailed statistics are available for Belgium on the proportion of secondary school graduates going on to the various forms of higher education.

If the number of certificates awarded each year in the humanities is related to the number of registrations for the first university year, the ratio, evaluated over an interval of several years, amounts to 64 per cent. The number of secondary school certificates awarded in 1961–62 was 15,900 (10,400 boys and 5,500 girls) and enrollment in the first university year in 1962–63 was 9,000 (6,800 boys and 2,200 girls). Thus, the percentage of graduates enrolled was 56.61 (65.3 per cent boys and 40 per cent girls).

Other graduates from the higher cycle of intermediate education, however, also proceed to higher technical education and middle teacher training schools along with graduates from technical schools and primary teacher training schools.

The proportion of women enrolling in university and technical education is relatively small but represents a majority in the case of teacher training.

In relation to the average of the eighteen- and nineteen-year age groups, higher education entrance rates in 1962 were as follows: university education, 8 per cent of the age groups; technical education, 3.9 per cent; middle teacher training, 4 per cent; middle technical teacher training, 1.1 per cent; and

TABLE 57   FIRST-YEAR ENROLLMENT IN VARIOUS TYPES OF HIGHER INSTITUTIONS, 1962–63, BY SEX—BELGIUM

	Boys		Girls		Total	
	NUMBER	PER CENT	NUMBER	PER CENT	NUMBER	PER CENT
University education	6,778	75.7	2,174	24.3	8,952	100
Technical education	2,995	67.7	1,423	32.8	4,418	100
Middle teacher training	2,354	52.0	2,175	48.0	4,529	100
Middle technical teacher training	185	15.1	1,042	84.9	1,227	100
Art education	305	75.5	99	24.5	404	100
Total	12,617	64.6	6,913	35.4	19,530	100

NOTE: It may be observed that enrollment in "university" institutions accounts for only 42 per cent of the total first-year enrollment.

art education, 0.35 per cent; or a total of 17.4 per cent of the age groups.

FRANCE

French higher education institutions still recruit primarily from secondary school graduates: the special entrance examination adds only a few hundred students each year and the faculties are only beginning to become accessible to holders of technical *lycée* certificates.

The ratio of new enrollments in the faculties to the number of secondary school (second part) graduates has been in the vicinity of 80 per cent over the last ten years. In 1960, the number of secondary school graduates was 59,300, and the new enrollments in the faculties in 1960–61 was 48,077; thus the ratio of new enrollments to secondary school graduates was 80.8 per cent. This high percentage demonstrates the pre-university nature of "long" secondary studies, but

TABLE 58   CHOICE OF HIGHER STUDIES, IN PERCENTAGE, ACCORDING TO SPECIALIZATION IN THE SECOND PART OF THE BACCALAURÉAT, 1960—FRANCE

	Type of Baccalauréat		
	PHILOSOPHY	EXPERI-MENTAL SCIENCE	MATHEMATICS, TECHNICAL MATHEMATICS
Law and economics	15.8	6.1	5.2
Science and technology	6.5	34.5	64.7
Arts	46.8	18.5	3.9
Medicine	8.1	17.0	4.9
Pharmacy	2.8	4.2	1.3
Total	80.0	80.0	80.0
Other	20.0	20.0	20.0

SOURCE: B.U.S. Statistics.

the number of double registrations[68] or successive enrollments in different faculties inflates this percentage to a considerable extent.[69] Conversely, it does not allow for access to higher institutions outside the university (in so far as their students are not enrolled in the faculties).

There are very marked differences in choice of faculty according to the type of *baccalauréat*. The philosophy *baccalauréat* represents a very distinct channeling toward the humanities, especially arts which is mostly chosen by girls.

The mathematics and technical mathematics *baccalauréats* provide a very strong channeling toward science and technology.

The experimental science *baccalauréat* would seem to be more polyvalent; one-third do science, but usually natural sciences which do not require a very advanced mathematical background.

Table 59 shows trends in higher education entrance rates separately for the public faculties, and for other public and private institutions.[70]

Part-time courses for the *promotion supérieure du travail* (advanced training) (Conservatoire National des Arts et Métiers and the university institutes) account for a maximum of 0.8 per cent of the age groups.

The enrollment of women in higher university education rose significantly between the two wars and has risen further since the last war. In 1920, women accounted for 10.1 per cent of the total enrollment; in 1939, 31.8 per cent; in 1950, 35.5 per cent; in 1960, 41.1 per cent;[71] and in 1963, 42.1 per cent.

[68] Fairly frequent between the faculty of arts and law and the political study institutes.

[69] The actual percentage is perhaps as little as 60 or 70 per cent.

[70] Students in the fourth year of the teacher training schools (educational training year after the *baccalauréat*) may also be included: 4,500 in 1951 and 6,600 in 1961, or about 1.3 per cent of the age groups.

[71] The enrollment of women, however, varies to a marked extent according to the disciplines involved; in 1961 there were

TABLE 59 ENROLLMENT TRENDS IN HIGHER EDUCATION— FRANCE

	1950–51	1955–56	1960–61	1963–64
Average of 18- and 19-year-old age groups	650,000	580,000	520,000	615,000
New enrollments				
Public faculties	25,500	29,150	48,077	72,635
Other[a]	6,500	7,500	10,000	12,300
Total rate[b]	5.0	6.3	11.0	13.8

[a] Estimate (less students enrolled in the faculties).

[b] These percentages are increased to a degree which is not easy to establish by double enrollments in the faculties; moreover, a proportion of first-year students come from other *propédeutique* courses and not directly from the *baccalauréat*.

ITALY

University enrollment in Italy changed to a relatively limited extent from 1950–51 to 1962–63 but a spectacular increase occurred at the beginning of the 1964–65 academic year (see Appendix Table A-4).

Since 1946, the percentage of first-year students (all disciplines) in relation to the corresponding age groups is as follows: 1946–47, 5.8 per cent;[72] 1954–55, 4.4 per cent; 1958–59, 5.7 per cent; and 1960–61, 6.0 per cent. First-year enrollments represent roughly 80 per cent of the number of secondary school graduates and holders of normal institute certificates from the previous year; recruitment from among graduates of the technical institutes, however, is tending to increase (2,162 admissions in 1961–62) and this partly explains the rise in enrollment from 1962 to 1965.[73]

The proportion of female students in the total enrollment

31.8 per cent in law; 64.0 per cent in arts; 33.6 per cent in science; 27.2 per cent in medicine; and 61.1 per cent in pharmacy.

[72] This inflation was due to enrollments delayed by the war.

[73] We have no information on either the extent or source of enrollments in recent years.

TABLE 60   SECONDARY SCHOOL GRADUATES, IN PERCENTAGE, PRE-
PARING FOR AN ACADEMIC EXAMINATION—THE NETH-
ERLANDS

	Boys	Girls	Average
Classical lycée			
Section A	79.0	71.0	76.0
Section B	92.0	78.0	88.0
Modern lycée			
Section A	30.0	10.0	24.0
Section B	62.0	37.0	58.0
Secondary technical	—	—	14.0
Secondary agricultural and horticultural	—	—	10.0

has not varied over the last decade: in 1951–52, 27 per cent,
and in 1958–59, 27 per cent.

THE NETHERLANDS

The mean percentages of secondary school graduates who
prepared for an academic examination (university education) in 1959, 1960, and 1961 are shown below.

Table 60 reveals that relatively few holders of technical
and agricultural certificates proceed to the universities. The
bulk of the enrollment comes from the classical secondary
schools and the scientific section of the modern secondary
schools.

The university entrance has shown a constant increase
since 1960 which is directly related to the development of
secondary education.

The proportion of women attending universities, however, remains relatively low: 16 per cent of the total enrollment in 1950–51, and 18 per cent of the total enrollment in
1962–63. This is due to the small numbers graduating from
the classical and modern pre-university secondary schools[74]

[74] Modern colleges for girls do not prepare for the university.

TABLE 61   Trends in University Enrollment Rate—The Netherlands

	1937	1950	1960	1961
Number (in thousands)				
Boys	2.1	3.7	5.9	6.9
Girls	0.5	0.7	1.3	1.5
Percentage of 18-year-old population				
Boys	2.9	4.5	6.8	7.5
Girls	0.7	0.9	1.6	1.7
Total	1.8	2.7	4.3	4.6

and also to the fact that they are less inclined than boys to continue their education.

GENERAL RECAPITULATION

Table 62 provides a general recapitulation of the situation in the individual countries. These details should be cautiously interpreted since they are not strictly comparable. It should be remembered that the first two years of college in the United States are not regarded as equivalent to European higher education; three of the nine countries (Germany, England, and the United States) provide training for primary school teachers in institutions which are classified as higher; and the advanced part-time courses under English further education do not really correspond to preparation for the first university degrees.

NUMBER OF GRADUATES FROM HIGHER EDUCATION BY MAJOR DISCIPLINES

NUMBER OF GRADUATES (FIRST LEVEL)[75]

Table 63 shows the number of higher education graduates for each country by major disciplines over the most recent

[75] See note 6 to Table 63.

years for which figures are available (1962 or 1963). For the United States and the U.S.S.R., the situation in 1959 is also noted.

It was difficult to obtain comparable data for this table because of reasons already mentioned:

1. The training of elementary school teachers is included in higher education in only three of the countries concerned (United States, Great Britain, and Federal Republic

TABLE 62   GENERAL RECAPITULATION, IN PERCENTAGE: RATE OF ACCESS TO HIGHER EDUCATION[a] AND PERCENTAGE OF WOMEN ENROLLED

| | | Rate of Access | | Percentage of Women in Universities or Other Higher Institutions |
	YEAR	FULL TIME	PART TIME	
United States	1963	34.0	—	38.0 (1961)
U.S.S.R.	1963	7.3	9. 7	42.0 (1962)
England and Wales				
University		4.0	—	25.0 (1962)
Further education	1961	2.0	6.6	—
Training Colleges		2.5	—	70.0 (1962)
		8.5		
Federal Republic of Germany				
University	1963	5.8	—	24.0 (1963)
Pedagogic institutes		1.5	—	62.5 (1963)
Belgium	1963	17.4	—	24.0 (1963)
France	1963	13.8	0.8	42.1 (1963)
Italy	1960	6.0	—	27.0 (1959)
Netherlands	1961	4.6	—[b]	18.0 (1962)

[a] Ratio between the number of first-year enrollments and the eighteen- or nineteen-year age groups.

[b] Not including part-time courses for secondary and technical school teachers.

of Germany), and this inflates the number of graduates for these countries. To make allowances for this, Table 65 shows the number of graduates from teacher training schools and the number from higher education.

2. In certain countries, secondary teacher training is provided to a greater or lesser extent in special higher schools (teacher training colleges or higher pedagogical institutes) whereas in other countries it is provided in the arts and science faculties (future teachers in these countries are included among the graduates of these faculties).

3. Certain classes of postsecondary leaving level (senior technicians, engineer technicians) may be included under higher education (Belgium, Great Britain) or under secondary technical education. To take account of the particular situation in Belgium and Great Britain, Tables 63 and 65 make distinctions between first-level certificates and those awarded on completion of short higher educational courses.

Table 64 shows the breakdown of the various types of graduate as percentages of the total. However, the comparison has little significance since the data under certain important headings is not comparable.

NUMBER OF GRADUATES IN RELATION TO
GENERATIONS

From Table 63 the following can be deduced: the percentage of graduates in higher education in relation to the average of the twenty-two–twenty-three and twenty-three–twenty-four age groups; and the relative proportion of graduates from the different disciplines in relation to age groups.

The significance of the two series of observations presented in Table 65 will be discussed in the Conclusion.

DEVELOPMENT OF POSTGRADUATE EDUCATION

As already stated, some of the countries organize courses or studies following the first higher education diploma as an introduction to scientfic research or to encourage original

TABLE 63   NUMBER OF GRADUATES FROM INSTITUTIONS OF HIGHE[R]

Disciplines	Federal Republic of Germany 1963	Belgium 1963	France 1964	Great Britain 1962[b]
Human sciences				
Law, economics, political science, commerce	6,172	I 1,449 [c] / II 393	5,200	I 5,573 / II 4,215
Arts, social sciences, biology	5,798	1,285	5,800	I 9,38◦ / II 447
	11,970	I 2,734 / II 393	11,000	I 14,959 / II 4,66◦
Natural and applied sciences				
Natural sciences	2,518	858	5,650	I 7,70◦ / II 1,31◦
Technology	I 3,081 / II —	I 560 / II 1,421	5,930	I 9,38◦ / II 8,77◦
Agronomy and veterinary science	692	I 182 / II 109	580	I 65◦ / II 2◦
Medical sciences (medicine, pharmacy, dentistry)	3,940	I 907 / II 280	4,150	I 2,56◦ / II 44◦
Architecture and the fine arts	1,184	I 4 / II 306	440	I 1,1◦ / II 9◦
	11,415	I 2,511 / II 2,116	16,750	I 21,4◦ / II 11,5◦

EDUCATION, BY MAJOR DISCIPLINES[a]

Italy 1963	*Nether-lands* 1962	*U.S.S.R.*		*United States*	
		1959	1963	1959	1963
7,384	595	25,000	24,800	66,924	68,398
4,436[d]	641	25,500	—	97,280	135,514
12,270	*1,236*	*50,600*	—	*164,214*	*203,842*
2,297	385	21,000	—	39,628[e]	51,615[e]
2,405	687	108,600	121,100	38,135	37,535
583	149	34,500	31,400	7,576	6,063
3,546	538	29,500	31,500	23,479	25,914
379	—	2,400	3,100	14,435	16,566
,910	*1,759*	*196,000*	—	*123,352*	*137,693*

(Continued on pp. 182–183)

TABLE 63   NUMBER OF GRADUATES FROM INSTITUTIONS OF HIGHE

Disciplines	Federal Republic of Germany 1963	Belgium 1963		France 1964	Great Britain 1962[b]	
Education[t]	14,514	I 4,030	II 602	127	I —	II 4,59(
Miscellaneous	—	—		—	I 1,08'	II 1,32:
Total	37,899	I 9,275	II 3,111	27,877	I 37,51(	II 22,08(
Average population of 22–23 and 23–24 year age groups	923,000[k]	115,000		550,000	660,0(	

 ª This table generally includes foreign students who could not alwa be distinguished from the total in national statistics.

ᵇ For Great Britain, category I includes: degree-level diplomas ; diplomas in technology; diplomas of the same level, e.g., membership professional association, art teacher's diploma, etc., are classified un category II (nondegree level); training college diplomas, H.N.I H.N.C.'s, Membership of Commercial Association, etc. This is the cla fication adopted by the Robbins Commission.

ᶜ I = University education or equivalent (first level). Diplomas, e neering diplomas, diploma of doctor of medicine, etc., are awarded a complete higher education; subsequent diplomas or degrees obtained preresearch or postgraduate courses are therefore excluded.

II = Short courses.

ᵈ Includes the *magistero* faculties.

ᵉ Biology, mathematics, and physics; more than 25 per cent of th graduates become high school teachers.

DUCATION, BY MAJOR DISCIPLINES[a] *(Continued)*

Italy 1963	*Nether- lands* 1962		*U.S.S.R.*		*United States*	
			1959	1963	1959	1963
729	I II	21 [h] 1,961	91,400[i]	86,500	87,877	102,796
110	—		—	—	7,808	6,263
3,019	I II	3,016 1,961	338,000	331,700	383,151	450,594[i]
2,000	169,000		4,100,000[i]	3,860,000[i]	2,150,000	2,300,000

[f] This line does not include teacher training in Belgium, France, Italy, e Netherlands, and the U.S.S.R.; in the other countries (Federal Relic of Germany, Great Britain, and the United States), this training is luded in the above statistics.

[g] In 1962, the number of graduates from the training colleges was forously reduced because of the extension from two to three years decided in 1960; in 1959 the number in this category of graduates reached 500.

[h] Secondary certificate (*M.O.-akten,* A level) and technical certificate aar nijverheidsonderwijs jongens, A level). These figures relate to the rs 1963 and 1964.

[i] Includes approximately 40,000 science teachers.

Includes 2,970 graduates from Puerto Rico (outlying area); for 1963– the total number of graduates is estimated at 487,860.

Population of twenty-six to twenty-seven age group.

Average of twenty to twenty-four age groups.

scientific work; for example, in the United States and Great Britain, preparation for the Master's degree and Ph.D.; in the U.S.S.R., preparation for the degree of candidate; and in France, preparation for the third-cycle doctorate and the state doctorate. These post-graduate courses are tending to occupy a more and more imoprtant place in higher education institutions.

In the other countries, training for scientific research is not systematically organized in a special university cycle[76] and, in any case, is not covered by published statistics.

In the United States, more than 10 per cent of the total enrollment in the colleges or universities continue their studies with the purpose of obtaining a Master's degree or doctorate (including three-fifths on a part-time basis). The number of graduates at these two levels is steadily increasing. For the Master's degree, in 1940, there were 26,700 graduates (1.1 per cent of the age group); in 1950, 58,100 graduates (2.5 per cent); in 1960, 75,700 graduates (3.6 per cent); in 1963, 91,300 graduates (4 per cent); and in 1964 (estimated), 95,000 graduates (4.2 per cent). For the doctorate, in 1940, there were 3,290 graduates (0.13 per cent of the age group); in 1950, 6,633 graduates (0.28 per cent); in 1960, 9,829 graduates (0.45 per cent); in 1963, 12,800 graduates (0.55 per cent); and in 1964 (estimated), 13,200 graduates (0.57 per cent).

The graduates receiving the Master's degree in 1960 were distributed among the major disciplines as follows: science and technology, 19.4 per cent; agriculture, 1.6 per cent; architecture, 0.4 per cent; medical sciences, 2.5 per cent; and

[76] It is partly combined with preparation for the first diploma, while the university training of research workers merges with assistants' careers in the faculties. Young research workers are also trained by the research institutes themselves. Few statistics are available on this subject.

The example of the Federal Republic of Germany, however, shows the importance of training for research through assistants' posts: the number of assistants and assistant masters (*Assistenten* and *Oberassistenten*) rose from 5,700 in 1960 to 15,970 in 1964.

TABLE 64 GRADUATES FROM INSTITUTIONS OF HIGHER EDUCATION, BY MAJOR DISCIPLINES, AS A PERCENTAGE OF THE TOTAL

Disciplines	Federal Republic of Germany	Belgium	France	Great Britain	Italy	Netherlands	U.S.S.R. (1959)	United States (1959)
Human sciences								
Law, economics, commerce	16.3	14.9	17.6	16.4	34.0	11.9	7.3	17.4
Arts, social science, theology	15.3	10.4	19.0	16.5	19.3	12.9	7.5	25.3
Natural and applied sciences	*31.6*	*25.3*	*36.6*	*33.0*	*53.3*	*24.8*	*14.9*	*42.8*
Natural science	6.7	6.9	20.3	15.1	13.0	7.7	6.2	10.3
Technology	8.1	16.0	22.3	30.6	10.5	13.8	32.1	10.0
Agronomy and veterinary science	1.8	2.3	2.3	1.1	2.5	2.9	10.2	2.0
Medical sciences	10.4	9.6	16.5	5.0	15.4	10.8	8.6	6.1
Architecture and fine arts	3.1	2.5	1.3	3.5	1.6	?	0.7	3.7
	30.1	*37.3*	*62.7*	*55.3*	*43.0*	*35.2*	*58.0*	*32.2*
Education	*38.3*	*37.4*	*0.6*	*7.7*	*3.2*	*39.9*	*27.0*	*22.9*
Miscellaneous	—	—	—	4.0	0.5	—	—	2.0
Total	100.0	100.0	100.0	100.0	100.0	100.0	100.0	100.0

TABLE 65 PERCENTAGE OF GRADUATES FROM INSTITUTIONS OF HIGHER EDUCATION AND FROM TEACHER TRAINING SCHOOLS, BY AGE GROUPS AND BY MAJOR DISCIPLINES[a]

	Federal Republic of Germany (1963)	Belgium (1963)		France (1964)	Italy (1963)	Netherlands (1962)		Great Britain (1962)		United States (1963)	U.S.S.R. (1959)
		I	I + II			I	I + II	I	I + II		
Graduates from higher institutions specializing in teacher training	1.40[b]	3.50	4.00[c]	0.02[d]	0.09[d]	0.01	1.20	—	0.70[e]	4.60[f]	2.20[g]
Other graduates											
Science and technology[h]	0.68	1.30	2.70	2.20	0.65	0.70		2.68	4.22	3.90[i]	4.00[j]
Human sciences	1.30	2.40	2.70	2.00	1.53	0.70		2.26	2.93	8.90	1.20
Medical sciences	0.43	0.80	1.00	0.76	0.44	0.30		0.38	0.45	1.10	0.70
Fine arts	0.13	0.00	0.20	0.08	0.04	—		0.17	0.32	0.70	0.06
	2.54	*4.50*	*6.90*	*5.04*	*2.70*	*1.80*		*5.68*	*8.30*	*15.00*	*5.96*
Total	3.94	8.00	10.90	5.06	2.86	1.80	3.00	5.68	9.00	19.60	8.20
Graduates from teacher training schools	—	—	2.00[k]	1.20	1.20[l]	2.50[m]		—	—	—	1.20[n]

NOTE: Given the variable content of lines 1, 2, and 3, this table must be interpreted with considerable caution. As already mentioned, the main difficulty lies in the different types of training for teachers in the various countries.

[a] Some of these percentages are slightly inflated since they include foreign graduates.

[b] This percentage includes the training of primary school teachers and *Realschulen* teachers, and has been calculated on the basis of the twenty-three- and twenty-four-year-old age groups.

[c] Includes the training given in middle teacher training schools and middle technical teacher training schools.

[d] Higher schools of physical education and special diplomas in education.

[e] Includes the training of primary school teachers (approximately two-thirds) and secondary school teachers (one-third). It was exceptionally low in 1963 but amounted to 2.4 per cent in 1959.

[f] Includes the training of primary school teachers (60 per cent) and high school teachers (40 per cent).

[g] This percentage basically comprises the training of teachers for secondary classes 5 to 10.

[h] Natural sciences, technology, agronomy.

[i] Includes 2 per cent in pure science and 1.9 per cent in applied science.

[j] Includes 0.5 per cent in pure science and 3.5 per cent in applied science.

[k] Estimated.

[l] Estimate of teacher recruitments.

[m] 1964.

[n] 1963.

human sciences, 76.1 per cent. Those receiving the doctorate in 1960 were distributed as follows: science and technology, 42.1 per cent; agriculture, 4.5 per cent; architecture, 0.2 per cent; medical sciences, 1.1 per cent; and human sciences, 52.1 per cent.

In the U.S.S.R., the training of young research workers *(aspirants)* with the purpose of obtaining the degree of candidate *(Kandidat Nauk)* is provided in higher institutions (V.U.Z.) and in research institutes on either a full-time or part-time basis.

The number of trainees and graduates has greatly increased since 1960 as shown in Table 66.

Analysis shows that a substantial priority is given at this stage to the natural sciences and technology. In 1963, the 73,105 *aspirants* were distributed as follows: natural sciences, 25.6 per cent; technology, 37.6 per cent; agriculture and veterinary surgery, 8.1 per cent; medical sciences, 6.5 per cent; social science, economics, law, 20.5 per cent; and fine arts, 1.7 per cent.

TABLE 66   TRENDS IN ENROLLMENT IN HIGHER EDUCATION AND NUMBER OF GRADUATES—U.S.S.R.

	1940	1950	1960	1963
Total enrollment (in thousands)	16.8	21.9	36.7	73.1
Higher education institutions				
Full time	11.5	11.2	13.4	27.5
Part time	1.6	1.2	6.9	15.7
Research institutes				
Full time	2.9	6.9	9.5	15.3
Part time	0.7	2.4	6.8	14.5
Number of graduates				
Total	1,978	—	5,517	11,660[a]
Higher education institutions	1,472	—	3,020	6,854
Research institutes	506	—	2,497	4,806

[a] Approximately 0.3 per cent of the average of the 25- to 29-year age group.

In Great Britain, of the 107,000 full-time students attending universities in 1960–61, more than 17,800 (16.7 per cent) went on to postgraduate courses. The number of higher degrees and diplomas awarded has increased steadily. In 1951, there were 2,410 (0.33 per cent of the age group); in 1959, there were 3,088 (0.44 per cent); and in 1962, there were 3,350 (0.49 per cent).

In 1959, these degrees were distributed among the main disciplines as follows: human sciences, 32 per cent; natural sciences, 43 per cent; technology, 15 per cent; medical sciences, 8 per cent; and agronomy, 2 per cent.

In France, courses or training following the first degrees or certificates awarded by the higher education institutions are also becoming more important: the enrollment is distributed as follows: in law and economics, 11 per cent; in science and technology, 13 per cent; in arts and human sciences, 13 per cent; and in medicine, 15 per cent.

In arts and sciences, however, a large proportion of this enrollment represents preparation for the higher studies certificate leading to the examination for the *agrégation de l'enseignement secondaire;* in medicine, it primarily represents preparation for specialist certificates.[77]

The rate at which certificates are awarded on completion of courses providing an introduction to research (doctorate level of the third cycle) or on completion of research (state or university doctorate) is still relatively low (1961).

YIELD OF HIGHER EDUCATION

RELATIVE NATURE OF THIS CONCEPT

With the growth in European university enrollment has come an increasing concern with the problem of the "yield," that is, the ratio between the number of new enrollments and the number of graduates three, four, or five years later. For

---

[77] Report on the number enrolled in the first year and the eighteen- or nineteen-year age group.

TABLE 67   RATE OF SUCCESS, IN PERCENTAGE, IN BRITISH UNI-
VERSITIES, 1960–61—GREAT BRITAIN

Discipline	Success after Course of Normal Duration	Success after Longer Period	Still Studying	Failures
Arts and social sciences	86.3	—	2.1	11.9
Pure science	82.9	—	2.3	14.7
Applied science	72.5	—	7.5	20.8
Agriculture	83.4	—	4.4	14.2
Medicine and dentistry	57.2	30.0	2.8	10.0
Veterinary medicine	56.9	25.9	2.7	15.0

SOURCE: *Report of the University Grants Committee, 1960–1961.*

a variety of reasons—repeaters, complexity of the study pattern, diversity of students' aims—the statistics are not of much help in forming a clear opinion on this subject.

In making international comparisons, it is essential to bear in mind the various factors involved: (1) *the more or less selective nature of initial recruitment:* an institution which recruits on the basis of strict selection will obviously have a better rate of success than another at the same level which accepts all candidates;[78] (2) *the relative difficulty of studies leading to degrees:* it is difficult to make comparisons because of problems of equivalence (see remarks in the introduction); and (3) *the quality of the teacher-student ratio* is a key factor governing success in higher studies; as will be shown later, the disparities are considerable.

From another angle, this concept of the yield from higher education is in itself somewhat vague. Has a student who, for intellectual, family, or economic reasons, drops out of a higher course before completing it in fact wasted his time?

[78] As in universities in all the Common Market countries.

TABLE 68 RATE OF SUCCESS IN SOVIET HIGHER EDUCATION, 1950 to 1955—U.S.S.R.

	Number Enrolling in 1950 (in thousands)	Number of Graduates in 1955 (in thousands)	Rate of Success (in percentage)
Total	*349.1*	*245.7*	*70.3*
Full-time or evening classes	237.6	183.5	77.2
Correspondence courses	111.5	62.2	55.7
By Specialization (examples):			
ENGINEERING: *Total*	*86.0*	*65.9*	*76.6*
Full-time classes	70.1	62.2	88.7
Correspondence courses	15.9	3.7	23.3
AGRICULTURE: *Total*	*28.5*	*24.1*	*84.5*
Full-time classes	23.8	23.0	96.6
Correspondence courses	4.7	1.1	23.4
EDUCATION: *Total*	*185.4*	*123.3*	*66.1*
Full-time classes	108.7	73.1	66.6
Correspondence courses	76.7	50.2	65.4

SOURCE: Nicholas DeWitt, *Education and Professional Employment in the U.S.S.R.* (Washington, D. C.: Government Printing Office, 1961), page 343. The ratio of enrollment in 1950 to successes five years later is taken as representing the rate of success.

Are incomplete, interrupted, or "failed" higher studies a waste, as contended by certain economists specializing in problems relating to the economics of education? It would not seem that there can be any cut and dried answers to these questions.

In any case, all the statistics confirm what common sense alone would indicate, namely, that there is a close correlation between success and the selective nature of recruitment and the quality of the teacher-student ratio.

TABLE 69   RATE OF SUCCESS IN HIGHER EDUCATION IN THE COMMON MARKET COUNTRIES

	Number Admitted (as a percentage of age groups)	Number of Graduates (as a percentage of age groups)	Rate of Success
Federal Republic of Germany[a]	4.2 (1957–58)	2.5 (1963)	60.0
Belgium[b]	—	—	60.0
France[c]	6.7 (1956–57)	3.8 (1960–61)	57.0
Italy	4.4 (1954–55)	2.8 (1958–59)	63.0
Netherlands	3.4 (1956–57)	2.0 (1962–63)	58.0

[a] Universities only.

[b] Middle teacher training courses and engineer-technician courses only.

[c] Universities and *grandes écoles*.

DISPARITIES IN YIELD

In countries where students are recruited on a selective basis, the percentages of success are high (at any rate, in full-time education) as may be seen in the following tables for Great Britain and the U.S.S.R.

In the U.S.S.R., it will be observed that there is a high average yield (77.2 per cent) for full-time studies and evening courses; a much lower yield, although still remarkable, in correspondence courses (55.7 per cent), this yield apparently varying to a large extent according to the branch involved.

For the United States, a comparison of enrollments in the first year and the number of first degrees four years later gives an average yield of between 63 and 65 per cent. However, this does not allow for certificates obtained in two or three years in the junior colleges and technical institutes (48,000 in 1959). The yield is relatively satisfactory, especially if the extremely variable level of recruitment is borne in mind, and is partly facilitated by the differences in the level of studies from college to college, at any rate for certain categories of certificate.

In the Common Market countries, statistics do not always make it possible[79] to obtain a precise picture.

A comparison of the admissions in the first year and the number of degrees awarded five years later is shown in Table 70.

What is striking is the relative homogeneity which emerges even though the pattern of studies may differ from one country to another.

In France, the yield from those schools which recruit on the basis of an examination (engineering schools, certain business schools, and the like) is excellent and, generally speaking, almost 100 per cent. The problem of success for this category of student arises in the special preparatory classes of the *lycées,* that is, before they have been included in the statistics for higher education.

In the faculties, the propédeutique or first year is the one in which the basic selection takes place. Allowing for repeaters, the rate of success in the first cycle is only between 45 and 60 per cent.[80] Subsequently, progress is more satisfactory: 75 to 85 per cent of students enrolled in the first year complete their studies within the normal period or with a delay of one or two years. Finally, the percentage of success in relation to the initial enrollment varies, according to the discipline involved, from 35 to 45 per cent.[81]

In Belgium, the process is roughly the same: the strictest

[79] Particularly in Germany, where there are no annual examinations.

[80] Rate calculated in relation to students sitting for the examination.

[81] The results of the 1963 examinations in medicine confirm this.

The rates of success were, for the first year, in examination A, 63.8 per cent, and in examination B, 55.8 per cent; for the second year, 79.7 per cent; for the third year, 94.9 per cent; for the fourth year, 93.9 per cent; and for the fifth year, 95.2 per cent.

TABLE 70   RATE OF ADMISSION, IN PERCENTAGE, AT 21 YEARS
OF AGE TO FULL-TIME HIGHER EDUCATION, AND
NUMBERS INVOLVED,[a] BY OCCUPATION OF FATHER,
1961–62—GREAT BRITAIN

Occupation of Father	Rate of Admission			Numbers Involved[b]	
	DEGREE LEVEL	OTHERS	TOTAL	FIGURES	PER-CENT-AGE
BOYS AND GIRLS					
Nonmanual					
Higher professional	33.0	12.0	45.0	15,000	2.8
Managerial and other					
professional	11.0	8.0	19.0	87,000	16.5
Clerical	6.0	4.0	10.0	38,000	7.2
Manual					
Skilled	2.0	2.0	4.0	248,000	47.2
Semi and unskilled	1.0	1.0	2.0	137,000	26.1
BOYS					
Nonmanual	15.0	4.0	19.0	70,000	
Manual	3.0	2.0	5.0	189,000	
GIRLS					
Nonmanual	9.0	10.0	19.0	70,000	
Manual	1.0	2.0	3.0	196,000	

SOURCE: *Robbins Report*, p. 50.
NOTE: Notwithstanding the low rate of attendance of children
of manual workers, 30 per cent of the new full-time students come
from such families which represent 73 per cent of the total.

[a] Universities, further education, training colleges.

[b] Excluding indeterminate professions.

selection is effected by the examinations for the candidature;
subsequently, the rate of success comes close to the maximum.
For example, the rates of success in the 1959–60 examinations were as follows: In the first test for the *candidature,* 39
per cent in the arts and 40 per cent in the sciences were

passed successfully; in the second test, 65 per cent in the arts and 64 per cent in the sciences were successful. In the first test for the *licence,* 91 per cent in the arts and 88 per cent in the sciences were successful; in the second test, 88 per cent in the arts and 95 per cent in the sciences were successful.

In The Netherlands, the percentage eliminated is relatively high in the later years and this explains both the low percentage of success and the very marked prolongation of studies.

SOCIAL ASPECTS OF ACCESS TO HIGHER EDUCATION

SOCIAL INEQUALITIES AT SECONDARY LEVEL
AGGRAVATED IN HIGHER EDUCATION

The tremendous disparities in the rate of admission to general secondary education and in the chances of success in relation to the social background of the children concerned were discussed above.

Earlier in this section, it was noted that, notwithstanding the development of other types of recruitment, especially through technical education, long general secondary studies are still the normal channel leading to higher education or, at any rate, the one followed by an overwhelming majority of candidates.

These two factors imply that the social differentiations observed at the entrance to secondary education and, even more, at its completion will recur unchanged at the higher education level, further aggravated by family difficulties in financing this new study cycle and even from the need for a further intellectual choice. Available national statistics on the social background of students in higher education confirm this. The following may be cited as examples.

SOME NATIONAL STATISTICS

The ideal basis for proper comparisons would be standardized data on rates of attendance or enrollment in higher education by social groups.

TABLE 71   PERCENTAGE OF STUDENTS COMPLETING HIGH SCHOOL
            WHO PROCEED TO HIGHER EDUCATION, BY OCCUPA-
            TION OF PARENTS—UNITED STATES

Occupation of Father	Boys	Girls
Professional and technical	67.0	61.0
Business	51.0	52.0
Farm	28.0	21.0
Skilled and semi-skilled labor	24.0	15.0
Others	27.0	18.0

SOURCE: Survey undertaken by the Educational Testing Service for the College Entrance Examination Board.
NOTE: The above percentages do not genuinely represent enrollment rates by social category. They apply only to that section
of young people which, in the United States, is very numerous
(69 per cent of the age group in 1964), who have completed high
school. The real rates of entrance to higher education for the
eighteen-year-old population are really lower.

Moreover, the enrollment rate in the terminal classes in the
United States is not absolutely the same for all social groups (it
is very probable that most of the students who have not successfully completed high school (31 per cent) come from the families
of manual workers). The result is that the social differentiations
among entrants in American colleges are more pronounced than
the above percentages indicate.

In fact, the most commonly published national statistics
merely give a breakdown of student numbers in absolute
terms and by percentages according to social background (cf.
figures below for the Federal Republic of Germany, Belgium,
The Netherlands, and France).

For Great Britain and, with certain qualifications, for some
parts of the United States, we show the rates of admission by
social groups. For France, we give the breakdown of students by social origin, the number per 1,000 persons actively
employed, and the rates of attendance in higher education between nineteen and twenty-four years of age by social groups.

Some observations are made regarding the Soviet Union,

and some more precise information is given on regional disparities in higher education.

In other words, no attempt is made to do more than set out the heterogeneous factual elements available, and note the conclusions which can be drawn.

SOME DATA ON THE SOVIET UNION

Following the Revolution, a systematic effort was made in the Soviet Union to provide access to higher education for children from manual workers' (workers and peasants) families. In 1932–33, the proportion of students from such families is thought to have reached 72 per cent.[82] Subsequently, this percentage dropped and the report on educational reform submitted to the Central Committee of the Soviet Communist

TABLE 72 BREAKDOWN OF UNIVERSITY ENROLLMENT, 1962–63, BY SOCIAL BACKGROUND—FEDERAL REPUBLIC OF GERMANY

	As a Percentage of the Total	
Occupation of Parents	BOYS	GIRLS
Farmers (owners)	3.6	3.0
Tradesmen and industrialists	14.6	13.8
Liberal professions	11.3	15.5
Officials	32.8	36.5
Office employees[a]	30.0	27.0
Workers	6.0	2.8
No occupation	1.7	1.3
	100.0	100.0

[a] This probably includes medium and higher cadres in the private sector.

[82] This seems reasonable in view of the development of education under the first Five-Year Plan and the increased numbers of medium-grade and senior cadres.

TABLE 73 BREAKDOWN OF ENROLLMENT, IN PERCENTAGE, IN
THE UNIVERSITY OF LOUVAIN, 1959–60, BY SOCIAL
BACKGROUND—BELGIUM

| | Students Enrolled | | |
Profession of Parents	FLEMISH SECTION	FRENCH SECTION	General Average
Farmers	6.8	4.5	5.74
Industrial and Commercial employers	26.6	22.0	24.40
Heads of firms	7.0	11.2	9.00
Tradesmen and small shopkeepers	19.6	10.8	15.40
Liberal professions and senior cadres	24.2	43.3	33.31
Liberal professions and professions requiring a university degree	15.4	26.1	20.48
Senior officials, magistrates	6.9	14.7	10.59
Teachers	1.9	2.5	2.24
Senior cadres in the private sector[a]	—	—	—
Medium-grade cadres	20.8	18.7	19.77
Public service	4.5	5.8	5.13
Teachers	7.5	2.9	5.27
Private sector	8.8	10.0	9.37
Office employees	10.4	5.6	8.20
Industrial workers and junior cadres	8.4	3.0	5.77
Other categories or occupation unknown	2.8	2.8	2.81
Total	100.0	100.0	100.00

SOURCE: Survey by the research service of the Universitaire
Werkgemeenschap of Louvain for 1959–60.
[a] Data for this item are included with those for liberal professions, etc., two lines above.

TABLE 74 BREAKDOWN OF ENROLLMENT, IN PERCENTAGE, IN HIGHER EDUCATION, 1947–48 AND 1958–59, BY SOCIAL BACKGROUND—THE NETHERLANDS

Occupation of Parents	1947–48	1958–59
Farmers (owners)	4.3	5.0
Heads of firms	8.6	8.9
Tradesmen and shopkeepers	17.8	15.1
Officials		
Cadres	23.9	23.8
Clerical Staff	11.9	9.0
Liberal professions	12.1	13.4
Commercial and industrial office employees		
Cadres	6.9	6.4
Others	11.3	11.4
Industrial and agricultural workers	1.0	5.2
No occupation or occupation unknown	2.2	1.8
Total	100.0	100.0

Party in 1958 gave the proportion of workers' and peasants' children attending Moscow University as only about 40 per cent. Given the structure of the working population in the Soviet Union (see Table 4), this scarcely reflects complete equality of access to higher education but is not surprising, since the influence of family background on attendance at secondary and higher institutions certainly operates in the U.S.S.R. as in all other countries.

The extent of social disparities in access to higher education cannot be deduced from current Soviet statistics. Regional disparities are of the same order of magnitude as those noted earlier concerning the second secondary cycle, and the trend toward equalization is pronounced because of the rapid progress made in the more backward republics during the 1950's. This trend is clearly apparent in Soviet statistics for the numbers of students per 10,000 inhabitants. For the en-

TABLE 75   BREAKDOWN OF ENROLLMENT, IN PUBLIC FACUL-
TIES, 1961–62, BY SOCIAL BACKGROUND—FRANCE

Occupation of Parents	Percentage of Active Population (1962 census)	Percentage for All Faculties[a]	Number of Students per 1,000 Persons Actively Employed
Farmers	15.7	5.6	3.9
Agricultural workers	4.3	0.6	1.4
Industrial and commercial employers	10.4	17.7	—
Industrialists	0.4	4.0	107.0
Shopkeepers	6.6	9.8	16.0
Artisans	3.3	3.9	13.0
Liberal professions and senior cadres	4.0	28.5	—
Liberal professions	0.7	9.9	168.0
Professors[b]	0.7	5.8	91.0
Senior cadres[b]	2.6	13.2	55.0
Medium-grade cadres	7.8	17.8	—
Teachers[b]	2.2	5.8	39.0
Medium-grade cadres[b]	5.6	12.0	24.0
Office employees	12.6	7.9	7.0
Workers	36.7	6.4	—
Foremen	1.6	1.6	11.0
Workers	27.8	4.2	1.4
Unskilled	7.3	0.6	0.8
Service personnel	5.4	0.9	1.8
Other categories or not known[c]	3.1	14.6	11.0
Total	100.0	100.0	—

[a] *Information Statistiques*, No. 53–54.

[b] Public and private.

[c] Including persons of independent means, army, clergy, and police.

NOTES: (1) The social background of students in the *grandes écoles* is not, on the average, significantly different.

(Continued on p. 201)

TABLE 76   HIGHER EDUCATION DEGREES GRANTED, 1961— FRANCE

Discipline	Degree Level	Third-cycle Doctorate[a]	State Doctorate[b]
Law and economics	716	244	—[c]
Arts	1,738	64	42
Science	1,243	358	237
Technology	—	146	—
Medicine	1,614[d]	—	—[c]
Pharmacy	365[d]	107	28
	5,676	919	307
As percentage of age groups	0.9	0.15	0.05

[a] Does not include the secondary *agrégé.*

[b] Level which gives access to teaching posts in higher education.

[c] Allowance should be made for the fact that university professors may be recruited by examination (law faculty *agrégation,* and so on).

[d] Special study certificates.

NOTES to TABLE 75 *(cont.)*

(2) The rates shown in the last column are not absolutely comparable because of variations in the birth rate and the duration of working life in the different social groups.

(3) Ignoring the variations noted above, it is possible, on the basis of Table 75, to establish the enrollment rates in university education (evaluated in relation to the five nineteen- to twenty-four-year age groups) for the various social groups: agricultural workers, 1.0 per cent; farm owners, 3.0 per cent; industrial workers, 1.4 per cent; office employees, 5.0 per cent; artisans and tradesmen, 11.0 per cent; medium-grade cadres, 18.0 per cent; and liberal professions, senior cadres, industrialists, 58.0 per cent.

It will be noted that these figures do not cover enrollment in the *grandes écoles* and private faculties. The real rates for all higher education are therefore somewhat higher, that is, for the higher categories, they exceed 60 per cent.

tire U.S.S.R. there were 69 students for each 10,000 of the population, and in 1963, there were 144 students. For the four most advanced republics, the numbers of students were 64, 88, 93, and 97 in 1950, and 142, 143, 158, and 161 in 1963. For the four most backward republics, the numbers were 36, 41, 44, and 47 in 1950, and 89, 94, 101, and 102 in 1963.

3. The Human, Material, and Financial Resources Devoted to Education

The extensive development of school attendance in the nine countries involves increasingly large human, material, and financial resources. In countries where progress has been particularly marked during the last decade (see Table 11), the recruitment of teachers, the building of schools and universities, and the financing problems have often presented great difficulties.

Chapter 3 of this study shows how the various countries have tackled the teacher problem, and the extent to which national resources are devoted to schools and universities.

EDUCATIONAL STAFFING

The increase in numbers who enter schools and in numbers who qualify represents only one aspect of the real stage reached in educational development. To obtain a picture which would allow true comparisons, it would be necessary to analyze all factors that affect the quality of the education that young people receive in each of the countries concerned: the quality of the teaching staff, the student-teacher ratio, methods, timetables, programs, what the examinations really involve, and so on.

It has already been indicated in the Introduction that the scope of the present study excludes a consideration of these factors. We shall merely consider, very succinctly, the vital problem of the teachers from two aspects: how they are recruited and trained; and the ratio of teachers to school population.

On the first point, in the deliberately restricted framework of this study, we shall deal only with teachers in general primary and secondary schools.

THE TRAINING AND RECRUITMENT OF TEACHERS FOR GENERAL PRIMARY AND SECONDARY EDUCATION

This subject was mentioned earlier in connection with higher education and the place which it allots to the training of teachers.

As pointed out, in certain countries (United States, Great Britain, Federal Republic of Germany), all teachers for general schools, including elementary, are trained in higher education institutions; in other countries (the other five Common Market countries and the U.S.S.R.), teachers for elementary classes are trained in special institutions (normal schools) which are classified as secondary. Again, secondary school teachers may be trained either in the universities or in schools or institutes for higher education studies which are independent of the universities.

For the sake of clarity and although the two are closely interconnected in certain countries, we shall deal separately with the training of primary and of secondary school teachers.

THE TRAINING AND RECRUITMENT OF PRIMARY SCHOOL TEACHERS

In all the nine countries primary classes (preschool and elementary) are generally taught by a single "polyvalent" teacher. Some countries, in schools of sufficient size to justify it (usually urban), have specialized teachers for drawing, music, and physical training. This will not be further considered here.

THE COMMON MARKET COUNTRIES

Except for the Federal Republic of Germany, training of public school teachers (and, in certain cases, private school teachers) is through normal schools or teacher training schools.[1] These specialized institutions generally accept students before they have completed their secondary schooling, and then provide supplementary general secondary education (which may or may not lead to a final secondary examination) and vocational training. However, this common denominator permits certain variations:

1. Preschool teachers are trained either in special schools or through special courses which will not be discussed here (Belgium, Italy, The Netherlands, Luxembourg) or with other primary school teachers (France).

2. The level of recruitment is traditionally at the end of the first cycle of long secondary education (Belgium, France, Italy) or after the short cycle.[2] In France, The Netherlands, and Luxembourg,[3] however, recruitment from among holders of the final secondary certificates has gradually been introduced.

3. The duration of studies and graduation are obviously related to the level at which students are recruited.

In France, studies last four years for students recruited after the first secondary cycle, with the first three years de-

---

[1] Sometimes also by promoting monitors or assistant teachers.

[2] In The Netherlands, the teacher training schools mainly enroll from the upper primary school (U.L.O.); somewhat less than 10 per cent of the students have completed the first three secondary classes.

[3] In Luxembourg, under a Law of 1958, this has become the only type of recruitment.

voted to the completion of secondary education and preparation for the *baccalauréat* while the fourth year is concerned with theoretical and practical vocational training. Students recruited after the *baccalauréat* merely take this final year.

On leaving the teacher training school, graduates are appointed as probationary teachers in public schools and are only confirmed in their posts after two years of practical teaching and after passing the tests for the *certificat d'aptitude pédagogique*. Student teachers enrolled in the vocational training year at present number some 8,500; certain private secondary institutions serve as teacher training schools for the recruitment of private elementary school teachers.

In Belgium, studies in the primary teacher training schools also last four years. The program for the first two years is equivalent to that of the third and second classical classes; the program for the third and fourth years is equivalent to the final classical year; lectures and exercises in education are also provided (ten hours a week). On completion of the final year, students sit for both the classical certificate and the teacher certificate.

Enrollment in the primary teacher training schools rose from 10,000 in 1953 to 14,900 in 1961.[4]

In Italy, courses in the teacher training schools only last four years (against five in the secondary schools); graduates from these institutions may sit for the state examination for primary teachers.[5] There were over 23,000 such graduates in 1963.

In Luxembourg, students attending the Institute of Education are recruited, as noted earlier, after the secondary school leaving examination and receive theoretical and practical training over a two-year period which leads to a teaching diploma.

---

[4] Teacher training schools for *gardiennes* (children's supervisors) had an enrollment of 4,200.

[5] As already mentioned, they also have access to the *magistero* faculties.

In The Netherlands, courses in the teacher training schools last a maximum of five years, divided into three cycles; the program for the first cycle (two years) is devoted solely to general education and leads to the final secondary examination level. The program for the second cycle lasts two years and is theoretical and practical; it leads to an elementary teaching certificate. The third cycle leads to a fully qualified teacher's diploma.[6] In 1960, the number enrolled for the teacher's course amounted to some 21,000 (total for the three cycles) and the number enrolled for the preschool teacher's course to 5,400 (total for the two two-year cycles); in 1963–64, 5,257 teachers' diplomas (second cycle) were awarded.

FEDERAL REPUBLIC OF GERMANY

The training of primary school teachers (elementary cycle and upper cycle) is organized in schools for higher educational studies *(Pädagogische Hochschulen und entsprechende Anstalten* or *Hochschulen für Erziehung* in Hesse) which, depending on the state, are known as pedagogic Academies or pedagogic university institutes. These are open to secondary school graduates *(Abiturienten)* or candidates who can prove that they are of equivalent level by passing a special examination (10.5 per cent of the 44,000 students concerned in 1963–64).

Courses last for six half-year terms. They comprise general and theoretical lectures (education, sociology, psychology, and the like, together with a subject taught in higher education) and practical training, and culminate in an examination. Successful students become assistant teachers and, after two or three years, sit for a state examination, after which their appointment is confirmed.

[6] This opens the way to headmasterships and is a precondition for extended primary teaching, special teaching, or senior primary teaching.

GREAT BRITAIN

There is no sharp distinction between the training of teachers for junior and senior classes. General teachers form two categories: "qualified" teachers, trained in teacher training colleges independent of the universities; and "graduate" teachers, trained in the universities. Both may teach junior or senior classes, but in fact the overwhelming majority of teachers in primary schools (93 per cent of men and 97.5 per cent of women) are "qualified" teachers. We shall therefore concentrate on this type of recruitment.

The training colleges are administered by the local education authorities and in principle their students are aged about eighteen and hold the G.C.E. (A); however, 39 per cent of entrants in 1961[7] only held the G.C.E. (O) or an equivalent.

Courses lasted two years until 1960 when they were extended to three years. The program includes general subjects (English, mathematics), special subjects (psychology, theory of education), and practical courses. At present, there is a movement to bring these institutions up to university level.

The number of first-year students in the training colleges rose from 12,400 in 1953 to 18,000 in 1962, over two-thirds of whom were women.

Graduates from the training colleges are recruited on a contract basis by the local education authorities and paid in accordance with a state-approved scale.

UNITED STATES

Preschool and elementary and secondary school teachers are recruited in accordance with standards established in each state by the state board or state department of education. The minimum requirements are four years of higher education in a state college of education or a teachers college for teaching in elementary or high school classes. Certain towns require a fifth year which may or may not lead to a Master's degree.

[7] England and Wales (see Table 56).

The first two years in the teachers colleges are devoted to general education; student teachers specialize in the last two years. The training of elementary school teachers allots an important place (one-quarter of the program) to methods, whereas prospective secondary school teachers concentrate more on the subjects they intend to teach.

SOVIET UNION

Teachers for the elementary classes (classes I to IV) and kindergartens are trained in teacher training schools which, administratively, are specialized secondary schools *(tekhnikums)*. Teachers must teach for twenty-four hours a week.

Recruitment is on the basis of an examination taken by students who have successfully completed the first secondary cycle (incomplete secondary). General courses and courses in educational theory last four years. This is largely the same as in the teacher training schools in the Common Market countries except that there is also a course for students who have completed their secondary studies; this course lasts two years only.[8]

In 1963, there were 57,800 graduates from the teacher training schools; this was lower than during the 1950's because the increased needs resulting from the increase in population had by then been fully satisfied.

In conclusion, it may be said that, notwithstanding differences in the administrative classification within the various countries (training in higher schools or in secondary teacher training schools), the training of elementary school teachers—except in Italy—generally transcends general secondary studies[9] by one year in France and Belgium, by one or two years in The Netherlands, by two years in Luxembourg, by two or

[8] Certain institutes of advanced education have introduced a four-year course of training for elementary school teachers.

[9] As already noted, however, prospective primary school teachers need not hold the final secondary certificate in Italy and The Netherlands.

four years in the U.S.S.R., by three years in Great Britain,[10] by three years in the Federal Republic of Germany, and by four years in the United States.[11]

TRAINING OF GENERAL SECONDARY SCHOOL TEACHERS

The training of secondary school teachers is always at a higher educational level but a more or less sharp distinction is drawn, except in Italy and the United States, between short (or first cycle) and long (or second cycle) courses. In principle, all teachers concentrate on one or a limited group of special subjects, the degree of specialization varying from one country to another, and especially between long and short courses.

COMMON MARKET COUNTRIES

1.   *Teachers for long secondary courses*   As a general rule, the scientific and job training of teachers for *lycées, athénées, Gymnasia,* and the like, is provided in the universities.

In the Federal Republic of Germany, prospective *Gymnasium* teachers take university courses, or courses in higher technical schools for certain science subjects, during at least eight or (usually) ten terms. This involves the following examinations: a preliminary examination: general knowledge in philosophy and education, generally taken during the sixth term; and a state examination in the specialized subjects to be taught (state scientific examination).

The prospective teacher must then spend two years as a *Student Referendar,* culminating in a state examination in educational theory and practice *(Pädagogische Prüfung).* He may then become a probationary teacher, and subsequently a full teacher. German teachers must teach for twenty-four hours a week up to the age of fifty-five; thereafter,

---

[10] Except in the case of those students (one-third) recruited on the basis of the G.C.E.(O) alone.

[11] Subject to what has already been said concerning the comparability of the high school diploma and European secondary school leaving certificates.

this timetable is reduced to twenty hours, and teachers in the terminal classes also benefit from this reduction.

In Belgium, teachers in *athénées, lycées,* and *collèges* must hold the degree of *licencié ès lettres, licencié ès sciences,* and so on, awarded after four years of university study, and they must have passed the *examen d'agrégé de l'enseignement secondaire supérieur* provided in all universities. This second examination may be taken in the same year as the *licence* or a year later.

While studying for the *licence,* candidates receive practical instruction in training courses in middle schools. First-cycle teachers are required to teach between twenty-one and twenty-four hours a week, this timetable being reduced to nineteen to twenty-two hours for the second cycle.

In France, teachers in the classical, modern, and technical *lycées* (for general disciplines) are trained in the arts or science faculties where courses last three or four years and culminate in a *licence d'enseignement.*

Student teachers recruited by the *Ecole Normale Supérieure* (see Chapter 2) also prepare for this initial university degree. Students in the arts and science faculties who have passed an entrance examination for the *Institut de préparation aux enseignements de second degré* (I.P.E.S.) [12] become student teachers [13] and receive a state salary like the students in the *ecole normale supérieure.*

State teachers are subsequently recruited through examinations [14] organized by the National Ministry of Education in the two following ways:

The *agrégation* examination *(professeurs agrégés des lycées)* is open to candidates holding a teaching diploma and a

[12] Each arts and science faculty has an I.P.E.S.; there were 4,000 first-year student teachers in 1964 and the figure rose to 4,600 at the beginning of the 1965–66 academic year.

[13] The examination covers the *propédeutique* program and students may then enter the I.P.E.S. from the beginning of the second faculty year.

[14] These examinations are open to I.P.E.S. students and all other *licenciées.*

diplôme d'études supérieures (*D.E.S.*: higher studies certificate). This examination includes written and oral tests and a test in practical teaching. Because the *D.E.S.* is required and because of the high level of the examination, a minimum delay of two years after the *licence* is considered essential for success.

Professeurs agrégés in the *lycées* are required to teach fifteen hours a week and are increasingly assigned to the secondary classes; they are also employed as *assistants* and *maîtres-assistants* (demonstrations) in the universities.

The *concours du certificat d'aptitude au professorat de l'énseignement secondaire* (C.A.P.E.S.) or *des lycées techniques* (C.A.P.E.T.) (certificated teachers) includes a theoretical section (generally taken one year after the *licence*) and a practical section; success in the theoretical section gives access to the regional education centers while the practical tests are taken after one year's training in those centers. Qualified teachers are required to teach eighteen hours a week.

In Italy, those wishing to teach general disciplines in secondary institutions of all kinds (first cycle, general, or technical second cycle) must first have obtained the degree of *Dottore* in a university (generally in a *magistero* faculty). They may subsequently become full teachers, provided they obtain the teaching certificate by passing a qualifying examination organized by the Ministry of Education (this certificate entitles the holder to occupy the post of assistant teacher), and provided they pass the recruitment competition for vacant posts.

The division of teachers into first-cycle schools (middle schools, *avviamento professionale* schools) and second-cycle schools *(gymnasia, lyceums)* is determined by the degree of difficulty in these two examinations; with this reservation, the conditions for recruiting teachers for general first cycle and second cycle schools are identical.

Teachers are required to teach a maximum of eighteen hours a week, but this is reduced to ten hours for certain subjects.

In Luxembourg, secondary school teachers are recruited on the basis of complete higher studies culminating after four years[15] in a doctorate awarded by a Luxembourg jury.

Doctors are subsequently required to complete a two-year educational course in a Luxembourg secondary school, after which they receive a diploma entitling them to teach. The weekly timetable for teachers is twenty-four hours.

In The Netherlands, the training of teachers for pre-university secondary schools is organized in two ways: either university training, or training in free institutions or by independent teachers.

University training involves complete studies in the subjects chosen (five to six years) and specific teacher training, supplemented by six months of practical training.

The other type of training (Opleiding Woor M. O. akten) is open to secondary school graduates who may sit for the special secondary teacher examination before a jury appointed by the Minister of Education in Arts and Sciences.

Full time teachers teach from twenty-six to twenty-nine hours a week; there are also part-time teachers.

2. *Teachers for short (or first cycle) secondary courses. In Italy,* as already mentioned, there is no basic difference in the qualifications required of teachers in first cycle and second cycle schools; in all the other Common Market countries, however, differences exist in two respects: teachers of short courses are generally less highly specialized; and they are not required to have the same level of qualifications in science.

Notwithstanding these, their more or less common features, conditions for recruitment are far from being the same.

In the Federal Republic of Germany, there are two distinct channels to teaching posts in the *Mittelschule:* the first is open to students, the second to practicing teachers only.

Students study in the universities for six terms, for a first state examination, in *two subjects,* for *Realschule* teachers. In most of the *Länder* they then spend one year in a higher

[15] Including one year of higher studies in Luxembourg and three years abroad.

institute of education, and may be appointed full teachers after two to three years as assistant teachers and a second examination in practical education.

Full teachers (those who have received the training already outlined in higher institutes of education) with adequate teaching experience may prepare for the *Realschule* teacher's examination either by a special course in the schools of higher education, or in some other way. Candidates passing the examination are considered to have acquired the necessary training and are directly posted to a *Realschule*.

Both systems involve *four years* of full-time study after the secondary school leaving examination.

In Belgium, teachers in middle schools are all *agrégés de l'enseignement secondaire inférieur*.

They are trained in middle teacher training schools which may be public or private. Recruitment for these schools is from practicing teachers and holders of the classical certificate and certain higher technical certificates. Studies last for two years. Training covers six groups.[16]

Courses in classical languages are given by *agrégés de l'enseignement secondaire supérieur*.

In France, teachers in the *collèges d'enseignement général* prior to the 1959 reform were selected from among the best teachers in the primary classes who specialized in the teaching of literature or science (depending on their aptitudes); the only theoretical and practical requirements at that time were the *baccalauréat* and the *certificat d'aptitude pédagogique*.

Following on the 1959 reform, a specific *certificat d'aptitude pédagogique* was introduced for teachers in the general *collèges* (with two main specializations: literature and science). Examinations for the *C.A.P.* are open to teachers in

[16] *French system:* mother tongue and history; modern languages; mathematics; science and geography; art; physical training and biology. *Netherlands system:* Netherlands and English; French and history; mathematics; science and geography; physical education; biology; art.

service and comprise written tests in the selected group (literary or scientific), at the level of the faculty *propédeutique* certificate; and practical teaching tests.

The *C.A.P.* for the general *collèges* is prepared on a full-time basis through one-year courses in specialized regional centers in the university towns; trainees attend the *propédeutique* arts or science courses in the faculties.

In Luxembourg, advanced primary education is provided by teachers holding the *brevet d'enseignement primaire supérieur,* a certificate awarded after a special examination.

In The Netherlands, teachers in the advanced primary schools *(U.L.O.)* hold the third cycle diploma of the teacher training schools (teacher-principal diploma) and have specialized in certain subjects included in the middle school program.

This specialization is obtained through evening classes, lasting from one to three years, in the teacher training schools, culminating in the award of the appropriate diplomas.

In conclusion, for this category of teacher, the Common Market countries provide three types of training: complete university training (Italy); short higher training open to students (Federal Republic of Germany, Belgium); and general complementary training at the level of full- or part-time higher education, limited to teachers in primary schools (France, The Netherlands, Luxembourg, and, in part,[17] the Federal Republic of Germany).

UNITED STATES

High school teachers are trained in state colleges, teachers colleges,[18] or universities.

The program lasts four years and leads to a bachelor's degree; it comprises supplementary general training, more advanced instruction in the subject(s) which the student wishes to teach, and theoretical and practical training. More and

[17] The second method of recruitment for *Realschule* teachers.
[18] These tend to be transformed into liberal arts colleges which train future teachers and other students.

more candidates for teaching positions in high schools continue their studies through a fifth year so as to obtain a master's degree. A growing number of states are making this second degree a condition for recruitment, and 44 per cent of secondary school teachers already hold it.

Service timetables are the same as in the elementary schools, that is, between twenty-five and thirty hours a week distributed over five school days.

GREAT BRITAIN

Secondary school teachers (modern, grammar, and technical schools) are trained either in teacher training colleges (qualified teachers), as already explained in respect of elementary class teachers, or in universities (graduate teachers).

Those wishing to become graduate teachers study for a Bachelor of Arts or a Bachelor of Science degree in the universities, generally an Honours degree.

Subsequently, they receive theoretical and practical training for one year in one of the twenty-four education departments in the universities. In 1962–63, 3,260 student teachers were being trained in this way.

In principle, graduate teachers may occupy posts in either primary or secondary classes, but in fact virtually all teach in secondary schools with the majority teaching in grammar schools. In 1953, of the graduate teachers 15.2 per cent taught in the modern schools, 78.9 per cent in the grammar schools, and 49.9 per cent in the technical schools. In 1962, the percentages were 17.0, 77.8, and 51.6, respectively.

In addition to teaching from twenty to twenty-seven hours a week, secondary school teachers have other required duties: supervision of meals, meetings with parents, postschool and sports activities, and so on.

SOVIET UNION

Secondary school teachers are trained either in universities or, and this applies to the majority, in institutes of higher education.

The universities train teachers specializing in a given subject (mother tongue and literature, physics, chemistry, mathematics). These teachers are employed in schools where the enrollment is heavy, and preferably in terminal cycle classes (IX and X). The period of training is the same as the university courses.[19]

The institutes of higher education generally prepare teachers who will teach one main and one supplementary subject (mother tongue and history, mathematics and physics, mathematics and industrial design). The duration of studies (theoretical and practical) was increased from two to four years in 1950 and to five in 1957.

Recruitment for both types of institution is on the basis of an examination for candidates holding the final secondary certificate. Generally speaking, the selection is very strict.

In 1963, there were 119,200 secondary school teachers with diplomas. Teachers in classes V to X are required to teach eighteen hours per week.

THE STUDENT-TEACHER RATIO

Quality may be judged not only in terms of the teacher's level of qualification but also by the student-teacher ratio.

No survey seems as yet to have clearly established how far teaching efficiency depends on the number of students in the class or on the number of students per teacher. In many countries, while there is a tendency to consider that twenty-five students per class is the optimum, regulations usually stipulate a maximum of thirty-five.

In any event, overloading beyond a certain limit certainly lowers the quality and efficiency of the teacher's work; the teacher can no longer individualize his teaching or adequately supervise the work of each child. This is obviously one of the main causes of backwardness in school. It particularly

[19] To an increasing extent, practical training in schools is also included.

TABLE 77   INCREASE IN THE NUMBER OF TEACHERS IN PUBLIC AND

	1950–51	1960–61	Percentage of Growth 1951–1961	1963–64
Federal Republic of Germany[a]				
Primary and special	132.2	137.2	+ 4	148.8
Middle	6.1	13.6	+123	17.3
Gymnasien	28.3	41.3	+ 46	44.6
Schools in Berlin, Bremen, and Hambourg	17.1	17.6	+ 3	17.7
Vocational and technical	19.7[b]	31.2	+ 58	31.3
Technical	6.8[b]	9.6	+ 41	10.7
Higher education[c]	—	16.0	—	25.0

	1950–51	1960–61	Percentage of Growth
Belgium[d]			
Primary	34.1	39.1	+ 15
Middle	9.5	15.5	+ 63
Technical	15.0	18.7	+ 24
Higher	1.9	2.3	+ 25

	1951–52	1961–62	Percentage of Growth 1952–1962	1962–63
France[e]				
Preprimary	11.7	26.5	+127	28.7
Elementary	128.9	178.2	+ 38	186.9
General *collèges*	11.1	25.1	+126	32.1
Classical and modern *lycées*	19.0	38.4	+102	42.3
Technical *collèges* and *lycées*	15.0	26.8	+ 79	30.1
Universities	4.5	10.4	+131	15.0[f]

PRIVATE EDUCATION, UNLESS OTHERWISE INDICATED *(in thousands)*

	1951–53	1963–64	*Percentage of Growth*
Italy[g]			
Primary	157.4	188.7	+ 19.9
Middle	28.3 ⎱	124.9 ⎱	+110.3
Vocational	31.1 ⎰	⎰	
Lyceums and gym-nasia	88.8	9.2	+ 4.5
Universities	7.6	13.8	+ 81.6

	1952–53	1962–63	*Percentage of Growth*
England and Wales[h]			
Elementary	139.9	139.0	− 0.6
Secondary	85.5	136.5	+ 59.0
Total	*225.5*	*275.5*	
Great Britain: Universities	10.0	15.7	+ 57.0

	1950–51	1961–62	*Percentage of Growth* 1951–1962	1962–63
U.S.S.R.				
Primary (I to IV)[i]	559.0	635.0	+ 13	644.0
Secondary (V to XI)[i]	527.0	835.0	+ 56	883.0
Total (including principals and specialized teachers)	*1,425.0*	*1,968.0*		*2,046.0*
Higher education	87.0	137.8	+ 58	

(Continued on p. 220)

TABLE 77   INCREASE IN THE NUMBER OF TEACHERS *(Continued)*

	1949–50	1961–62	*Percentage of Growth* 1950–1962	1963–64
United States[j]				
Elementary	665.6	1,009.9	+ 56	1,093.0
Secondary	366.3	643.9	+ 75	763.0
Higher education	190.3	310.7	+ 63	370.0

[a] In general, includes West Berlin and the Saar; SOURCE: *Statistisches Bundesamt.*

[b] Does not include the Saar.

[c] Includes teachers in the institutes of higher education.

[d] SOURCE: D'Hoogh, *op. cit.*

[e] Public education only, 1951: budgeted posts occupied by full teachers or assistants 1961–62 and 1962–63, posts in fact occupied.

[f] 1963–64.

[g] Public education only.

[h] Maintained primary and secondary schools; SOURCE: *Statistics of Education,* 1962.

[i] Does not include principals or specialized teachers.

[j] Public and nonpublic education.

prejudices children who get little help from their families, and adds to the handicaps of children from lower social strata.

The following observations and tables give certain data available on the teacher-student ratio at different educational levels, and on the present situation.

INCREASE IN THE NUMBER OF TEACHERS SINCE 1950, AND RECRUITMENT DIFFICULTIES

Table 11 and Appendix Tables A-1 to A-9 show trends in enrollment at various levels for each of the nine countries.

Because population changes after World War II vary from one country to another, the trend is not homogeneous. There is, however, a general increase in enrollments in secondary and higher education.

Accordingly, the decade which began in the early 1950's

was distinguished in all countries by an expansion in the number of teachers, more or less parallel with the increase in the number of students.

INCREASE IN THE NUMBER OF TEACHERS

Table 77 summarizes the data for a number of countries. A comparison of these figures with those in Table 11 will indicate the changes in the teacher-student ratio over the period in question.

The variations are far from absolutely parallel.

At primary level, countries with a declining birth rate have slightly improved the ratio (Federal Republic of Germany, U.S.S.R., Italy); where the postwar birth rate was expanding (United States, France, Belgium) the ratio has slightly worsened.

At secondary and higher levels, the increase in the number of teachers is particularly striking, ranging from 50 to 120 per cent or even 160 per cent; this, however, has not always been enough to match the growth in enrollment. This comparison of the two curves of growth is not especially significant in itself, since the point of departure is rarely the same. We must rather, in each case, examine end results. Let us first discuss the problem of teacher recruitment.

THE DIFFICULTIES OF RECRUITING TEACHERS

The recruitment of supplementary teachers because of the increase in the number of pupils and students has, from 1950 on, presented grave difficulties—not only quantitative. These difficulties varied from country to country because of the variety of demographic situations; the diversity of social or economic pressures which encouraged the growth of enrollment at secondary and higher levels; the diversity of government policies in education which speeded up or slowed down requirements; and the comparative attraction of teaching careers for young graduates.

Another fundamental question was whether, in the years following World War II, the rate of graduation from schools and universities was sufficient—in view of the needs in other sectors—to allow the recruitment of tens or even hundreds of thousands of additional teachers in so short a period. From this point of view also, the situations varied greatly and still do so.

Only a thorough analysis of the component elements in the situation of each country would enable us to resolve this problem, and that would be outside the scope of the present study. We shall revert to the problem in the conclusions. For the present, it can be said that the problem should not be in-definitely intractable for two reasons: the rate of increase in the needs of the most "dynamic" countries will tend to slacken; and the demand for teachers should become increas-ingly easy to satisfy by the very fact of the increase in the number of graduates which will result from the extension of schooling since 1950.

This is true in a general way but it is nonetheless evident that the situation in each of the nine countries has specific features of its own at the various educational levels.

TABLE 78   PUPIL-TEACHER RATIO AT THE
PRESCHOOL LEVEL

	Pupil-teacher Ratio
England and Wales	
Public schools	22 (1961)
Independent schools	16 (1961)
Belgium	34 (1961)
Luxembourg	34 (1960)
France	
Public schools	44 (1963)
Private schools	29 (1961)
Italy	37 (1961)
Netherlands	34 (1964)

PRESENT STUDENT-TEACHER RATIOS AT PRIMARY AND SECONDARY LEVELS

PRESCHOOL

The situation in France would appear to be less satisfactory than in the other European countries.

In the U.S.S.R. the pupil-educator ratio (thirteen) is extremely low since there are two teachers[20] for each class; the regulation establishing the number of pupils per class at twenty-five is observed.

At this level, the teachers are all women.

TABLE 79 PUPIL-TEACHER RATIO IN ELEMENTARY AND TERMINAL PRIMARY CLASSES, AND PERCENTAGE OF WOMEN TEACHERS

	Pupil-teacher Ratio[a]	*Pupils per Class*[a]	*Percentage of Women Teachers*
Federal Republic of Germany (1963–64)	30.5	32.3	45.5
Belgium (1959–60)	25.0	—	61.0[b]
France[e] (1962–63)	28.0	28.7	64.0
Italy[e] (1958–59)	24.0	—	—
Luxembourg (1959–60)	26.0	—	52.0
Netherlands (1963–64)	32.0	—	53.0
United States (1962)	28.4	—	87.0
U.S.S.R. (1962–63)	25.9[d]	—	87.0
England and Wales (1962–63)	29.3	32.2	73.0

[a] In most of these countries, the criteria are similar because of the system of a single "polyvalent" teacher per class.

[b] Catholic education only. SOURCE: C. D'Hoogh, *Problèmes économiques de l'enseignement* (Brussels, 1963).

[e] Public education only.

[d] Including principals and not including teachers of special subjects.

[20] The classes are generally open from 7 A.M. to 7 P.M.; this explains the need for two teachers for each class.

ELEMENTARY AND TERMINAL PRIMARY CLASSES

1. *The average pupil-teacher ratio*   Table 79 shows that in the Federal Republic of Germany and in The Netherlands the average pupil-teacher ratio is relatively unsatisfactory, although it was even worse in Germany in 1950 (it then was 48) but has improved, partly through the reduction in the number of pupils (see Table 11).

The average pupil-teacher rates in Belgium, Italy, Luxembourg, and the U.S.S.R. would seem to be satisfactory.[21]

The other countries—England, the United States, and France—occupy a position midway. In the latter two, the spectacular increase in elementary school enrollment after 1950 (see Table 11) made the national rate top-heavy; a contrary trend since 1960 has slowed down the increase in primary school enrollment.

2. *Classes with too few and classes with too many* The national averages do not reflect the real situation since they represent many classes with too few or too many pupils on either side of the average. The "too few" classes are mainly in underpopulated rural areas in certain parts of France and Italy. The solution gradually being applied in Europe, as originally it was in the United States, is to arrange school transport services.

The national statistics also show a high proportion of pupils in overcrowded classes (more than thirty-five to forty pupils). Table 80 shows two countries with average ratios (England and France) and two (Federal Republic of Germany and The Netherlands) where the ratios are high.

The data in this table indicate that at the time[22] the proportion of pupils in classes having more than thirty-five pupils amounted to 60 per cent in Germany, 50 per cent in The Netherlands, 49.9 per cent in England (junior classes), and 34 per cent in France. These figures reveal how much must

[21] Subject to a precise count of the number of full-time teachers in Belgium and Italy.

[22] The situation has definitely changed since the dates given here.

TABLE 80 PRIMARY CLASSES BY NUMBER OF PUPILS IN CLASS, AND DISTRIBUTION OF PUPILS BY SIZE OF CLASS (in percentage)

	Number of Classes, by Enrollment				Number of Pupils, by Class			
	1–25	26–35	36–40	OVER 40	1–25	26–35	36–40	OVER 40
France (1961–62)	27.8	51.6	16.4	4.2	17.5	48.5	24.0	10.0
England and Wales (1961–62)	20.4	39.1	26.6	13.9	12.5	37.6	31.3	18.6
Federal Republic of Germany (1962)[a]	8.8	39.7	23.1	28.4	5.3[b]	34.2[b]	25.2[b]	35.2[b]
	1–24	25–34	35–44	45 AND OVER	1–24	25–34	35–44	45 AND OVER
Netherlands (1963–64)	14.0	45.0	37.0	5.0	9.0	41.0	43.0	7.0

[a] SOURCE: *Statistisches Bundesamt.*
[b] Estimated.

be done before European school systems can operate under reasonable working conditions.

In the United States, despite an average teacher-pupil ratio of only 28.5, there were 914,000 children enrolled in 1962 in elementary classes that were above their normal capacity; however, the 1955 figure was 1,117,000, so the trend is downward.

3. *Women teachers in primary schools*   Table 79 shows the percentage of women teachers in primary schools (not including preprimary) for each of the countries concerned. This percentage is extremely high in the two English-speaking countries and in the U.S.S.R. This is probably explained by various circumstances, for example, the relative level of teacher salaries, the loss of men during the war, certain national traditions, and so on.

In the Common Market countries, the proportion of women teachers is much lower; indeed, most primary school teachers in the Federal Republic of Germany are men.

SECONDARY SCHOOLS (GENERAL, VOCATIONAL, AND TECHNICAL)

The number of students per class is almost impossible to use as a criterion for evaluating student-teacher ratios or for international comparisons in secondary schools because of the variety of courses involved.[23] The teacher-pupil ratio criterion is valid, provided that two things are genuinely comparable: the students' hours per week, and the teachers' duties.

Conditions vary so extensively from country to country that international comparisons based on the teacher-pupil ratio are deprived of much of their validity. Uncertainty regarding the exact number of full-time teachers in certain countries[24] (Belgium, Italy) also distorts comparisons.

Subject to these qualifications, Table 81 gives the teacher-

[23] Within a given day, children are regrouped for specialized and optional subjects; "class" remains to be defined.

[24] Statistics do not always draw a distinction between full-time and part-time.

pupil ratio for the various types of secondary school as shown by official statistics or individual surveys. It is practically impossible to draw any conclusions from this table because of the absence, already mentioned, of any real comparability in the data.

It should be noted regarding the proportion of women teachers in secondary schools that in all countries, it is much lower than at primary level, and that women are in the majority only in the U.S.S.R.; elsewhere, the number is the same as for men or lower—particularly in countries where secondary education for girls lags behind.

STUDENT-TEACHER RATIO IN HIGHER EDUCATION

STRUCTURE AND RECRUITMENT OF TEACHING STAFF

The hierarchic organization of the teaching staff in higher education is complex and varies from one discipline to another and from one country to another. Generally speaking, two categories may be singled out: professors and lecturers (senior grades), generally permanent members of the staff, more especially responsible for lectures, and who, in principle, must hold the highest university degree; and staff responsible for practical and supervised work (junior grades), with lower university degrees, frequently not permanently established.

Within a given discipline, however, the specific features of these two groups, their recruitment standards and respective duties, are not the same in all countries. As it is not possible here to enter into detail, we shall merely indicate the hierarchy among full-time staff for a certain number of countries, and give a quantitative breakdown.

Apart from the full-time staff, part-time staff (lecturers, practical demonstrators, and the like) are employed in varying proportions.

In certain countries (United States, U.S.S.R.), some members of the staff may devote all their time to research; this also helps to distort comparisons between student-teacher ratios. Other countries employ advanced students in connection with

TABLE 81 STUDENT-TEACHER RATIO IN FULL-TIME SECONDARY SCHOOLS AND PERCENTAGE OF WOMEN TEACHERS[a]

	General Education		Vocational Education	Technical Education
	SHORT OR FIRST CYCLE	LONG OR SECOND CYCLE		
Federal Republic of Germany (1963)	24.0 (43%)	19.0 (32%)[b]	19.0	17.0
Belgium (1960)	14.1 (52%)[b]		18.6 (57%)[b]	
France (1963)[c]	22.8 (52%)	20.2 (55%)	16.0 (39%)	14.0 (37%)
Italy (1963)[d]	12.1 (61.5%)	12.1 (61.5%)	11.9 (30.6%)	13.0 (45%)
Luxembourg (1959)	—	15.0	—	—
Netherlands (1963)[e]	27.0	—	—	—
United States (1962)	21.7 (51%)		—	—
U.S.S.R. (1962–63)[f]	23.0 (76%)	14.5 (68%)	—	—
England and Wales (1961–62)[g]	20.8 (43%)	18.0 (43%)	—	17.9 (43%)

[a] These percentages are given in parentheses.

[b] Catholic education only. SOURCE: C. D'Hoogh, *Problèmes économiques de l'enseignement* (Brussels, 1963).

[c] Public education only.

[d] All teachers, including religion, music, physical education; if we allow only for teachers holding university degrees, the figures are 19.8 for general and 18.5 for technical education; these rates involve some overlapping.

[e] The teacher-pupil ratio cannot be calculated for the other types of education for lack of information on part-time teachers.

[f] Does not include school principals and study directors, teachers of drawing, music, physical education, and the like.

[g] The proportion of women teachers is the average for all secondary schools.

TABLE 82 STRUCTURE OF THE UNIVERSITY TEACHING STAFF IN VARIOUS COUNTRIES

Great Britain	1949–50	1961–62
Professors, readers, senior lecturers	(29.3%)	(30.4%)
Lecturers, assistant lecturers, others	(70.7%)	(69.6%)
Total	7,682 (100 %)	12,786 (100 %)

France	1956–57	1960–61	1963–64
Professors, senior lecturers	3,152 (56.0%)	3,585 (45.0%)	4,903 (33.0%)
Demonstrators and assistants	2,479 (44.0%)	4,319 (55.0%)	10,195 (67.0%)
Total	5,631 (100 %)	7,904 (100 %)	15,098 (100 %)

Italy	1951–52	1962–63
Professors, senior lecturers	2,197 (29.5%)	5,275 (38.3%)
Assistants and other staff	5,265 (71.5%)	8,497 (61.7%)
Total	7,462 (100 %)	13,772 (100 %)

	1960	1964
Federal Republic of Germany[a]		
Full professors (ordinary or extraordinary)	3,098 (21.5%)	4,312 (16.8%)
Extraordinary professors, senior lecturers (*Privatdozenten*), honorary professors, and lecturers	2,058 (14.5%)	5,232 (20.4%)
Assistants	9,268 (64.2%)	16,113 (62.8%)
Total	14,424 (100 %)	25,657 (100 %)

		1958–59
Netherlands		
Professors and senior lecturers		942 (21.0%)
Extraordinary professors, readers[b]		575 (13.0%)
Monitors and assistants		2,958 (66.0%)
Total		4,475 (100 %)

	1946	1955
U.S.S.R.[c]		
Professors and associate professors	19,300 (28.8%)	31,100 (26.2%)
Assistants, instructors, others	47,900 (71.2%)	87,800 (73.8%)
Total	67,200 (100 %)	118,900 (100 %)

[a] SOURCE: *Ständige Konferenz der Kultusminister.*
[b] Mostly part time.
[c] SOURCE: Nicholas DeWitt, *Education and Professional Employment in the U.S.S.R.* (Washington, D.C.: Government Printing Office, 1961), p. 369.

231

the practical work (*moniteurs* in France); these are not included here as teaching staff.

Provided the major categories, and the proportion of teaching done by part-time staff are genuinely comparable, the structure of the teaching staff in the various countries seems to be tending toward a certain measure of uniformity.

COMPARATIVE STUDENT-TEACHER RATIOS

The expansion of the student population since the end of World War II has required a considerable increase in the number of teachers everywhere; at the same time, certain countries have endeavored to improve the student-teacher ratio. The present situation is still far from uniform; on the contrary, the differences are very substantial.

This analysis may be taken further and a comparison made between the student-professor ratio by major university disciplines in various European countries.

The data in Table 84 must be very cautiously interpreted as they are not really comparable; more especially, the inclusion—or noninclusion—of part-time teachers largely distorts the comparisons. Available statistics, however, do not permit anything better.

In any event, Tables 83 and 84 reveal a certain homogeneity in the ratio except in France and Italy where the situation is much less satisfactory, especially in law, arts, economics, and social science. It should, of course, be noted in the case of France that the above ratios take no account of the *grandes écoles* where the student-teacher ratio is generally good (but this does nothing to improve the situation of the faculties); do not allow for part-time staff (largely represented in the arts and law faculties); and are based on student figures artificially inflated by 10 to 15 per cent of invalid registrations.[25]

This, however, only attenuates the disparaties which remain considerable and largely explain the poor "yield" of the institutions concerned (cf. Chapter 2).

[25] Linked with the question of multiple enrollments.

TABLE 83 COMPARATIVE STUDENT-PROFESSOR RATIO IN THE UNIVERSITIES—ALL DISCIPLINES

	1945-46	1950-51	1954-55	1956-57	1960-61 (or 1959-60)	1962-63 (or 1961-62)	1963-64
Federal Republic of Germany	—	—	—	—	12.0[a]	—	10.0[b]
Belgium[c]	—	10.6	—	12.0	12.8	11.3	—
France[d]	—	—	—	29.0	25.8	23.0	21.6
Italy	—	34.0	—	—	27.0	22.6	—
Netherlands[a]	—	—	8.0	—	8.0	—	—
Great Britain[a]	9.8	8.4	—	7.5	7.6	7.5	—
United States[e]	—	—	—	12.0	—	13.0	—
U.S.S.R.[f]	13.0 (8.6)	—	—	—	15.6 (9.6)	16.3 (7.9)	—

[a] University institutions or equivalent.
[b] Universities and equivalent institutions and institutes of higher education.
[c] Includes part-time staff.
[d] Universities only; does not include part-time staff.
[e] Includes professors working full time on research.
[f] Figures in parentheses represent the ratio for full-time students only.

EXPENDITURE ON EDUCATION

In the Introduction, some of the difficulties and uncertainties involved in making international comparisons of expenditure on education were mentioned: differences in the definition of educational expenditure in national statistics; difficulty of saying how much exactly is paid, for example, by families, by various enterprises, and even by local authorities; and factors more or less external to the quantitative and qualitative development of education (demographic variations, teachers' salaries) which significantly affect the total expenditure.

In any event, and disregarding all such reservations, the rapid rise in expenditure on education has been a general phenomenon since the beginning of the postwar period and is attracting more and more attention from governments and economists.

As for the expenditure to be considered, preliminary surveys in each country to provide a basis for the present conspectus suggested these three categories: (1) operational expenditure of public and private schools and universities (salaries, pensions, equipment, upkeep, administrative and supervisory services); (2) capital expenditure (purchase of land, building, basic equipment); and (3) expenditure on measures to encourage attendance (scholarships, transport, canteens, boarding facilities).

We shall not here go into details (as was done in the notes established for each country) regarding the methods used to finance educational expenditure, and their distribution between state, public authorities, families, and individuals, or the trends in expenditure by educational level.

The following tables and observations indicate, for each of the countries,[26] a synthesis of trends since 1950 in expenditure on education, by capital and operational expenditure, further broken down, where necessary, for public and private edu-

---

[26] Except Luxembourg, where the information is not available.

cation; and the proportion of expenditure on education represents in the state budget (or total public expenditure) and in relation to the gross national product (G.N.P.).[27]

Also presented are comparisons of educational expenditure in relation to G.N.P. in the various countries, and summary analyses of the factors which may underlie the disparities observed.

TABLE 84   STUDENT-PROFESSOR RATIO BY MAJOR UNIVERSITY DISCIPLINES

Discipline	Federal Republic of Germany (1961)	Great Britain[a] (1962)	France		Italy	
			1958	1963	1952	1962–63
Literature and philosophy	15.0	8.5	58.0	53.0[b]	46.8	39.5
Law, economics, social sciences	27.5	9.3	60.0	50.0[b]	68.0	66.0
Natural sciences	10.0	7.0	27.0	17.0	24.0	12.8
Engineering sciences	18.0	8.8	—[c]	—[c]	25.0	39.0
Medicine and pharmacy	6.0	6.0	17.0	10.0	11.6	6.8
Average	8.8	12.0	29.0	23.0	27.6	22.6

[a] Does not include Oxford and Cambridge.

[b] Does not include a considerable number of part-time staff (lecturers, demonstrators).

[c] French statistics do not give these separately. A large proportion of engineering training is given in *grandes écoles* outside the universities where the student-teacher ratio is much lower than in the faculties.

[27] The G.N.P. is calculated on the basis of market prices; estimates (except for the U.S.S.R.) by OECD.

TRENDS IN EDUCATIONAL EXPENDITURE, BY COUNTRY

FEDERAL REPUBLIC OF GERMANY

Between 1950 and 1960 (for which period the data in Table 85 are homogeneous), there was an exceptional increase of 240 per cent. This, to a comparatively small extent only, is due to increases in the cost of living index (21 per cent) and the building costs index (57 per cent)[28] and is mainly due to the increase in the number of teachers (see previous section), especially in secondary and higher education; the considerable increase in capital expenditure; and the rise in teachers' salaries.

The increase continued at the same rate beyond 1960. However, the increase in educational expenditure, when compared with public expenditure and G.N.P., has been much less rapid.

Public expenditure has been divided between the various authorities as follows: in 1950, the *Länder* was responsible for 67.5 per cent and the communes for 32.5 per cent; in 1960, the *Bund* provided 1.2 per cent, the *Länder* 55.3 per cent, and the communes 32.5 per cent.

BELGIUM

Tables 87 and 88 reveal an exceptional growth in total expenditure (over 200 per cent) between 1950 and 1961, or, on the basis of constant prices, some 170 per cent. However, it is probably distorted by a very inadequate evaluation of private expenditure on education in 1950 when state subventions were low.

FRANCE

In new francs, expenditure on education rose by 270 per cent between 1952 and 1962 (public education: +290 per cent; private education: +125 per cent). During the same

[28] SOURCE: G. Palm and B. Trouillet "L'enseignement en R.F.A." Hochschule für Internationale Pädagogische Forschung, Frankfurt (1963).

TABLE 85 PUBLIC AND PRIVATE EXPENDITURE ON EDUCATION—FEDERAL REPUBLIC OF GERMANY[a]
(in millions of Deutsch Marks)

	1950	1952	1956	1958	1960	1961	1962	1963
Public financing[b,c]								
Current expenditure[d]	1,982	2,672	4,146	5,234		7,297	7,475	
Capital expenditure	360	694	1,303	1,423		2,378	2,830	
	2,342	3,366	5,449	6,657	8,080	9,675	10,305	
Private financing								
Current expenditure[e]	78	107	170	218	270	295	310	
Capital expenditure[f]	?	?	?	?	?	?	?	
Kindergartens								
Current expenditure[g]	120	150	230	300	350	370	410	
Capital expenditure[f]	—	—	—	—	—	—	—	
Total	2,540	3,625	5,840	7,175	8,700	10,340	11,025	

[a] Figures from 1950 to 1960 do not include the Saar and West Berlin; from 1961 to 1962, they include the Saar.

SOURCE: *Statistisches Bundesamt.*

[c] Includes subventions to private schools and does not include university clinics.

[d] Includes interest charges.

[e] Estimate in round figures (approximately 4 per cent of public current expenditure).

[f] Relatively small sums, the omission of which does not really change the order of magnitude of expenditure.

[g] Estimates based on a lump sum cost per pupil.

237

TABLE 86   PUBLIC EXPENDITURE ON EDUCATION IN RELATION TO
TOTAL PUBLIC EXPENDITURE,[a] AND TOTAL EXPENDI-
TURE ON EDUCATION IN RELATION TO THE GROSS NA-
TIONAL PRODUCT—FEDERAL REPUBLIC OF GERMANY

	[b]	G.N.P.[c]	Total Expenditure on Education[d]	Percentage of G.N.P.	Capital Expenditure as Percentage of G.N.P.
1950	8.8	97.20	2.54	2.61	0.36
1952	8.8	135.60	3.62	2.68	0.52
1956	9.6	196.40	5.84	2.96	0.66
1958	9.8	228.50	7.17	3.14	0.63
1960	9.8	277.70	8.70	3.10	—
1961[d]	—	310.40	9.84	3.17	0.76
1962	—	338.00	11.02	3.26	0.84
1963	—	—	—	—	—
1964	—	—	—	—	—

[a] *Bund, Länder,* Towns, Communes.

[b] Includes West Berlin.

[c] In thousand million Deutsch Marks.

[d] Includes the Saar as from 1961, and does not include West Berlin.

period, however, prices (I.N.S.E.S. retail price index) rose by approximately 55 per cent. The real increases in expenditure amounted to +143 per cent. Operational expenditure in public education rose, on the basis of constant prices, by 128 per cent.

This growth is significantly higher than that of school enrollment (+60 per cent) and reflects increased enrollment in secondary and higher education, and increased salaries (advantage derived by officials from the increase in national revenue).

ITALY

In eleven years, public expenditure on education increased by 218 per cent or, allowing for a price increase of 42 per

TABLE 87 PUBLIC AND PRIVATE EXPENDITURE ON EDUCATION—
BELGIUM[a]

(in thousands of millions of Belgian francs)

	1950	1955	1959	1960	1961	1962	1963	1964
Public institutions[a]								
Current expenditure	6.3	8.5	13.0	14.7	15.3	16.3	17.8	18.8
Capital expenditure	0.7	1.1	2.8	2.7	2.8	3.1	2.8	2.6
	7.0	*9.6*	*15.8*	*17.4*	*18.1*	*19.4*	*20.6*	*21.4*
Private institutions								
Current expenditure[b]	2.2	3.9	7.0	8.6	9.5	10.3	11.4	11.9
Capital expenditure[c]	?	?	?	?	?	?	?	?
Total[d]	9.2	13.5	22.8	26.0	27.6	29.7	32.0	33.3

SOURCE: Documentation provided by the Service des Statistiques of the Ministry of National Education.

[a] Financing by the State: 72 per cent in 1950, 87.2 per cent in 1961.

[b] The sums indicated represent state subventions which, since the law of May 29, 1959, cover a very large proportion of operational expenditure.

[c] No information available.

[d] This total does not exactly reflect all educational expenditure since capital expenditure in respect of private institutions and their own share of operational expenditure are lacking.

cent during this period, a growth of 125 per cent on the basis of constant prices. This is very much higher than the increase in enrollment during the same period (+18 per cent).

Operational expenditures on public education were borne as follows: in 1950, 84.7 per cent by the state, 13.7 per cent by the local communities, and 1.6 per cent by families; in 1951, the figures were, respectively, 80.3 per cent, 17.8 per cent, and 1.9 per cent. The share borne by the local authorities tends to increase. The total educational expenditure in 1961 was financed as follows: 72.9 per cent by the state, 18.7 per cent by the local authorities, and 8.4 per cent by families and private organizations.

TABLE 88 STATE EXPENDITURE ON EDUCATION IN RELATION TO THE BUDGET, AND TOTAL EXPENDITURE ON EDUCATION IN RELATION TO THE GROSS NATIONAL PRODUCT—BELGIUM

(in thousands of millions of Belgian francs)

	State Budget	State Expenditure on Education	Percentage of Budget	G.N.P.	Total Expenditure on Education[a]	Percentage of G.N.P.	Percentage of G.N.P. Devoted to Investment[a]
1950	85.3	7.2	8.5	363.5	9.2	2.54	0.19
1955	103.5	11.2	10.8	460.9	13.5	2.97	0.24
1959	148.1	20.5	13.9	535.9	23.0	4.28	0.52
1960	155.4	23.6	15.2	572.2	26.0	4.54	0.47
1961	142.0	25.3	17.9	601.2	27.7	4.68	0.56
1962	151.9	27.7	18.2	646.0	29.7	4.60	0.47
1963	167.09	29.8	17.8	695.0	32.0	4.60	0.40
1964	181.38	31.1	17.1	761.0[b]	33.3	4.37	0.34

[a] Not including capital expenditure in respect of private education.
[b] Estimate.

240

(in thousands of millions of new francs)

	1952	1955	1959	1960	1961	1962	1963	1964
Public education								
Current expenditure[a]	2.67	3.30	6.40	7.24	8.24	9.57	11.56	13.74
Capital expenditure[b]	0.37	0.65	1.76	1.63	1.87	2.44	2.82	3.20
	3.04	*3.95*	*8.06*	*8.87*	*10.11*	*12.01*	*14.38*	*16.94*
Private education								
Current expenditure[c]	0.58	0.71	0.93	1.00	1.15	1.30	1.40	1.50
Capital expenditure[d]	0.04	0.10	0.12	0.12	0.12	0.15	0.16	0.17
	0.62	*0.81*	*1.05*	*1.12*	*1.29*	*1.45*	*1.56*	*1.67*
Total	3.66	4.76	9.11	9.99	11.40	13.46	15.94	18.61

[a] Expenditure on public educational institutions and their common services financed from the budgets of the Ministry of National Education and other competent ministries, and by local authorities (primarily the communes); *includes* pensions (mostly not covered by contributions from actively employed staff), expenditure on physical training and sport (approximately 60 per cent of the budget of the Secretariat of State for Youth and Sport), but does *not include* scientific research, theaters, museums, youth welfare activities, and the like. State expenditure has been estimated on the basis of budgetary documents; expenditure by local authorities has been estimated at 15 per cent of state expenditure.

[b] Expenditure on school and university buildings and equipment (including physical training and sports equipment); expenditure by local communities has been estimated at 16 per cent of the total.

[c] Estimates based on unitary costs per pupil, calculated in a survey carried out by the Institut National de la Statistique on educational expenditure in France in 1955. These estimates certainly underestimate the real expenditure.

[d] Treasury evaluations up to 1962; estimates for 1963 and 1966.

TABLE 90 STATE EXPENDITURE ON EDUCATION IN RELATION TO THE TOTAL BUDGET, AND TOTAL EXPENDITURE ON EDUCATION IN RELATION TO THE GROSS NATIONAL PRODUCT—FRANCE

(in thousands of millions of new francs)

	State Budget	State Expenditure on Education[a]	Percentage of Budget	G.N.P.	Total Expenditure on Education	Percentage of G.N.P.	Capital Expenditure as a Percentage of G.N.P.
1952	30.6	2.86	9.3	144.04	3.66	2.54	0.28
1955	33.65	3.65	10.8	170.5	4.86	2.87	0.45
1959	54.8	7.14	13.0	267.3	9.11	3.41	0.70
1960	58.01	8.08	13.9	296.2	9.99	3.37	0.61
1961	62.96	8.85	14.1	319.6	11.38	3.56	0.62
1962	70.09	10.68	15.2	353.5	13.46	3.81	0.73
1963	76.88	12.74	16.6	391.8[b]	15.94	4.04	0.76
1964	86.31	15.00	17.3	427.75[b]	18.61	4.35	0.79

[a] Includes payments to private education (685 million francs in 1964), retirement pensions (that proportion not covered by contributions from actively employed staff), and the proportion of credits available through the Secretariat of State for Youth and Sport devoted to physical training and sports. State expenditure in 1964 (excluding pensions) was divided thus: Ministry of Education, 90.2 per cent; the Ministry of Finance, 7 per cent; the Ministry of Agriculture, 1.8 per cent; the Ministry of Health, 0.36 per cent; the Ministry for Cultural Affairs, 0.19 per cent; and the Ministry for Public Works, 0.16 per cent.

[b] Estimates.

TABLE 91 PUBLIC AND PRIVATE EXPENDITURE ON EDUCATION, OPERATIONAL AND INVESTMENTS—ITALY *(in thousands of millions of lire)*

	1950	1955	1958	1959	1960	1961	1962	1963
Public education[a]								
Operational expenditure	192.8	359.2	499.4	560.2	623.7	668.3	829.0	1,078.0
Capital expenditure	23.5	36.2	45.3	61.6	88.5	123.9	160.0	200.0
	216.3	*395.4*	*544.7*	*621.8*	*712.2*	*792.2*	*989.0*	*1,278.0*
Private education[b]								
Operational	24.6	37.8	49.6	52.3	55.0	57.7	60.0	65.0
Capital expenditure	1.3	2.3	3.4	3.6	4.2	4.8	5.0	5.0
	25.9	*40.1*	*53.0*	*55.9*	*59.2*	*62.5*	*65.0*	*70.0*
Total	242.2	435.5	597.7	677.7	771.4	854.7	1,054.0	1,348.0

[a] Institutions under the Ministry of Education
[b] Estimates

TABLE 92 STATE EXPENDITURE ON EDUCATION IN RELATION TO THE BUDGET, AND NATIONAL EXPENDITURE ON EDUCATION IN RELATION TO THE GROSS NATIONAL PRODUCT—ITALY

	State Budget	State Expenditure on Education	Percentage of Budget	G.N.P.	Total Expenditure on Education	Percentage of G.N.P.	Capital Expenditure as a Percentage of the G.N.P.
1950	1,716	176.0	10.25	8,768	242.2	2.79	0.27
1955	2,623	312.5	11.91	13,807	435.5	3.15	0.27
1958	3,323	431.7	12.99	17,114	597.7	3.45	0.28
1959	3,506	473.6	13.50	18,290	677.7	3.70	0.35
1960	4,005	554.1	13.83	19,937	771.4	3.85	0.46
1961	4,500	623.9	13.85	21,912	854.7	3.88	0.58
1962	4,850	759.7	16.70	24,789	1,054.0	4.25	0.66
1963	5,700	980.2	18.70	28,329	1,348.0	4.76	0.72
1964	6,350	1,178.2	19.80	30,950	1,557.0	5.03	—

THE NETHERLANDS[29] (Tables 93 and 94, pages 246–247)

In The Netherlands, almost all expenditure on education, public and private alike, is borne by the public authorities (state, provinces, communes).

UNITED KINGDOM (Tables 95 and 96, pages 248–249)

UNITED STATES (Tables 97 and 98, pages 249–250)

SOVIET UNION[30] (Tables 99 and 100, pages 250–251)

From 1950 to 1963, the price index in relation to 1940 dropped from 192 (1950) to 177 (1961). Accordingly, the increase in educational expenditure between 1950 and 1962 (approximately +100) is in no way attributable to price increases.

In 1961, approximately 90 per cent of this expenditure was borne by governmental organizations and 10 per cent by enterprises and families.

COMPARISON OF RECENT TRENDS AND EXISTING EXPENDITURE ON EDUCATION

For eight of the nine countries under consideration, the foregoing tables provide a synthesis of the trends in expenditure on education (current and capital) in absolute values, and then in relation to the state budget and G.N.P.

International comparisons of the percentage expenditure by states in relation to their own budgets is of limited interest since the breakdown of expenditure on education as between state, local authorities, and private individuals varies from one country to another. As pointed out in the Introduction, the only valid comparison is percentage expenditure in rela-

[29] Central Statistical Office, The Hague.

[30] SOURCES, 1950 TO 1960: Harold J. Noah, *Financing Soviet Schools* (New York: Teachers College Press, 1966). This study includes an estimate of private educational expenditure, not wholly incorporated in 1961 and 1962.

1961 AND 1962: Unesco annual statistics.

TABLE 93 PUBLIC AND PRIVATE EXPENDITURE ON EDUCATION, OPERATIONAL AND CAPITAL—THE NETH-
ERLANDS

(in millions of florins)

	1954	1956	1958	1960	1961	1962	1963	1964
Current expenditure[a]								
Public schools	264	347	430	502	578	668	790	920
Private schools	466	671	841	1,037	1,195	1,378	1,580	1,800
Administration, etc.	51	78	85	100	160	165	180	195
	781	*1,096*	*1,356*	*1,639*	*1,933*	*2,211*	*2,550*	*2,915*
Capital expenditure								
Public schools	75	93	119	177	205	229	265	310
Private schools	74	119	127	181	180	190	230	260
Administration, etc.	4	5	7	9	8	11	15	15
	153	*217*	*253*	*367*	*393*	*430*	*510*	*585*
Total	934	1,313	1,609	2,006	2,326	2,641	3,060	3,500

[a] Includes interest.

TABLE 94 STATE EXPENDITURE ON EDUCATION IN RELATION TO THE BUDGET, AND NATIONAL EXPENDITURE ON EDUCATION IN RELATION TO THE GROSS NATIONAL PRODUCT—THE NETHERLANDS
(in thousands of millions of florins)

	State Budget	State Expenditure on Education	Percentage of Budget	G.N.P.	Total Expenditure on Education	Percentage of G.N.P.	Capital Expenditure as a Percentage of the G.N.P.
1954	6.8	0.59	8.7	27.0	0.93	3.4	0.57
1956	7.8	0.88	11.3	33.6	1.31	4.0	0.67
1958	8.1	1.11	13.7	35.9	1.60	4.5	0.70
1960	9.5	1.52	16.0	42.7	2.00	4.7	0.86
1961	11.3	1.81	16.2	45.3	2.32	5.1	0.87
1962	11.6	2.12	18.3	48.1	2.65	5.5	0.91
1963	12.4	2.50	20.1	52.2	3.06	5.9	0.98
1964	14.2	2.94	20.7	60.1	3.50	5.8	0.97

TABLE 95 PUBLIC AND PRIVATE EXPENDITURE ON EDUCATION, OPERATIONAL AND INVESTMENTS—UNITED KINGDOM

(in millions of pounds)

	1953–54	1955–56	1957–58	1959–60	1960–61	1961–62	1962–63	1963–64
Public expenditure[a,b]								
Operational	394.7	470.5	615.8	738.4	807.4	903.7	1,014.3	1,121.9
Capital	75.5	91.3	134.6	138.7	141.7	180.1	208.6	232.2
	470.2	561.8	750.4	877.1	949.1	1,083.8	1,222.9	1,354.1
Private expenditure								
Operational[c]	51	60	75	88	95	105	112	118
Capital	—	—	—	—	—	—	—	—
Total	521.2	621.8	825.4	965.1	1,044.1	1,188.8	1,334.9	1,472.1

[a] SOURCE: *Statistics of Education, Part One, 1964.*

[b] Budget for state schools and subventions to private schools do not include expenditure on school canteens and milk, nurses, public libraries. Expenditure on school canteens and milk annually represents approximately 0.3 per cent of the G.N.P.

[c] Estimate. The Central Statistical Service of the Ministry of Education and Science of London estimated this expenditure at 4 or 5 per cent of the Gross National Product (factor cost).

248

TABLE 96 EXPENDITURE ON EDUCATION IN RELATION TO THE GROSS NATIONAL PRODUCT, TOTAL EXPENDITURE AND CAPITAL EXPENDITURE—UNITED KINGDOM
(in millions of pounds)

	G.N.P.	*Total Expenditure*	*Percentage of G.N.P.*	*Capital Expenditure as Percentage of the G.N.P.*
1953–54	16,912	521.2	3.10	0.44
1955–56	19,155	621.8	3.20	0.47
1957–58	21,944	825.4	3.68	0.61
1959–60	24,004	965.1	4.02	0.57
1960–61	25,424	1,044.1	4.11	0.55
1961–62	27,112	1,188.8	4.38	0.66
1962–63	28,238	1,334.9	4.73	0.73
1963–64	30,001	1,472.1	4.90	0.77

TABLE 97 PUBLIC AND PRIVATE EXPENDITURE ON EDUCATION—UNITED STATES
(in thousands of millions)

	1951[a]	1955[a]	1959[a]	1961[b]	1962[c]	1963[c]
Public institutions						
Current expenditure	—	10,542	16,139	18,400	20,800	22,700
Capital expenditure	—	2,809	3,308	4,600	4,100	4,400
	—	*13,351*	*19,447*	*23,000*	*24,900*	*27,100*
Private institutions						
Current expenditure	—	2,828	4,463	4,800	5,200	5,700
Capital expenditure	—	630	811	1,000	900	900
	—	*3,458*	*5,274*	*5,800*	*6,100*	*6,600*
Total	11,312	16,809	24,721	28,800	31,000	33,700

[a] SOURCE: *Statistical Summary of Education, 1955–1956.*

[b] Statistics communicated to Unesco by the United States Department of Health, Education and Welfare.

[c] SOURCE: *Digest of Educational Statistics,* O.E. 10024-64.

TABLE 98   EXPENDITURE ON EDUCATION IN RELATION TO THE
GROSS NATIONAL PRODUCT—UNITED STATES
(in thousands of millions of dollars)

	G.N.P.	Total Expenditure	Percentage of G.N.P.	Capital Expenditure as Percentage of G.N.P.
1951–52	328.9	11,312	3.44	—
1955–56	398.9	16,809	4.23	0.86
1959–60	484.2	24,721	5.10	0.85
1961–62	519.4	28,800	5.55	1.08
1962–63	556.1	31,000[a]	5.57[a]	0.90[a]
1963–64	585.0	33,700[a]	5.80[a]	0.91[a]

[a] SOURCE: *Digest of Educational Statistics,* O.E. 10024-64.

TABLE 99   EXPENDITURE[a] ON EDUCATION—U.S.S.R.
(in thousands of millions of old rubles)

	1950	1955	1959	1960	1961	1962	1963
Current expenditure	—	—	69.4	—	78.8	86.9	—
Capital expenditure	—	—	8.1	—	12.7	13.5	—
Total	53.2	62.2	77.5	84.4	91.5	100.4	—

SOURCES: From 1950 to 1960, *Financing Soviet Schools,* by
Harold J. Noah (New York: Teachers College Press, 1966). For
1961 and 1962, Unesco *Annual Statistics.*
[a] Not including expenditure on scientific research proper.

EXPENDITURE ON EDUCATION IN RELATION TO THE STATE BUDGET,[a] AND IN RELATION TO THE GROSS NATIONAL PRODUCT[b]—U.S.S.R.

(in thousands of millions of old rubles)

	State Budget	State Expenditure on Education	Percentage of Budget	G.N.P.	Total Expenditure on Education	Percentage of G.N.P.	Capital Expenditure as Percentage of the G.N.P.
1950	413	48.7	11.8	—	—	—	—
1955	539	56.8	10.5	940	62.60	6.60	—
1959	704	68.2	9.7	1,359 *1,677*	77.50	5.70 *4.60*	0.60 *0.49*
1960	731	74.2	10.2	1,466 *1,794*	84.40	5.76 *4.70*	
1961	763	81.3	10.7	1,561 *1,848*	91.50	5.94 *4.94*	0.81 *0.68*
1962	827	85.4	10.3	1,660 *1,994*	100.43	6.05 *5.04*	— *0.68*
1963	870	93.1	10.7				

[a] Federal state, federated republics, and local administrations.

[b] The Soviet G.N.P. is not calculated in the same way as in Western countries (O.E.C.D. evaluations). It excludes a large proportion of tertiary activities and is therefore approximately 20 per cent lower in relation to the O.E.C.D. estimates. This results in a relative increase in the percentage of the Soviet G.N.P. devoted to education as compared with Western countries. To permit a genuine comparison, the present table indicates the official Soviet G.N.P. (*United Nations Statistical Yearbook*) and the percentage of expenditure on education; and the re-estimated Soviet G.N.P. (SOURCE: A. S. Becker, *Soviet National Income, 1958–1962*) and the corresponding percentage of expenditure on education (the numbers and percentages in italics).

251

TABLE 101 COMPARATIVE RATIOS OF EXPENDITURE ON EDUCATION TO THE GROSS NATIONAL PRODUCT

	Federal Republic of Germany	Belgium[a]	France	Italy	Nether-lands	United Kingdom	United States[b]	U.S.S.R.
1950								
Current expenditure	—	2.35	—	2.42	2.56	—	2.90	—
Capital expenditure	—	0.19	—	0.27	0.36	—	0.54	—
	—	2.54	—	2.69	2.92	—	3.44	—
1952								
Current expenditure	2.16	—	2.26	—	2.64	2.63	—	—
Capital expenditure	0.52	—	0.28	—	0.37	0.47	—	—
	2.68	—	2.54	—	3.01	3.10	—	—
1961								
Current expenditure	2.41	4.12	2.94	3.30	4.27	3.72	4.47	4.26
Capital expenditure	0.76	0.56	0.62	0.58	0.87	0.66	1.08	0.68
	3.17	4.68	3.56	3.88	5.14	4.38	5.55	4.94

1962								
Current expenditure	2.42	4.50	3.08	3.59	4.60	4.00	4.67	4.36
Capital expenditure	0.84	0.48	0.73	0.66	0.91	0.73	0.90	0.68
	3.26	*4.98*	*3.81*	*4.25*	*5.51*	*4.73*	*5.57*	*5.04*
1963								
Current expenditure	—	4.20	3.28	4.04	4.88	4.13	4.89	—
Capital expenditure	—	0.40	0.76	0.72	0.98	0.77	0.91	—
	—	*4.60*	*4.04*	*4.76*	*5.86*	*4.90*	*5.80*	—
1964								
Current expenditure	—	4.03	3.56	—	4.85	—	—	—
Capital expenditure	—	0.34	0.79	—	0.97	—	—	—
	—	*4.37*	*4.35*	*5.03*	*5.82*	—	—	—

[a] The percentage of capital expenditure is deliberately reduced because of the absence of any estimate for private education.

[b] For 1950, the breakdown between current and capital expenditure was estimated by the rapporteur.

tion to G.N.P.[31] We shall therefore limit ourselves to this comparison.

Table 101 shows expenditure on education (current, capital, total) in relation to G.N.P. in 1950 and 1952 and 1961 and 1962[32] for the eight countries for which adequate data

Table 101 calls for some remarks.

CURRENT EXPENDITURE

1. *Disparities in the growth of current expenditure*   In 1950 and 1952, the proportion of current expenditure did not vary to any significant extent in the Common Market countries, the United Kingdom, or even the United States. Only the U.S.S.R. seems to have had a relative advance at that time.

In 1961 and 1962, the disparities between the Western countries increased substantially (United States: 4.47; Federal Republic of Germany: 2.42%) while in the U.S.S.R., the ratio would seem to have been stationary although at a relatively high level.

There should have been a relatively close correlation between growth in current expenditure as a percentage of G.N.P. and growth in enrollment figures. In fact, the two were far from being parallel (see Table 102). In many countries[33] (Federal Republic of Germany, Belgium, Italy, Great Britain) the increase in the ratio is greater than the increase in enrollment. This is due[34] to the particularly rapid—and expensive —expansion[35] of secondary and higher education and, in some cases, to the lower pupil-teacher ratio in primary schools. In France, for the period under consideration,[36] the growth in enrollment was more rapid than that of the proportion of the G.N.P. devoted to current expenditure on education.

2. *Causes of disparities in the current expenditure on ed-*

[31] Or other national accounting aggregate.

[32] And, for certain countries, in 1963 and 1964.

[33] Except in France.

[34] Irrespective of variations in the rate of growth of the G.N.P. which may to some extent distort comparisons.

[35] See Table 11.

[36] The trend was reversed in 1963 and 1964 (see Table 91).

TABLE 102   GROWTH IN ENROLLMENT AND GROWTH IN RATIO
OF CURRENT EXPENDITURE TO GROSS NATIONAL
PRODUCT[a]

	Extreme Years	Growth of Expenditure as a Percentage of G.N.P.	Growth of Enrollment, All Levels
Federal Republic of Germany	1951–1961	+11	−10
Italy	1951–1961	+36	+15
England and Wales	1952–1962	+40	+22
U.S.S.R.	1951–1961	?	+32
Belgium	1952–1962	+75[b]	+32
Netherlands	1952–1962	+74	+33
United States	1951–1961	+54	+49
France	1952–1962	+37	+51

[a] Data for this table was taken from Appendix Table A-11.

[b] The exceptional increase in expenditure in Belgium is basically due to the unduly low level in the initial year and the rapid increase resulting from application of the agreement regarding teachers' salaries.

ucation   The considerable divergences in 1961 and 1962 and after (see Table 101) can be explained mainly by a combination of three factors: the level of teachers' salaries in relation to the per capita G.N.P. (this study unfortunately provides no data on this far from insignificant factor); the pupil-teacher ratios (see previous section); and the size of the school-age population and its distribution by educational level.

Chapters 1 and 2 indicate the extent of enrollment at various levels. Figure 1 synthesizes all the earlier information and shows the full-time enrollment rate between five and twenty-five years of age for each country.[37] Given the extent

[37] This virtually covers all educational levels other than the first years of preschool education.

TABLE 103 THE SCHOOL-GOING POPULATION OVER 5 YEARS OF AGE IN RELATION TO THE TOTAL POPULATION BETWEEN 5 AND 24 YEARS OF AGE

	Total Population (in millions)	Population between 5 and 24 Years of Age (in thousands)	Population over 5 Years of Age Attending Full-time Educational Institutions, 1961–62 (in thousands)	Percentage of School-going Population in Relation to the Population Between 5 and 24 Years of Age[a]
Federal Republic of Germany (6/6/61)	53.975	15,632	7,225[b] (8,804)[c]	46.2 56.3
Belgium (12/31/61)	9.189	2,557	1,635	64.1
France (3/7/62)	46.530	14,090	9,208	65.3
Italy (10/15/61)	50.623	15,744	7,591	48.2
Luxembourg (12/31/60)	0.314	83	45	54.2
Netherlands (7/1/61)	11.638	4,060	2,562	63.1
England and Wales (4/23/61)	46.071	13,070	7,915	60.5
U.S.S.R. (1/1/62)	219.763	77,295	41,612[d] 47,489[e]	55.7 61.4[e]
United States (7/1/61)	183.642	62,229	48,000	77.1

[a] It will be noted that these percentages are unfavorable in some countries (the U.S.S.R. and the Federal Republic of Germany) where enrollment during the period of compulsory education was affected by a drop in births due to the war.

[b] Assumes that 400,000 children aged more than 5 years are enrolled in kindergartens.

[c] Includes part-time vocational schools.

[d] Assumes that 1.5 million of the 3,627 million in primary schools were under 5 years of age.

[e] Includes part-time and correspondence courses.

257

FIGURE 1 CURRENT EXPENDITURE ON EDUCATION AND ENROLLMENT
BETWEEN 5 AND 25 YEARS OF AGE

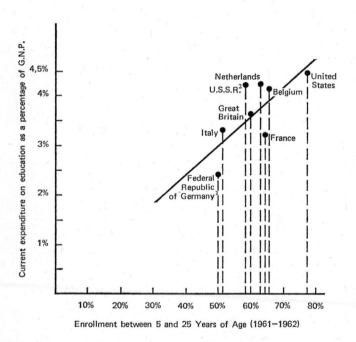

[1] Federal Republic of Germany: assuming one-quarter enrolled part time.

[2] U.S.S.R.: assuming one-half enrolled part time.

of the variations in enrollment rates between five and twenty-five years of age, this factor must largely explain the divergences in expenditure.

Figure 2 shows a fairly close correlation between the percentage of the G.N.P. devoted to education and total enrollment.

In several countries, however, there are reasonably striking divergences from the general trend:

In the U.S.S.R., expenditure is particularly high in relation to the enrollment rates, partly, it would seem, because of the relatively low enrollment in preschool and elementary classes as compared to the total[38] and partly because of a relatively satisfactory student-teacher ratio together with the exceptionally high expenditure on scholarships (40 per cent of the individual cost in vocational schools, and 33 per cent of the cost per student in the *tekhnikums* and higher institutions).[39]

In Germany the contrary phenomenon exists: expenditure seems low in relation to enrollment, apparently because of the high pupil-teacher ratios at primary level and the more limited development of secondary and higher education.

France and The Netherlands, with similar enrollment rates, come respectively below and above the average expenditure curve; any attempt to explain these differences lies outside the scope of the present study.

CAPITAL EXPENDITURE

There was a general but varying increase in capital expenditure.

In 1951 and 1952, certain countries (Great Britain, the United States, the Federal Republic of Germany) devoted approximately 0.5 per cent of their G.N.P. to school and university buildings, as against 0.28 and 0.27 per cent respectively by France and Italy.

---

[38] A factor which increases the average cost per student.
[39] Never found to the same extent in the other countries.

FIGURE 2   ENROLLMENT RATES, BY SOCIAL BACKGROUND[1] – FRANCE

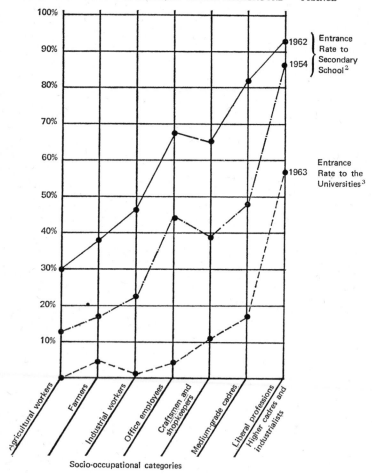

Socio-occupational categories

[1] Ratio between number of young people by social background and number of enrollments by social category.

[2] In relation to the average of the two age groups of 11 and 12 years.

[3] Average rate in relation to the five age groups of 12 to 22 years.

In 1962, the situation was much better balanced: from 0.64 per cent[40] (Great Britain) to 0.90 per cent (United States). In France, where the expansion in enrollment was most rapid between 1952 and 1962, expenditure on school and university buildings still represented only 0.73 per cent of the G.N.P. in 1962, that is, less than the Federal Republic of Germany or The Netherlands where enrollment did not develop at the same rate. Nevertheless, as we have seen, French classrooms were less, not more overcrowded than those in the two other countries.

To be really valid, international comparisons would need a preliminary study of norms in the construction and equipment of schools and universities, and the resulting unit cost per pupil or student. These obviously differ. Again, certain countries go further than others in their efforts to rationalize and standardize school building and to reduce costs.

For these two reasons, a comparison of total capital expenditures does not necessarily provide an accurate relative picture of the number of school places which have been provided or of the quality of the installations. This matter unquestionably deserves investigation.

[40] As already noted (see Tables 88 and 89), the data on Belgium is incomplete.

Conclusions

The question was raised in the Introduction about the capacity of the "old countries" which make up the European Economic Community to adapt their educational systems to the human, social, democratic, and economic imperatives of our time. An answer has been sought by comparing their educational systems and those of three other major industrialized countries: the United States, the U.S.S.R., and Great Britain.

The information provided above shows how difficult it is to find clear and unequivocal answers, and the care which must be taken in making international comparisons in education. National structures lend themselves unwillingly to comparative evaluation, and there is always a temptation to contrast quantitative and qualitative. Spirit and methods involved have been completely ignored and this omission to some extent limits the scope of our analysis.

Subject to these reservations, the observations or conclusions which may be drawn from the data assembled and compared are many and of varying importance. Some have already been given, and we shall not revert to them here.[1] Others

---

[1] For example, comments concerning the comparison of timetables in "long" education (Chapter 1) and regional and social differences in secondary enrollment and their causes (Chapter 1).

are obvious from a comparison of the statistics and have not merited further comments. We do not try in this concluding chapter to review everything, but rather to underline the points of major economic and social importance.

The main points which emerge show, economically, the relatively slow rate at which senior cadres are trained in the Common Market countries and, socially, the extremely limited access to extended studies of children from the lower classes.

THE TRAINING OF SENIOR CADRES IN THE EUROPEAN ECONOMIC COMMUNITY AND THE INADEQUATE DEMOCRATIZATION OF ACCESS TO HIGHER EDUCATION

The tables in Chapter 2 give comparative national statistics for graduates from institutions of higher education from which we shall now make a synthesis. In regard to the qualitative aspect of these comparisons, please refer to what has already been said in the Introduction.

THE SLOW RATE OF TRAINING OF SENIOR CADRES IN COMMON MARKET COUNTRIES

TOTAL FIGURES

Table 65 shows the total number of graduates from institutions of higher education (first level) by main disciplines for each of the countries concerned[2] in the last year for which statistics are available.[3]

Taking the three major economic units (Common Market, U.S.S.R., the United States) the total numbers of graduates (first level) are: in the Common Market countries, 101,000 graduates for 180 million inhabitants; in the United States, 450,000 graduates for 190 million inhabitants;[4] and in the

[2] Except Luxembourg.
[3] 1962, 1963, or 1964.
[4] As pointed out in the Introduction, American bachelor de-

U.S.S.R., 331,000 graduates for 223 million inhabitants. In other words, the Common Market figure is barely a quarter of the American and a third of the Soviet figures.

An estimate of the number of graduates in relation to age groups corrects the effects of population differences, especially in birth-rates, but substantial disparities remain: for the Common Market countries,[5] 4 per cent of age groups; for Great Britain, 5.68 per cent of age groups (9 per cent including the nondegree level); for the U.S.S.R., 8.2 per cent of age groups; and for the United States, 19.6 per cent of age groups.

As already explained at length in Chapter 2, national statistics on higher education are not entirely comparable since some include primary teacher training (Great Britain, United States, Federal Republic of Germany) or training of senior technicians or technical engineers (Great Britain, Belgium). Even excluding these, however, the differences between the Common Market countries, the United States, and the U.S.S.R. are still very significant, while the differences with Great Britain would remain substantial, as shown by the data below (1962, 1963, or 1964):

Common Market countries: 101,000 graduates (first level) + 29,000 teachers + 23,000 graduates at a level higher than the secondary school leaving examination[6] = 153,000 graduates, or 6 per cent of the age groups.

United States: 450,000 graduates (first level) + 50,000 graduates from junior colleges or technical institutes = 500,000 graduates, or 22 per cent of the age groups.

U.S.S.R.: 331,000 graduates (first level) + 58,000 teachers = 389,000 graduates, or 10 per cent of the age groups.

---

grees cannot be automatically taken as the equivalent to European degrees, so that the quantitative comparison is not really meaningful.

[5] General average.

[6] Including 14,600 graduates from the German *Ingenieurschulen,* 3,300 graduates from short higher education institutions in Belgium, 2,400 French senior technicians, and 1,960 Netherlands teachers *(M.O.-Atken).*

The problem is further illuminated by an analysis by main specialization groups.

In the scientific and technical disciplines (see Table 65), the rate of graduation is as follows: in the Common Market countries, 25,000 graduates,[7] or 1.1 per cent of the age groups; in Great Britain, 17,000 graduates, or 2.68 per cent of the age groups;[8] in the United States, 78,000 graduates, or 3.9 per cent of the age groups;[9] and in the U.S.S.R., 130,000 graduates,[10] or 4 per cent of the age groups.

Estimated as a percentage of the age groups, the training rate for scientists (first level) and engineers in the Common Market countries is barely 40 per cent of that in Great Britain and 30 per cent of that in the United States and the U.S.S.R. In reality, the gap is even greater if we allow for the fact that, in most of the Common Market countries, graduates from the science faculties include future teachers in secondary schools, *Gymnasia, athénées,* and so on, whereas, in the U.S.S.R. and the United States, these are largely included under the heading "education" in Table 65. To make the figures genuinely comparable, therefore, 25,000 to 30,000 science teachers should be added to the U.S.S.R. and United States figures.

It will be noted that, contrary to a widely held opinion, the American effort in scientific and technical training, evaluated as a percentage of the age groups, is on the same level as that of the Soviet Union. The breakdown between pure

[7] Not including the Belgian short courses.

[8] 27,700 including the nondegree level, or 4.22 per cent of the age groups.

[9] The remarks concerning the nonequivalence of American degrees are, generally speaking, much less applicable to the American scientific and technical bachelor degree. On the whole, the American figures here are comparable.

[10] In 1959. This total undoubtedly increased to a very significant extent in 1964, when 133,000 engineers were trained.

and applied science, however, is very different: the U.S.S.R., relatively speaking, trains many more engineers and fewer scientists (see footnotes 8 and 9 to Table 67).

In the human sciences (arts, philosophy, social science, economics), the Common Market countries are in a relatively better but by no means leading position: the Common Market countries, 38,000 graduates, or 1.5 per cent of the age groups; the U.S.S.R. (1959), 50,600 graduates, or 1.2 per cent of the age groups; the United States, 203,300 graduates, or 8.9 per cent of the age groups; and Great Britain, 14,500 graduates,[11] or 2.26 per cent of the age groups.

The comparison with the United States is obviously of little significance since American colleges provide courses leading to degrees (Bachelor's degrees in social science,[12] home economics, and the like) for which there is virtually no equivalent in European universities.

Again the U.S.S.R. rate for the human sciences is not lower than the European average; and would even be slightly higher if prospective teachers in arts disciplines, included under "education" in Table 65, are counted.

DIFFERENCES AMONG THE COMMON
MARKET COUNTRIES

Statistics for the Common Market countries are grouped together above to facilitate comparisons with the United States and the U.S.S.R. The averages for the Common Market countries as a whole, however, conceal variations which, while not as pronounced as those indicated above, are nonetheless noteworthy (see Tables 65 and 67).

Generally speaking, the Federal Republic of Germany, The Netherlands, and then Italy have the lowest rate of graduation.

---

[11] Degree level only.
[12] Nearly 3 per cent of the age groups obtain this degree.

DO TECHNICAL GRADUATES IN THE
COMMON MARKET COUNTRIES REPRESENT
SOME COMPENSATION?

This question would not be necessary if the boundaries between training in institutions of higher education and secondary technical institutions were clearly marked but, as already noted, this is not the case and certain courses (in the technical or medical disciplines, for example) may or may not be included in higher education.

In the technical disciplines, if the 14,600 graduates from the German *Ingénieur Schulen,* the 1,400 Belgian engineer-technicians, and the 2,200 French senior technicians were included with graduates in higher education, the percentage of scientific and technical graduates would amount to between 1.1 and 1.8 per cent of the age groups for the Common Market countries as a whole, that is, still very markedly less than the percentages in the U.S.S.R., the United States, and Great Britain (4.22 per cent).

This nullifies any qualitative arguments which might be advanced in regard to American or Soviet graduates: even if short European courses are included in the comparison with the first level in the U.S.S.R and the United States,[13] the lower rate of the Common Market countries still remains manifest. On the other hand, the position of the Federal Republic of Germany (scientific and technical graduates of university level representing 0.68 per cent of age groups) would be very definitely improved (2.2 per cent of age groups) and, on this basis, would almost reach the level of France (2.5 per cent) and Belgium (2.7 per cent).

Leaving aside this marginal zone between secondary and higher education and taking into account only graduates from long technical courses (technical assistant or technician level), the present rates of training are as shown in the tabulation on page 268.

[13] This would imply a parity of level which is far from being established.

	All Degrees %	Industrial Courses %
Federal Republic of Germany	?	1.2[a]
Belgium	11.2	?
France	4.8	1.8
Italy	6.9	1.1
Netherlands	3.6	1.1
England and Wales	4.0	3.2
U.S.S.R.	13.0[b]	6.0

[a] Graduates from *Technikerschulen;* no German statistics for the other categories are available.
[b] Graduates of the *tekhnikums* (which include primary teacher training).

Here again, the Common Market countries as a whole very definitely lag behind the U.S.S.R. and England, especially in the training of industrial technicians. Whereas industries in the U.S.S.R. at present employ more than two technicians (trained in the *tekhnikums*) for one engineer and plan to raise this ratio to three or four to one in 1970, the Common Market countries on the average train scarcely any more technicians than engineers.

It is true that, in this respect, the situation even in the United States is far from satisfactory: the vocational and technical courses in the junior colleges and technical institutes account for barely 2 per cent of the age groups, and the courses given in the vocational and technical high schools do not provide this level of training. The Federal Government, incidentally, is very much concerned with this problem and Congress has voted funds for several important programs.

To sum up, engineer-technician training in the Common Market countries cannot compensate for the lag at the level of the first higher education diploma; furthermore, the training of specialists at the technician level[14] would seem to be

[14] On the other hand, the Common Market's effort to train workers and skilled employees within the educational system (full-

very inadequate, at any rate when compared with the U.S.S.R. and Great Britain.

TRAINING OF RESEARCH WORKERS

Comparisons are particularly difficult here, since the effort to train advanced students is not necessarily reflected in the statistics on graduates; except for France, the Common Market countries have not systematically organized postgraduate courses which prepare for research and lead to degrees.

If the degrees awarded (as a percentage of the age groups) in the United States, the U.S.S.R., and France are compared, the differences are still more pronounced: the United States (1963), 0.55 per cent[15] on the Ph.D. and D.S. level; the U.S.S.R. (1963), 0.30 per cent[16] on the *Candidature* level; and France (1961), 0.15 per cent[17] on the *Doctorat de troisème cycle* level.

It will be noted that the rapid expansion in the number of Soviet aspirants between 1960 and 1964 should lead to a doubling of the above percentage within a few years.

Except perhaps in the Federal Republic of Germany, it would not seem that the training of young research workers in the other Common Market countries is proceeding any more rapidly than in France. Accordingly, at this vital stage at the beginning of careers in scientific research, the training of cadres in the Common Market countries is still lagging sharply behind.

---

time or part-time) is relatively greater—Belgium, 24 per cent of age groups, and France, 21 per cent, against 22 per cent in the U.S.S.R. and 16 per cent in England. The efforts of the Federal Republic of Germany and The Netherlands (not shown in the statistics on graduates) are very extensive if we may judge from current enrollments. Apart from official training, there is also the training provided by various enterprises at this level (of great importance in the U.S.S.R. and Germany) but it is difficult to make any comparative evaluation.

[15] Including 46 per cent of doctorates in science and technology.
[16] Including 71 per cent of doctorates in science and technology.
[17] Including 55 per cent of doctorates in science and technology.

SOCIAL INEQUALITIES IN ACCESS TO HIGHER EDUCATION ARE PARTICULARLY PRONOUNCED IN THE COMMON MARKET COUNTRIES

Statistics were given in Chapter 2 on the social aspects of access to higher education. Whatever may be the difficulty of comparing and interpreting these statistics, certain general conclusions may be drawn.

LIBERAL PROFESSIONS, SENIOR CADRES, AND INDUSTRIALIST CATEGORIES

The highest enrollment is in these categories and the figures are remarkably homogeneous: approximately 60 per cent in the United States, France, and the other Common Market countries. In the United Kingdom, the proportion is lower (45 per cent), but the classification of professional categories may not be the same. It is also possible that this lower proportion is a consequence of the relatively severe selection made by the eleven-plus examination even among the higher social groups (see Chapter 1).

For children whose parents are themselves mostly graduates in higher education, access to the university has become a family standard and failure would mean a loss of caste. Setting aside the possible limitations imposed by the entrance examinations for universities and other institutions of higher education,[18] it is probable that rates very much higher than the average are also to be found among children of senior cadres in the Soviet Union.

On the question of securing the maximum percentage of young people equipped for higher education, it should be pointed out that enrollment rates may be high if family and social background provides real intellectual and economic assistance and very strong motivation.

These social groups, however, are relatively small (4 to 5 per cent of the active population in the Common Market countries) and it must be recognized that their attitudes

[18] This qualification is obviously very important.

form an exception in relation to the whole. Nevertheless, given the extent of their entrance rates, the children of the higher social categories form a substantial proportion of the total number of students (from 32 to 45 per cent of enrollment in the Common Market countries).

MANUAL WORKERS

The children of manual workers (industrial workers, agricultural workers, service personnel) form the other extreme.

Their entrance rates are particularly low: 3 per cent for the children of farmers and 1.4 per cent for the children of industrial workers in France (1962); and 4 per cent for skilled workers and 2 per cent for semi-skilled and unskilled workers in Great Britain, or percentages which are slightly but definitely higher than in France.

Because of these low rates and although these social groups represent a substantial proportion of the active population— 73 per cent of manual workers in Great Britain and 56 per cent of industrial workers and farmers in France—their children occupy a relatively low place in the student population: 30 per cent in Great Britain,[19] 12.6 per cent in France, 11.5 per cent in Belgium,[20] 10 per cent in The Netherlands, and 7.5 per cent in the Federal Republic of Germany. These latter two percentages would seem to indicate that the enrollment rates for children of workers and farmers in The Netherlands and the Federal Republic of Germany are even lower than in France.

Table 56 indicates that, in the United States, the lowest rates of access to higher education are approximately 15 per cent for children of farmers and 10 to 12 per cent for children of industrial workers, that is, rates which are between three and five times higher than in the Common Market countries.

---

[19] This percentage represents all manual workers; the figures for the Common Market countries represent only industrial workers and farmers.

[20] University of Louvain only.

Enrollment rates in higher education for the children of manual workers cannot be determined from the statistics published in the U.S.S.R. The rates of admission are only half those of the United States (17 per cent as against 34 per cent), and it is therefore probable that, despite the systematic effort made by the Soviet authorities and the fact that the state pays for almost 80 per cent of the full-time students, enrollment rates for children of manual workers have not yet reached the levels prevailing in the United States.[21] In any case, they are very much higher than those for the Common Market countries.

INTERMEDIATE SOCIAL GROUPS

In the intermediate social groups (shopkeepers, craftsmen, medium grade cadres, office employees) statistics indicate a very large difference between these and the higher cadres: enrollment rates for the children of medium-grade cadres, for example, are only half those for children of higher cadres (France).

However, enrollment rates for these categories are between three and eight times higher than in workers' and peasants' families. As was pointed out in connection with long secondary studies, these differences may relate more to the relative strength of family ambitions than to their living standards.

DIVERGENCIES IN ENROLLMENT
IN HIGHER EDUCATION

Thus it may be seen that there are extreme divergences in enrollment rates in higher education. They are approximately from 1 to 60 or more in the Common Market countries; from 1 to 15 or 20 in Great Britain; and from 1 to 5 or 6 in the United States.

The U.S.S.R. probably resembles[22] the United States, and the variations may even be still more limited if the enrollment

---

[21] It is true that the systems of admission are very different.

[22] This view is borne out by the results of the sociological surveys carried out in the Novosibirsk region which were published in

rates for children of higher cadres is significantly lower than in the West.

Analyzing access to higher education from the social angle, therefore, it will be seen that in the Common Market countries as a whole, or even individually, access to higher education for children of the lower social strata is the most limited.

THE LAG OF THE COMMON MARKET COUNTRIES IN RELATION TO THE UNITED STATES, THE U.S.S.R., AND GREAT BRITAIN

The situation outlined above does not represent a static phase in the educational history of each of the countries but rather a period of rapid evolution. Consequently, the elements used in the comparisons may very rapidly change. In what direction? Will the Common Market countries, given the impetus already operating everywhere, improve their present relative situation?

Precise answers to these questions would imply an analysis of all the plans or forecasts which may have been drawn up in the various countries but which cannot be dealt with here. In any event, to a large extent the development of higher education in the Common Market countries over the next ten or fifteen years is still latent in the secondary schools and, short of action which would radically alter the rules governing recruitment for higher education,[23] the limits of possible growth are already perceptible.

THE FORESEEABLE LIMITS OF DEVELOPMENT IN HIGHER EDUCATION IN THE COMMON MARKET COUNTRIES

As already observed, the demographic and social trend toward secondary and higher education is apparent in all the

---

the journal of the Institute of Philosophy of the Academy of Sciences of the U.S.S.R., *Voprossy Filosofii*.

[23] This would seem improbable and, in any case, could only take place on a large scale at the expense of technician training.

Common Market countries (see Appendix Tables A-1 to A-4) and, in many countries, the development of long secondary courses has not yet borne fruit in higher education either in the training of cadres or from the social point of view; progress may therefore be expected at the higher education level over the years ahead.

The most typical example of this dynamic evolution is undoubtedly provided by France. Table 105 shows the rates of access to secondary schools *(classes de sixième)* in 1954 and 1962 and the university enrollment rates in 1963, all by social categories.

University enrollment in 1963 was largely determined by the enrollment in the first secondary classes nine or ten years previously (1954). Enrollment in the first secondary classes in 1962 will determine university enrollment in 1970–1972. The noteworthy increase in the first class in secondary schools among the various social groups between 1954 and 1962 and later will therefore very greatly alter the situation in higher education up to 1975. French officials already expect over 600,000 students in 1972[24] and a significant increase in the number of graduates from higher education which should affect between 8 and 9 per cent of the age groups at that date.[25] This rise in enrollment will primarily benefit the children of medium-grade cadres and manual workers,[26] and will lead to some reduction in the disparities in access.

In the Federal Republic of Germany, the number of students between 1974 and 1979 has already been largely determined by the enrollment in the *Gymnasien* in 1964–65, since secondary school courses last nine years. As previously noted, the rate of access to pre-university secondary schools is still low (14.5 per cent in 1963) and has scarcely varied in recent years. Accordingly, the number of secondary school graduates, which conditions the number of university students,

[24] As against 280,000 in 1962.

[25] As against 5 per cent in 1964.

[26] Since the enrollment in higher education of children of higher cadres is already close to the maximum level.

will not significantly increase between now and 1972 (8 to 9 per cent of age group). Substantial progress in the rate of training of cadres could only be achieved through such measures as improved "yield" from the *Gymnasien* (more especially by reducing drop-outs after the tenth class); extension of access to *Gymnasien* for *Realschule* pupils (as already pointed out, the Conference of Ministers of Education suggested the systematic organization of such transfers); and extension of access to higher education through the "second channel," that is, technical education and special examinations.

Efforts along these lines will probably give results[27] but, in view of the virtual stabilization of the essential element which, short and medium term, will still consist of secondary school graduates, it seems unlikely that there will be any very substantial increase in the percentage of young Germans continuing their studies at university level over the next ten years.

In The Netherlands, the situation is not very different from that in the Federal Republic of Germany since the rate of access to pre-university secondary studies has remained virtually unchanged over recent years and was still very low in 1963 (13.9 per cent). Whatever contributory action may be taken, it is unlikely that the present low rate of training of higher cadres (1.8 per cent) can be significantly changed in the years ahead.

In Italy, the number of new secondary school graduates increased only very slightly from 1950 to 1963. However, the rapid development of middle schools until recently should soon have an effect at secondary school level, while the opening of the faculties to students from the technical institutes (as decided in 1961) will bring about an immediate increase in enrollment in Italian universities.

The rate of graduation from higher education at the present time is low (2.86 per cent in 1963), especially in the sci-

---

[27] An extensive program for the development of *Ingenieurschulen* is designed to raise enrollment to 70,000 by 1970.

entific and technical disciplines (0.65 per cent) and, notwithstanding the probable improvement, Italy will still be at a modest level after 1970.

Belgium would at present seem to be the Common Market country with the highest rate of graduation from higher education (10.9 per cent). A large proportion of this, however, represents the training of teachers for middle schools. The Belgian situation in respect of scientific and technical training is satisfactory in relation to the Common Market countries (if engineer-technicians are included) but is not equal to that of the other three countries.

It is impossible to foresee the effects of the Law of June 8, 1964, establishing a maturity examination on the quantitative development of higher education in Belgium. In any case, the very extensive development of the first and second secondary school cycles in Belgium, together with the development of technical education, represents a solid basis for a rapid extension of higher education.

IMMEDIATE PROSPECTS FOR THE DEVELOPMENT
OF HIGHER EDUCATION IN THE UNITED STATES,
THE U.S.S.R., AND GREAT BRITAIN

In the United States, the present extensive development of higher education does not represent a ceiling; on the contrary, all official forecasts are based on an increase in population and a further increase in enrollment rates after eighteen years of age.

Nearly 6,500,000 students are expected in 1970 and this would represent 875,000 bachelor's degrees per year (25 per cent of the age groups), including 135,000 graduates[28] in mathematics, physics, and engineering.[29]

In the U.S.S.R., the rate of enrollment in higher education

[28] Report by the Chairman of the Science Advisory Committee on December 12, 1962.

[29] If graduates in biology are added, the number of graduates in these disciplines would amount to more than 5 per cent of the age groups.

has significantly increased since 1960 (593,000 in 1960, 814,-000 in 1963) and accordingly the number of graduates should represent between 12 and 13 per cent of the age groups toward 1970. In addition, under the program of the 22nd Congress of the Communist Party, the number of students is to be raised to 8,000,000 in 1980 for all forms of education. This total would represent more than 1,000,000 graduates a year, or approximately 20 per cent of the twenty-four– to twenty-five–year age group.

In Great Britain, the report by the Robbins Committee (October 1963) estimated that full-time enrollment in higher education would rise as follows: in 1962–63, 216,000 (40 per cent in science and technology); in 1973–74, 392,000; and in 1980–81, 558,000 (47 per cent in science and technology).

This estimate is based on the increase in the eighteen-year-old age group and on an increase from 7 per cent in 1961 to 12.9 per cent in 1980 in the number of students who will obtain the necessary qualifications to proceed to higher education.[30] If these forecasts prove accurate, and there is every reason to think that they will, the already high rate of graduation in Great Britain will increase very rapidly.

THE LAG IN THE COMMON MARKET COUNTRIES

Except for France, and probably Belgium, which should, respectively, be able to improve or maintain their relative positions, the rate at which senior cadres are trained in the Common Market countries will not come appreciably nearer to the rate in the United States, the U.S.S.R., and even Great Britain; on the contrary, the existing gap will probably become still more pronounced.

From the point of view of their human capital in highly qualified manpower, it is safe to say that the relative position of the Common Market countries as a whole will be less good in 1970 and 1975 than it was in 1940 or 1950.[31]

[30] This increase certainly represents a minimum.

[31] In the U.S.S.R., the total number of actively employed persons who had completed higher education rose from 403,000 in

This is, of course, in purely quantitative terms, and some will reject it on qualitative grounds. We shall not revert to this argument (see Introduction) except to express our own belief that, even if the above quantitative comparisons could be weighted by an evaluation of the relative traditional quality[32] of higher education in the old European countries—in which respect it is all too easy to nourish illusions—the lag in the Common Market countries would still be incontestable. This is borne out by the fact that, even if we consider the level of advanced studies (studies in preparation for scientific research) only, the lag is equally pronounced, at any rate in pure science and technology.

THE NEED TO RECTIFY THIS SITUATION

At this stage, the obvious question is whether this situation has serious implications and whether it really demands an attempt to rectify it.

ECONOMIC ARGUMENTS

From a purely economic viewpoint, the problem really is to decide whether the continuous and rapid development in the production of goods and services depends on having cadres on the scale at which the United States and the U.S.S.R. are aiming.

It is certain that economic development does not depend only on the human capital factor, and that growth is governed by a number of other factors (investment rates, currency, foreign trade, the spirit of enterprise). Again, the extensive development of secondary and higher education is costly and the expenditure involved may, from a purely economic viewpoint, be weighed against other forms of expenditure which would seem more immediately profitable.

However, as noted in the Introduction, the qualifications

1932 to 4,282,000 in 1963; the number of specialists trained in the *tekhnikums* rose from 575,000 to 6,200,000. This growth should accelerate during the next decade.

[32] In relation to American, British, or Soviet education.

of the active population and, more especially, the extent to which medium-grade and senior cadres are available, play a decisive part in the continuous progress of the more advanced economies. What precisely is the extent of these requirements? Is it essential for rapid growth to carry the training of cadres and specialists as far as the United States and the U.S.S.R. have done and are proposing to do?

It should be noted that the development of higher education in these two great federations is far from following the same path.

The American effort is largely spontaneous and, so to speak, anarchic. The social impulsion toward extended education provides the basic driving force; at the same time, the economic "needs" which are readily reflected in the programs of American universities and colleges[33] direct this impulsion—more or less correctly, it is true—along lines which correspond to realities in the employment market. In the face of this superabundant production of bachelor's degrees, it might seem reasonable to anticipate substantial intellectual unemployment but, on the contrary, experience proves that the 450,000 college and university graduates find work more easily than those young people (30 per cent) who have not completed secondary school.

The Soviet effort is geared to the most detailed forecasts possible of requirements in terms of cadres and specialists. These forecasts are based on short- and medium-term economic plans and on more distant prospects (fifteen to twenty years). They are also based on a determination to transform and modernize the most backward economic sectors by providing them with senior personnel on the same scale as the sectors that are now most advanced. Studies by Soviet planners are made with a view to the objectives we have summarized.

In actual fact, some of the work done in the Common Market countries with very different methods and, above all, with

---

[33] Thanks to the close relationship between the universities and business enterprises.

very different means, lead to not very dissimilar conclusions. In Italy, the work done by the "S.V.I.M.E.Z." from 1960 onward on requirements in senior staff in 1975 led to the conclusion that the percentage of cadres and specialists in the active population should represent 12 per cent at university level and 19 per cent at the level of technical institutes and secondary school leaving certificate. In France, various studies recently carried out by the Planning Commission have led to similar conclusions: between now and 1980, recruitment needs demand over 30 per cent of medium-grade cadres (technicians or secondary school graduates) and senior cadres (graduates from short higher educational courses and university graduates).

In none of the Common Market countries will the rates of training described above suffice to satisfy such requirements.

It is true that a case may be made for the view that the Common Market's economy may well continue to advance with a minimum proportion of cadres, and that the high rates in the United States and the high Soviet norms are not absolute imperatives.

In other words, it would be possible to "economize" in cadres. Experience shows, it is true, that the possibilities of adapting and promoting staff on the job are considerable but they are nonetheless limited. It is certain that such an approach would mean that the already inadequately satisfied needs of European scientific research—and development here is vital to the economic independence of the Common Market countries—together with the needs of the most backward economic sectors and the possibilities of assisting the developing countries would have to be deliberately sacrificed.

While, from an economic viewpoint, the problem of cadres seems to be of particular importance and has accordingly been particularly stressed here, the intellectual improvement of workers generally is in itself a condition of high productivity. The two objectives, in fact, are inseparable.

There are other aspects, however, in addition to the purely economic.

THE HUMAN, SOCIAL, AND DEMOCRATIC ARGUMENTS

The desire to give men a better education involves more than purely economic considerations. Its justification is equally—if not more so—human, social, and democratic.

Now that systematic efforts are being made with growing success in all the advanced industrial societies represented by the nine countries to reduce disparities in standards of living, to give all families proper housing, to make the community responsible for covering the most expensive forms in medical care, and to provide leisure and holidays, education extended to the secondary and higher levels cannot continue, as at present, to be the least equitably distributed "consumer item."

It is undeniably necessary and urgent to seek social justice by ensuring everyone access to consumer goods and certain services, but this would still be a poor and unsatisfactory result if it ignored what might well be considered the essential—namely, to guarantee all an opportunity to make the most of their natural capacities and to make all forms of culture accessible to the whole population.

Moreover, in a world where specialized techniques occupy an increasingly important place in training and work, schools and educators must do more and more to protect the right of all people to their own thoughts and inner life.

In the Common Market countries however, as we have seen, not nearly enough is done to make long secondary studies or higher education—and hence, education and culture—generally available. In spite of recent progress, the opportunities for access to higher education that are available to children from the lower classes are much more limited than in the United States, the U.S.S.R., or even Great Britain.

The recognition of profound inequalities in the enjoyment of prolonged schooling has undoubtedly impelled the authorities in all the Common Market countries to try to provide a new chance for adolescents or young adults who could not proceed to higher education through the normal channels. Whatever the value and even the immediate or continuing necessity for such efforts (examples are given above for Germany and France), they should not give rise to any illusion: the number of those who benefit at the level of higher education is very limited and, furthermore, those who reach that level generally have already had some secondary education.

The basic problem, therefore, is to make prolonged schooling available to all social groups at the normal age for full-time studies. In this connection, the systematic access of all young people to general secondary education should be one of the basic aims of social policy in the economically advanced countries.

These ideas are generally accepted; the difficulty begins when it comes to applying them.

THE KEY TO THE PROBLEM: STRUCTURAL REFORMS IN SECONDARY EDUCATION IN THE COMMON MARKET COUNTRIES

We have noted the lag in the Common Market countries in their rate of training cadres (especially scientific and technological) and in regard to the democratization of extended education, and the reasons which make it essential to rectify this situation. The question now is: how?

As pointed out in the Introduction, the aim of the present study is to use comparisons with other advanced countries in order to assess the relative situation of education in the Common Market countries and isolate certain factual elements which, once recognized, may suggest solutions. In other words, it is not our purpose to submit recommendations; they would have to fit a wide variety of national situations and this would constitute a tremendous separate task.

In all the Common Market countries, those responsible for education are alive to the shortage of senior cadres (research workers, teachers, engineers) and the problem of the "democratization" of further studies, and decisions have already been taken, if not to solve them, at any rate to achieve rapid progress. Our comparative study may help to set out the problem more clearly and to give a new dimension to the proposed solutions or objectives.

Among the various types of action taken or likely to be taken, however, the structural reform of secondary schools would seem to be of particular importance.

The key to the problem of increasing and democratizing the rate of training for senior cadres does not lie primarily at the level of higher education—although specific measures at this level are required and will be discussed—but at the level of secondary education.

All the statistics show close correlations between rates of admission to long secondary education, the number of secondary school graduates, and the number of graduates from institutions of higher education. If the latter is to be increased, the bottleneck to be eliminated is the restricted access to pre-university secondary studies.[34] This has social implications: the extension of access to long secondary studies for the benefit, above all, of the social categories which are still largely excluded.

At the stage of economic and social development which the Common Market countries have now reached, however, the problem of providing wide access to pre-university secondary studies is only one aspect of a more far-reaching problem: under any policy for raising general cultural standards all young people should have access to secondary education, at any rate up to a certain level. Hence, all reforms concerning access to secondary education and its organization are central to the problems raised in this study. It would therefore seem essential to know what the various European countries have done and what are the main difficulties.

[34] This naturally includes long secondary education, and more specialized courses in technical secondary schools if they give access to higher education.

The effort at the secondary level is not autonomous but would have to be extended both above and below that level.

BELOW SECONDARY LEVEL

As indicated in Chapter 1, primary schools have a vital role to play in any policy to democratize access to extended studies. The basic problem is to reduce the educational backwardness which particularly impedes children from the lower social strata.

A solution should be sought in more individualized instruction and more direct assistance to such children. This implies the elimination of overcrowded classrooms, the extent of which in three Common Market countries is shown in Table 80; and improved teaching methods, and better general and pedagogic training for teachers which, except in the Federal Republic of Germany, are still relatively brief in the Common Market countries (see Chapter 3).

ABOVE SECONDARY LEVEL

This involves problems specifically related to higher education. The conclusions which emerge from our comparisons clearly indicate the main points on which the effort should be concentrated:

1. *A better "yield" from higher education*   There must be a substantial reduction in the proportion of failures. An improved teacher-student ratio would seem to be the key problem[35] here in such countries as France and Italy (see Table 83). New methods and modern teaching aids[36] must, however, also play a part.

2. *More social assistance for students*   We have not elaborated on this point in the consolidated report but the basic studies carried out for each of the countries concerned demonstrate that this is an area in which the Common Market countries still lag far behind: the number of scholarship-holders amounts to only 20 or 30 per cent of the total num-

[35] "Yield" also depends, of course, on the selection of students.
[36] Audio-visual aids, programmed education, and the like.

ber of students against 80 to 85 per cent in Great Britain and the U.S.S.R., while the value of the scholarships is on the average less.

It is true that the high percentage of scholarship-holders in Great Britain and the U.S.S.R. is closely related to a relatively selective system of access to higher education,[37] but it will also be noted that there is a close correlation between these percentages and the fact that children of manual workers have greater access to higher education.

STRUCTURAL REFORMS IN SECONDARY EDUCATION IN THE COMMON MARKET COUNTRIES

COMMON BASES

All secondary education reforms in European countries since the end of World War II reflect a dual concern: educational and social.

From the educational angle, it is the whole problem of guidance for children passing from childhood to adolescence which is involved. The traditional system of parallel courses is criticized because it means—subject to catching up later— that children's futures are decided by an examination taken at ten, eleven, or twelve years of age when they enter secondary school, at a stage in their lives when, in the overwhelming majority of cases, it is hopeless to try to make a definite appraisal of their capacities as a basis for either promotion or elimination. This has given rise to the idea that a more or less common course should be organized in the early (or first cycle) secondary classes, when children, while working and learning, could be more thoroughly observed and guided if necessary, if only through advice to their families, (1) toward different courses.

This is in line with the views of those who favor greater social justice in educational selection. As already explained at

[37] Even though the rates of access to higher education are higher than in the Common Market countries.

length, unduly early selection favors children from well-to-do
and cultivated social backgrounds. The mere fact of raising
the age of selection until after a common period of secondary
studies does not of itself eliminate the inequalities specifically
related to the social and family background—which will still
be apparent even if the selection is made at a later stage—but
it reduces such inequalities by the very fact of the school's
wider scope of action.

From another angle, systematic access to secondary studies
should very substantially reduce the wastage of gifted children
who at present still drift to the virtual dead-end of terminal
primary classes.

These two ideas are complementary and, since the end of
the war, have given rise to a series of reforms which, after
lengthy discussion, are gradually being applied or tried out on
a more or less extensive scale. The range of solutions adopted
in the Common Market countries alone is very extensive since
the aggressiveness of the reformers is more or less proportionate to the difficulties they must overcome: the effort to make
secondary studies accessible to all children raises very considerable short-term practical difficulties and these invite criticism;
and from a purely educational viewpoint, the idea of a more
or less common period of secondary studies also gives rise to
objections to which we shall revert later.

What are the main features of the reforms at present being
applied or tried out?

REFORMS AND EXPERIMENTS IN THE COMMON MARKET COUNTRIES

Reforms and experiments lie between two extremes: a
common secondary cycle accessible to the whole school age
population[38] by merging the previous parallel courses in a
single type of school and maintaining the parallel courses but
providing facilities for transfer (transitional classes, preliminary classes, and so on) between them.

The French reform lies between these extremes.

[38] Subject to a minimum level of qualification.

These reforms and experiments are obviously not solely related to structures but also relate to programs and methods, problems whose importance has already been stressed from one of the angles with which we are concerned: the access to secondary studies for children of manual workers (see Chapter 1). As pointed out in the Introduction, it is impossible in the present study to deal with this aspect.

1. *The common secondary cycle* (1962 Italian reform, Belgian experiments)   In Italy, since the Bottai reform of 1940, there have been two secondary cycles (see Chapters 1 and 2) following on the five-year elementary school: the middle school, and the school for vocational guidance. Over the last ten years, a certain number of postelementary primary classes have been added in areas where school enrollment between eleven and fourteen years of age is poor.

The Law of December 31, 1962, which is now being applied[39] merges the various courses, for eleven- to fourteen-year-old students, which previously existed in a single type of institution *(scuola media statale)*. Access to the new state middle school (first-level secondary studies) is open to all holders of the elementary certificate *(licenza elementaire);* the three-year course in the state middle school leads to a terminal examination *(licenza)* which gives access to all second-level secondary education. The programs include compulsory common subjects, and optional subjects (Latin, applied technology, music).[40]

In Belgium, the programs of the middle school's three classes for twelve- to fifteen-year-olds) are the same as those of the first three classes in the *lycées* and *athénées;* together they represent the lower level of the secondary school which, as noted earlier, is already broadly accessible to Belgian chil-

---

[39] This reform is to be applied at the beginning of the 1966–67 school year in communes with over 3,000 inhabitants.

[40] The teaching of "rudiments of Latin" is incorporated in the study of Italian during the second year; the study of applied technology and music is compulsory in the first year and is optional thereafter.

dren; in addition, the lower cycle in the technical schools (for the same age group) is very similar to the middle school in regard to the level of general studies. It can already be claimed that in fact the trend in the Belgian educational system is toward a first secondary cycle accessible to all, although the system of sections (classical, modern, technical) is retained.

Since 1959, however, an observation and orientation cycle has been introduced experimentally into a number of middle schools and this cycle does not include the traditional sections. Pupils may choose between a certain number of optional subjects (Latin, technology) but are never isolated from each other as a result.

Under the new Italian or experimental Belgian structure, the choice between differentiated courses (long general, long technical, vocational) is postponed until the second secondary cycle (as in the U.S.S.R.).

2. *Easier transfer between parallel courses* (Federal Republic of Germany, Netherlands)   Secondary structural reform has been extensively discussed in the Federal Republic of Germany in recent years. Various reform projects have been published: the *Rahmenplan* of the German Committee for Education and Culture, the Bremen plan prepared by a study group set up by the teachers' union. Decisions are a matter for the *Länder* and so far the main effort has been concentrated on facilitating transfers[41] between parallel courses through introductory classes *(Aufbauform)* in the *Realschulen* and *Gymnasien*. The text of the Hamburg Convention, however, expressly provides for the possible organization of an orientation cycle.

In The Netherlands, the Law of February 14, 1963, on the reform of extended education stipulates that the first-year programs in the various types of general secondary school (short or long) should be identical. This year will therefore serve as

---

[41] Transfer from the *Hauptschule* and *Realschule* to the *Gymnasium,* and transfer from the *Hauptschule* to the *Realschule.*

an orientation year by making horizontal transfers possible between one type of school and another.[42]

This law also aims at ensuring better general education before vocational training starts.

3. *The intermediate French solution*   The reform of secondary structures in France was brought before the public as early as 1947 with the tabling of the Langevin-Wallon Committee report, but the first reform was effectively introduced only in January 1959. This provided that, within the framework of ten years' compulsory schooling, all children having normally completed elementary school would enter an *observation cycle* class lasting two years (from eleven to thirteen years of age) in the *lycées* and general *collèges*. Organized within the traditional institutions, this orientation cycle which, incidentally, could not be fully extended to the two age groups concerned, failed to serve its purpose in spite of the establishment of orientation boards.

The new reform of August 1963 extended the observation cycle and the role of the orientation boards to all four years of the first secondary cycle. This cycle is organized either in the *lycées* (classic and modern sections) or in the general *collèges* (ordinary modern sections and terminal sections). The most original aspect of the reform is the proposal that schools known as *collèges d'enseignement secondaire (C.E.S.)* should group all the sections of the first cycle. These common first-cycle schools are to be set up under the Fifth National Plan (1966–1970).

With the application of a ten-year period of compulsory schooling, therefore, all French children will now take the first secondary cycle, and very often in an independent first-cycle institution *(C.E.S.)*. Unlike the Italian reform, however, the

[42] The Law of February 14, 1963, also provides that the entrance selection for secondary schools may be accomplished by means (including tests) other than the traditional school examination.

French reform preserves the system of parallel sections[43] in toto.

The Teaching Profession: Obstacle and Key to Reform of Secondary Education

Within the framework of compulsory schooling lasting nine or ten years, toward which all the Common Market countries, except Italy, are already moving, it would seem normal that the period of compulsory general education should include the elementary cycle, and a secondary cycle open to all and comprising either a common course (possibly with optional subjects) or even a course broken up into sections.

We will not argue the merits of these two systems: identity of programs in the European countries is made difficult by the time devoted to Latin. The minimum aim is equality of level and equal facilities for transfers between the classic and modern sections.

The reform of secondary structures, however, cannot take place in a void; the reform must also allow for the existing educational, social, and even political conditions. The range of approaches adopted in the Common Market countries alone is due to the variable effect of these different factors. Accepting the similarity of the economic and social structures in these countries, the social and political factors cannot account for all the differences. To a large extent, it would seem that these solutions are, consciously or unconsciously, largely determined in the minds of the authors of the reforms by factors relating to the teaching profession.

With the system of parallel courses following on the elementary school in the Federal Republic of Germany, Belgium, France, Luxembourg and The Netherlands, children between eleven or twelve and fourteen or fifteen years of age are taught (see Chapter 2) in *lycées, Gymnasien, athénées,* and the like,

---

[43] A system whose possible disadvantages from the orientation viewpoint are offset by the concentration of the various sections in a single institution *(C.E.S.).*

by teachers trained in the universities; in short secondary courses, by teachers trained, at best, in short higher courses; in terminal primary classes, by primary teachers; or in the first cycle or first level of vocational or technical courses (Belgium and The Netherlands).

We have already seen that the breakdown is far from being the same (Tables 16 and 49) within the Common Market countries.

If it is decided that pupils from eleven or twelve to fourteen or fifteen years of age should now be taught in a common secondary cycle (Italian solution) or in a first cycle with differentiated sections (French solution), what teachers in the immediate future will be able to teach in this cycle? The only teachers competent are obviously those at present in charge of the corresponding classes in the *lycées, collèges,* primary schools, and the like, or, in varying proportions, three or four categories of teachers including, in certain countries, a more or less substantial majority of primary teachers.

As a result, the rapid organization of a common secondary cycle between eleven or twelve and fourteen or fifteen years of age would mean in certain countries that this cycle would be entrusted to a majority of primary teachers. In itself, this is not wholly disadvantageous—in the first and second classes, it would facilitate the transition between elementary and secondary education—but it nonetheless involves enormous difficulties. From the educational viewpoint,[44] the most serious is the impossibility of continuing to provide education by specialists—allowing for any reforms that may be introduced at this level—and the regression which this represents in relation to the present first-cycle classes of the pre-university secondary school.

For these reasons, the common cycle is criticized, and very often violently criticized, as a "primarisation" of the secondary school, a regression which could endanger the traditional secondary culture of the "old" European countries. The scope

---

[44] Not to mention the trade union and political aspects.

of these objectives may be partly reduced and their transitional aspect[45] demonstrated but, objectively, it is difficult to rule them out completely, especially if one bears in mind the need to train the intellectual elite which scientific research so urgently requires. In any event, these objections are widely shared by those who have been educated in *lycées* and, of course, by the *lycée* teachers.

It is not, therefore, so much the common secondary cycle itself which is questioned, especially if the system of sections is adopted, but primarily the conditions, from the viewpoint of the teaching profession, in which the transition from the old structures to the new is to take place. It is very much to the point that in France the *lycée* teachers' associations supported the common core (without sections) of the Langevin-Wallon plan because it provided (if only on paper) that courses should be given by specialized teachers with a university background.

The obstacle is all the more difficult to overcome in that the present size of terminal primary classes, or similar classes, is larger, and vice versa.

This explains the feasibility of the Italian reform. The middle school and the *avviamento professionale* school were both secondary schools; their general teachers were therefore trained together in the universities. Accordingly, the merging of these two schools did not raise any major problems as far as the teaching profession was concerned.[46]

In the U.S.S.R., the difficulty did not arise as in the "old" European countries; given the low enrollment immediately after the Revolution, the problem of merging parallel courses scarcely existed. The first common secondary cycle was gradually introduced, with teachers trained for the purpose,[47] and

[45] It is true that the period of transition may be a long one.

[46] Teachers responsible for practical work are re-employed either in the teaching of optional subjects or in vocational and technical schools.

[47] These teachers have been trained on a much higher level since 1945 (see Chapter 3).

this cycle only became compulsory in the rural areas in 1949.

In the United States, where the system of parallel courses was never introduced, this difficulty only arose when the 8 + 4 educational system was replaced by the 6 + 3 + 3 system (see Chapter 1), but was very much attenuated by the fact that elementary school and high school teachers are trained in the same teachers colleges.

The reforms adopted in Great Britain (in 1944 and 1945) and in France (1959–1963) have also had to make due allowance for this factor.

The English reform of 1944 (Education Act) provided that, after six years of elementary schooling, all children of eleven years of age should enter secondary school (as distinct from elementary school), but provision was made for three types of secondary school (see Chapter 1). Notwithstanding the reformers' wish to give the three branches (classic, modern, technical) the same standing (parity of esteem), the grammar schools in fact occupy a pre-eminent position. This is primarily due to the quality of their teachers: 78 per cent of university-trained teachers against only 17 per cent in the modern schools. For a long time many of these new schools were no more than converted terminal primary classes. It was only very gradually (through the arrival of university-trained teachers and the improvement of the training colleges)[48] that the modern schools raised their level of teaching and began to send pupils to the first G.C.E. examinations. The results, more especially in the development of the comprehensive schools and the multilateral schools, are gradually making themselves felt.

In France, the reform of 1963, like the 1959 reform, while retaining the system of sections, makes it possible to use different categories of staff in first-cycle courses without introducing a complete "mixing"; the establishment of the *C.E.S.*, however, will encourage a gradual "amalgamation" of staff.

[48] Studies were extended from two to three years since 1961, and efforts were made to bring studies closer to the university level.

Under this system, as under the English reform, children are obviously not yet on a footing of true equality, from the point of view of teachers, but the main criticisms which we have outlined are partly met.

In any case, the merit of the English and French reforms is to have created a situation containing the potentials of development: the foundations have been laid on which, through a suitable staff policy, to construct a genuine, common secondary cycle.

To sum up, the organization of a secondary cycle in the Common Market countries which should be open to all and which should offer similar possibilities to all is largely conditioned by the present *de facto* situation: the structure of the teaching profession at this level.

A solution to this major difficulty implies protracted efforts and cannot be produced through a single operation; it is essential to apply transitional measures and, above all, to initiate a dynamic policy of teacher training by developing training at university level; and by improving existing "short" courses which might to some extent facilitate the promotions of teachers in the elementary classes.

In fact, in the early stages, the implementation of such a policy in certain countries comes up against a sort of material impossibility resulting from the present unduly low rate of graduation from secondary school. In other words, a broader access to long secondary studies is, in a sense, a preliminary to any genuine reform of secondary school structures, and in certain countries—for example, the Federal Republic of Germany[49]—this represents a really vicious circle: In order to train more teachers, more students must graduate from secondary school, but in order to enable more students to graduate from secondary school, it is essential first of all to train more teachers.

---

[49] The difficulty is further aggravated in Germany by the fact that there is at the same time an increased need for primary school teachers to handle the one million additional pupils expected in the elementary classes between now and 1970.

France has succeeded in extricating itself from this impasse (33,000 secondary school graduates in 1950, nearly 100,000 in 1965) notwithstanding considerable difficulties which, in certain cases, may have led to a lowering of standards, and thanks to an increased effort by the teaching profession. Having satisfied that precondition, it is now in a position to ensure, within a reasonable time and through an active policy of recruitment and training, an adequate teacher-pupil ratio for the new structures established in 1963. This example shows that in order to break the vicious circle it may be necessary, at any rate provisionally, to abandon an undue respect for certain traditional standards.

THE NEED FOR A LONG-TERM POLICY AND THE MAIN ALTERNATIVES FOR THE FUTURE

The observations regarding the conditions for a reform of secondary structures and the policy for recruiting and training teachers demonstrate the importance of the time factor in the evolution of educational systems and the difficulty of rapidly catching up where such relative lags as have been noted exist. These inevitable delays can be reduced to a minimum only through long-term forecasting of objectives and of human, material, and financial resources, and effective planning to ensure their proper use.

We shall now briefly consider some aspects of the problem of choosing objectives.

THE MAJOR EDUCATIONAL TRANSITION STAGES IN FUTURE

With the introduction of a common secondary cycle and the development of advanced higher studies, the three existing educational transition stages in the Common Market countries (end of elementary studies, end of the first secondary cycle, end of the second secondary cycle) will shift and will now occur at the end of the first secondary cycle; at the end of the second cycle; and after the first degree or diploma in higher education.

Educational development will tend to determine, for each of these three levels, the desirable or probable distribution of pupils or students between the various possible alternatives, thus: (1) At the end of the first secondary cycle, between the classic and modern secondary schools; the technical secondary schools; the vocational schools; and employment (with or without part-time studies).[50] (2) After the secondary school leaving examination (or the technical diploma), between higher education at the university level; short higher education; possibly,[51] the training of skilled workers; and employment (with or without part-time studies). (3) After the first university degree or diploma between advanced studies; and employment (with or without part-time study).

DETERMINING FACTORS AT EACH STAGE

At each stage allowances will have to be made for both economic and social factors.

ECONOMIC FACTORS

These are the manpower requirements at various vocational, technical, and scientific levels.

We shall not detail here the ways in which changes in technology and production structures in the industrialized countries continually increase the demand for skilled and highly skilled staff. In any case, we have already indicated very significant orders of magnitude regarding future requirements for medium-grade and senior cadres.

To allow for these requirements in the choices made by pupils and students, they must be foreseen in sufficient detail and sufficiently ahead of time to allow for the long periods required for training.

---

[50] Part-time studies include day, evening, or correspondence courses.

[51] Depending on the number of graduates and the type of sec-

The forecasting of trends in the structure and qualifications among the active population is difficult, and implies collaboration between the specialized survey and research services in the manpower sector and the firms themselves to determine the optimum correlations between jobs, and types and levels of training; and to determine the ratios of senior personnel required in the various branches of the economy.

None of these correlations or ratios is permanent. They are constantly changing in relation to technological progress, and so must be studied and forecast—difficult work which implies an expansion of the very tentative efforts so far made.

On the basis of the results, and without trying to be over-accurate,[52] a desirable distribution between the above stages can be worked out, and hence, an estimate of the training requirements that must be employed can be determined.

These forecasts in no sense imply imposing an authoritarian policy on young people. The provision of the training facilities (new institutions, new sections in existing institutions), itself attracts recruits. Moreover, educational and vocational guidance services can advise families and students and this should ensure a more accurate adjustment between the supply and demand for education and training, with due regard to individual capacities and tastes.

SOCIAL FACTORS AND THEIR LONG-TERM
CONSEQUENCES

To a lesser or greater extent, however, social factors will invariably interfere with the technocratic and somewhat inhuman structure which would result from an educational pyrmid primarily based on an evaluation of economic requirements.

It is true that it is in the general interest, and in the inter-

---

ondary leaving certificate decided on, consideration may be given to the training of skilled manpower at this level (see pages 297 ff.).

[52] Common sense suggests, and experience shows, that a person cannot be the absolute prisoner of whatever specialized training he may have received initially.

est of the individual, to try to adjust admission to vocational and technical schools (which may, of course, be full time or part time) (1) as nearly as possible to estimated requirements for skilled workers and technicians. At the level of the first transaction stage, some of the objectives will have to make fairly substantial allowance for the economic factor.

On the other hand, the question arises at this stage of whether to satisfy the spontaneous demand by families for admission to the second secondary cycle (leading to the secondary school leaving examination) or, conversely, whether admission to this cycle should also be adjusted to the need for cadres or specialists, trained after leaving secondary school.

Given the extent of the need for cadres, it is in fact by no means certain that the spontaneous demand will be in line with requirements[53] in all the countries for a long time to come; in this case, it will be necessary to encourage the demand. In other countries, however, where the population is becoming rapidly conscious of the value of extended studies, it is possible that the demand will very soon outstrip the objectives as determined from an economic viewpoint. In this event, which will not be exceptional if economic development continues at the same rate as it has since 1950, the question arises whether the spontaneous demand should be allowed to develop, or whether it should be held in check.

On the specific problem of the policy to be adopted in regard to the accessibility[54] of the second secondary cycle, it would be as well to begin by recalling the situation of two countries which have tried out a first cycle open to all. In the United States, 70 per cent of the relevant age groups complete the full secondary course, and the authorities are trying to bring enrollment at this level up to 100 per cent. In the U.S.S.R., more than 40 per cent of the age groups

[53] In certain East European countries, for example—though this does not apply to the U.S.S.R.—the spontaneous movement of young people toward the second secondary cycle is inadequate in relation to the planners' objectives.

[54] On the basis of a first common cycle.

enroll in the ninth class and the program of the 22nd Congress of the Communist Party provides that full secondary studies, including schools for young workers and farmers and technicians, should be available to all young people by about 1970. Accordingly, the policy in the United States and in the U.S.S.R. is to make the second cycle fully accessible, with complete secondary schooling the common basis for the training of all young people.

In the Common Market countries, the situation has not advanced to anything like the same extent (see Table 49). For certain social groups (liberal professions, senior cadres), enrollment in the second cycle has virtually reached saturation point. With the continued raising of living standards and the social consequences which this implies, the attitudes of other socio-occupational categories are tending to follow suit. This phenomenon will undoubtedly be encouraged by the reforms under way or due to be initiated. A certain equality will initially benefit such categories as the medium-grade cadres, office employees, and the like, and we have already noted the strong and understandable tendency for the families of manual workers to try to advance their children's interests through vocational and technical training (see Table 50) rather than through courses leading to the secondary school leaving certificate.

It is therefore quite certain that the trend will be slow and will differ in rate even within the Common Market countries; but it is nonetheless certain, and we do not feel that any economic arguments justify running counter to it.

In the long run, therefore, the development of second secondary cycle could exceed the "needs" so long as the latter continue to be evaluated on the basis of the present employment-training correlations.

This prospect represents the consequence and culmination of a policy for the democratization of access to extended studies and is in no sense disturbing from the point of employment openings.

The history of all advanced industrial societies, in fact,

shows that for any given occupation the level of general training tends to rise steadily. There are, of course, those pessimists who will see this as a sort of down-grading of education whereas, in fact, this phenomenon is the result of the progress of education and the rise in the cultural level of the population at large.

In all probability, therefore, in the more or less long term, the number of secondary school graduates, depending on the country, will exceed the estimated "needs" in respect to entrants to higher education.

This situation raises two important problems concerning the role of the secondary school leaving examination, and the development of higher education.

In accordance with the tradition of the Common Market countries, the secondary school leaving examination has so far remained a pre-university examination.[55] The number of secondary school leavers, although increasing, is still relatively low (between 6 and 12 per cent of the age groups) and explains the fact that the examination has continued to be pre-university in type. The situation is not very different in Great Britain. On the other hand, in the United States and the U.S.S.R., only a minority (between 40 and 45 per cent) of secondary school graduates proceed to higher education.

The expansion of the second cycle therefore implies that, for a growing number of students, the secondary school leaving certificate has become a terminal school rather than a pre-university certificate. To facilitate the integration into the economy of those full secondary school graduates who are not proceeding to higher education, the Soviet authorities have been impelled to undertake the December 1958 reform (see Chapter 1). The United States, for its part, has no difficulty in adjusting to this situation, given the practical nature of high school education and the fact that it offers direct employment openings.

The Common Market countries have first to decide

[55] This is borne out by the details given in Chapter 2.

whether the traditional long secondary school leaving certificate should represent a major transition toward specialized training at very different levels or direct access to employment. This does not seem to involve any major difficulty since there are many training courses and many forms of employment which can only benefit by recruiting secondary school graduates.

It may be asked, however, whether secondary school graduates, having become much more numerous (between 30 and 40 per cent of the age groups), might not continue to proceed in the main to higher education, as at present. It is not easy to say.

Such a development would raise no problems if the results remained proportionate to "needs"; with judicious guidance[56] between the various special branches at this level there is no reason to think that such would not be the case in the Common Market countries for a long time to come.

If, however, over a very long period, "needs" seemed likely to be substantially exceeded, might it not be desirable to make admission to higher education subject to other regulations? This question can be answered in the negative if it is considered that, after all, this would merely be a continuation at a higher education level of the process which we have noted in respect to general secondary education, that is, a rise in the level of qualifications required for a given occupation.

This, of course, is only partly valid since absorbing a limitless number of graduates from higher education into the economy is not the same as absorbing secondary school graduates.

Secondary education provides general training which, in principle, does not determine the occupation subsequently chosen, but higher education is invariably specialized, and many courses lead to very specific professions (engineering, medicine, architecture). It would hardly be conceivable that a large number of students should be allowed to complete

[56] This can only be ensured by detailed studies of trends in the employment market.

protracted and expensive specialized courses without subsequently being able to make use of their training in their special branches. However, it is humanly very difficult to apply a numerical limitation in order to exclude from higher education candidates who have the required qualifications.[57]

To a certain extent, it may be agreed that supply and demand will ensure the necessary adjustments both in the total number of students and in the breakdown by speciality. But it is not desirable that young people should pay the price of such adjustments.

If the Common Market countries wish to retain their liberal traditions, it would perhaps be as well to draw a distinction between specialized degrees, holders of which cannot be absorbed into the active population to a limitless extent; and courses of a more general type which can accordingly be adapted to a wide range of occupations or levels of occupation.

In any case, such a policy could only be based on a thorough knowledge of the active population and its trends and, as already pointed out, this presupposes a considerable extension of the means available in each of the countries for carrying out surveys.

The necessary expansion of school and university systems in the Common Market countries implies that the human, material, and financial means needed for that development are assembled.

We have already emphasized the vital aspect of the teacher problem: only by an active policy of teacher recruitment and training, and a parallel effort to renovate and improve teaching methods, can the necessary quantitative expansion be obtained while still preserving the traditional quality of the education provided in the "old" Common Market countries.

---

[57] In discussing the "selection" process for admission to higher education, a distinction must be drawn between mere insistence on adequate qualifications (the British system) and the numerical limitation system (U.S.S.R., French engineering schools, and so on).

Any such policy for schools and universities must obviously be expensive.

We shall not revert to the analyses devoted to educational and training expenditure in all the Common Market countries (see Chapter 2). Since 1950, expenditure has risen more rapidly than the national product and it is certain that this will continue in the future.

The burden on the economy will accordingly increase substantially. But who doubts that such expenditure is in the highest degree profitable humanly, socially and economically?

Appendix

TABLE A-1 FEDERAL REPUBLIC OF GERMANY AND WEST BERLIN: ENROLLMENT TRENDS
(number of pupils or students, in thousands)

			Variations 1951–1961		
				1961	
			ABSOLUTE	INDEX	
	1950–51	1960–61	VALUE	(1951 = 100)	1963–64
PRIMARY					
Primary classes (*Volksschulen*)	6,715.6	5,229.1	−1,486.5	78	5,439.2
Special schools (*Sonderschulen*)	97.7	133.1	+ 35.4	136	160.2
Subtotal	6,813.3	5,362.2	−1,451.1	79	5,599.4
SECONDARY					
General					
Middle schools (*Realschulen*)	237.6	430.7	+ 193.1	181	497.4
Secondary Schools (*Höhere schulen*)	666.1	853.4	+ 187.3	128	861.0
Technical and vocational					
Full-time vocational schools (*Berufsfachschulen*)	88.2[a]	139.2	+ 51	158	142.3
Part-time vocational schools (*Berufsschulen*)	1,699.2[a]	1,661.9	− 37.3	98	1,699.0

Technical schools (*Fachschulen* including *Ingenieurschulen*)	112.5ᵃ	185.1	+ 72.1	165	195.3
Subtotal:					
Including the *Berufsschulen*	2,803.6	3,270.3	+ 466.7	117	3,395.0
Excluding the *Berufsschulen*	1,104.4	1,608.4	+ 504.0	146	1,696.0
HIGHER EDUCATION					
Universities and higher technical schools	111.3ᵃ	184.5	+ 73.2	166	219.1
Institutes of education	11.4ᵃ	33.1	+ 21.7	290	44.0
Subtotal	122.7ᵃ	217.6	+ 94.9	177	263.1
TOTAL					
Including the *Berufsschulen*	9,739.6	8,850.1	− 989.5	91	9,257.5
Excluding the *Berufsschulen*	8,040.4	7,188.2	− 852.2	89	7,558.5

SOURCE: *Statistisches Bundesamt.*
ᵃ Not including the Saar.

TABLE A-2   BELGIUM: ENROLLMENT TRENDS
(number of pupils or students, in thousands)

	1952–1953			1962–1963			Variation	
							ABSOLUTE VALUE (1,000)	1962 INDEX (1952 = 100)
	PUBLIC	PRIVATE	TOTAL	PUBLIC	PRIVATE	TOTAL		
PRIMARY								
Preschool	102	221	323	152	271	423	100	131
Elementary	—	—	753	443	492	935	182	24
Primary school leaving classes (4th primary level)	33	62	95	13	21	34	—61	36
Subtotal	—	—	1,171	608	784	1,392	22	119
SECONDARY								
General:								
Lower cycle	—	—	*138.8*	*107*	*155*	*262*	*123.2*	*188*
Upper cycle	—	—	105	81	112	193	88	183
Upper cycle	14.3	19.5	33.8	26	43	69	35.2	203
Vocational and technical:			*127.7*	*96*	*167*	*263*	*135.3*	*207*
Lower cycle	29	74	103	75	135	210	107	203
Upper cycle	9.4	15.3	24.7	21	32	53	28.3	214
Art training	—	—	*0.8*	*0.7*	*1.0*	*1.7*	*0.9*	*212*

Teacher training:							
—	—	*13.9*	*12*	*13*	*25*	*11.1*	*173*
Preprimary teachers							
—	—	3.9[a]	3	4	7	3.1	154
Primary teachers							
—	—	10[a]	9	9	18	8	180
Subtotal							
—	—	281.2	216.4	337.0	553.4	270.5	196.8
HIGHER EDUCATION							
University							
7.7	14	21.7	11	24	35	13.3	161
Higher technical training							
2.4	4.6	7.0	6	9	15	8	214
Teacher training							
—	—	5.4[a]	4	7	11	5.6	203
Art training[b]							
—	—	1.4	1	—	1	−0.4	71
Subtotal							
—	—	35.5	22	40	62	26.5	174
TOTAL							
—	—	1,488.6	846	1,161.0	2,007.4	518	134.9

SOURCES: *Annuaire statistique de l'enseignement* and statistics provided by the educational and statistical department of the Ministry of National Education.

[a] In 1953–54.

[b] Art training includes the plastic arts and architecture only; it does not include music.

TABLE A-3 FRANCE: ENROLLMENT TRENDS
(number of pupils or students, in thousands)

Courses[a]	1951–1952		
	PUBLIC	PRIVATE	TOTAL
PRIMARY			
Preprimary and infant classes	1,000	221	1,221
Elementary and primary school-leaving classes[b]	3,336	80	4,137
Subtotal	4,336	1,022	5,358
SECONDARY			
General:			
General *collèges*	218	60	278
Classical and modern *lycées*	348	186	534
Technical and vocational:[c]			
Technical *collèges* (short courses)	148	70	216
Technical *lycées* (long courses)	101	35	136
Teacher training[t]	15	—	15
Subtotal	830	351	1,181
HIGHER EDUCATION			
Public and private faculties	137	3.7[g]	140.7
Other public and private higher educational institutions[h]	14.8	6.3	21.1
Subtotal	151.8	10	161.8
TOTAL	5,317.8	1,383	6,700.8

SOURCE: Statistics supplied by the Ministry of National Education (*Informations Statistiques* and publications by the B.U.S.).

[a] Does not include enrollment in the national correspondence course center.

[b] Includes the elementary *lycée* classes and special education.

[c] Only full-time public and private institutions under the Ministry of National Education.

[d] Including the vocational sections of the general *collèges* and courses leading to the *C.A.P.* in the technical *lycées* which were previously included with the general *collèges* and the technical *lycées*.

1761–1962			Variation 1952–1962		1963–1964		
			ABSOLUTE VALUE	1961 INDEX (1951 = 100)			
PUBLIC	PRIVATE	TOTAL			PUBLIC	PRIVATE	TOTAL
1,221	178	1,399	+ 178	114	1,358	238	1,597
4,955	948	5,903	+1,766	142	4,808	859	5,268
6,176	1,126	7,302	+1,544	136	6,167	1,098	7,265
629	141	770	+ 492	275	818	158	977
812	317	1,129	+ 595	212	1,016	352	1,368
219	107	326	+ 108	149	336[d]	178[e]	514
200	60	260	+ 120	188	147	43	190
29	—	29	+ 14	193	31	—	31
1,789	625	2,514	1,329	212	2,349	732	3,081
245	7[h]	252	+ 111.3	179	326	8[h]	334
19	11	30	+ 8.9	140	26	12	38
264	18.6	282	+ 120.2	174	352	20	372
8,329	1,779.0	10,098	+3,394	151	8,869	1,850	10,719

[e] Includes 28,000 girls enrolled in domestic economy institutions.

[f] Student teachers studying for the *baccalauréat* and engaged in vocational training.

[g] Students in the private faculties not included among those enrolled in the public faculties.

[h] Estimate of enrollment in various schools not included among university institutions.

TABLE A-4 ITALY: ENROLLMENT TRENDS
(number of pupils or students, in thousands)

Courses	1938–1939	1952–1953	1962–1963	Variation 1953–1963 ABSOLUTE VALUE	Variation 1953–1963 1963 INDEX (1953 = 100)	1964–1965
PRIMARY						
Preschool	766	1,012	1,169	+ 157	116	1,217
Elementary	5,094	4,447	4,403	− 74	98	4,472
Postelementary	—	—	37[a]	+ 37	—	—
Subtotal	5,860	5,489	5,609	+ 120	102	5,689
SECONDARY						
General:						
First cycle:						
Middle schools	257	444 ⎫ 864	842 ⎫ 1,506	+ 398	190	⎫ 1,730
Vocational orientation schools	288	420 ⎭	664 ⎭	+ 244	158	⎭
Second cycle and upper cycle:						
Ginnasio—classical secondary school	105	125	154	+ 29	123	173
Scientific secondary school	13.8	41	74	+ 33	—	93

312

Technical and vocational:

Short courses:					
Technical schools	15.8	47	16	− 31	34	8.7
Vocational institutes	—	17[b]	136	+ 119	800	169.0
Long courses:						
Technical institutes	63	149	393	+ 244	264	502.0
Midwifery schools	—	3.5	0.6	− 2.9	17	0.8
Teacher training	86	91	125	+ 34	137	178.5
Art education						
Art schools and institutes	6.8	9.7	16.7	+ 7.0	172	12.5
Secondary art schools	—	1.7	3.2	+ 1.5	188	3.5
Conservatoriums and music institutes	3	5.8	4.9	− 0.9	84	5.8
Subtotal	838.4	1,354.7	2,429.4	+1,074.7	179	2,876
HIGHER EDUCATION	236	224	273	+ 49	122	350
TOTAL	6,934.4	7,067.7	8,311.4	+1,243.7	118	8,916.0

SOURCE: *Italian Educational Statistical Yearbook.*
[a] In 1961–62.
[b] In 1953–54.

TABLE A-5 LUXEMBOURG: ENROLLMENT TRENDS
(number of pupils or students, in thousands)

Courses	1950–1951			1961–1962			Variation	
	PUBLIC	PRIVATE	TOTAL	PUBLIC	PRIVATE	TOTAL	ABSOLUTE FIGURES	INDEX 1950–1951 = 100
Preschool	2,997	396	3,396	—	—	4,516	1,118	133
Elementary:								
Elementary	28,850	799	29,649	30,711	11,445	32,126	2,477	108
Upper primary	—	—	—	358	302	660	—	—
Subtotal	31,847	1,195	33,045	—	—	37,300	4,255	113
Secondary:								
Classical and modern	2,957	600	3,557[a]	4,928	1,269	6,197	2,640	174
Vocational	2,744	—	2,744	3,481	—	3,481	737	127
Subtotal	—	—	6,301	—	—	9,678	3,377	154
Teacher training	100	—	100[b]	84	—	—	−16	84

| Higher Education | 98 | — | 98 | 116 | — | 116 | +18 | 118 |
| TOTAL | — | — | 39,544 | — | 47,178 | 7,634 | 119 |

SOURCE: Statistics provided by the Ministry of National Education.
[a] Estimate: Public education in 1951–1952, 2,957; no statistics available on private education.
[b] Estimate: Teacher training was different in 1951–1952.

TABLE A-6 THE NETHERLANDS: ENROLLMENT TRENDS
(number of pupils or students, in thousands)

Courses	1951–1952	1961–1962	Variations 1952–1962		1963–1964
			ABSOLUTE FIGURES	1962 INDEX 1952 = 100	
PRIMARY					
Preschool	*364.5*	*411.6*	*47.0*	*113*	*435.4*
Primary:	*1,306.1*	*1,496.1*	*189.9*	*115*	*1,493.7*
Elementary primary	1,239.7	1,397.8	158.0	113	1,395.4
Extended primary	31.0	42.1	11.0	136	39.1
Special courses	35.3	56.1	20.8	159	59.1
Subtotal	1,670.7	1,907.7	237.0	114	
SECONDARY					
General					
Short courses:					
Upper or intermediate primary	*132.4*	*274.5*	*142.0*	*207*	*276.2*
Long courses:					
Upper secondary	*83.5*	*178.3*	*94.7*	*213*	*194.1*
Gymnasiums	11.7	20.6	8.9	176	21.0
Modern collèges	30.9	50.6	19.7	164	52.5
Secondary schools	32.3	80.4	48.1	249	89.1
	6.9		17.5	252	20.0

Business schools	1.6	2.1	0.4	128	2.3
Technical and vocational					
Short courses:					
Primary technical[a]	82.3	179.9	97.5	219	196.2
Elementary domestic economy[b]	64.5	120.3	55.8	187	121.8
Long courses:					
Intermediate and secondary technical schools	15.0	29.1	14.1	194	33.8
Courses in the arts and applied arts	1.2	2.3	1.1	191	2.5
Agricultural and horticultural education	4.1	22.5	18.3	540	23.7
Intermediate and secondary domestic economy	—	—	—	—	—
Welfare assistants' schools	0.8	1.9	1.0	214	3.4
Teacher training for:					
Preprimary schoolmistresses	5.8	5.2	0.5	90	7.0
Primary schoolmasters and schoolmistresses	11.3	23.5	12.2	208	25.7
Subtotal	401.4	837.9	436.5	209	884.7
HIGHER EDUCATION	29.8	43.9	14.0	147	52.4
TOTAL	2,102.0	2,789.7	687.6	133	2,866.2

SOURCE: Publications issued by the Central Statistical Bureau of The Netherlands, The Hague.
[a] Includes enrollment in the apprenticeship system.
[b] Includes intermediate and secondary domestic economy.

TABLE A-7 ENGLAND AND WALES: ENROLLMENT TRENDS
(number of pupils or students, in thousands)

Courses	1946–1947	1951–1953	1961–1962	Variation 1952–1962 1962 INDEX (1952 = 100)	1962–1963
PRIMARY	**3,803**	**4,357.6**	**4,402**	**101**	**4,417.4**
Nursery schools	*19*	*23.4*	*27*	*116*	*29.7*
Primary schools	*3,743*	*4,288.7*	*4,307*	*100*	*4,318.3*
Maintained:					
Junior and infants	2,601	3,386	3,959	117	4,014.0
All age	1,099	816.9	170	21	130.0
Direct grant	—	—	—	—	—
Independent[a]	43	68	177	260	174.2
Special schools	*41*	*52.5*	*68*	*130*	*69.4*
SECONDARY	**1,538**	**2,010.0**	**3,261**	**162**	**3,200.7**
Maintained schools	*1,335*	*1,837.0*	*2,836*	*154*	*2,780.7*
Modern	764	1,138.0	1,676	147	1,609.3
Grammar	505	506.3	708	140	722.5
Technical	66	74.3	97	131	92.5
Others[b]	—	37.4	354	947	356.3
Direct grant schools	*81*	*87.5*	*113*	*129*	*114.9*
Independent schools[c]	*122*	*166.5*	*312*	*187*	*305.1*

FULL-TIME EDUCATION

TEACHER TRAINING	18[d]	26[d]	37	142	51.0
University, department of education	—	—	3.2	—	3.2
Training colleges	—	—	34.3	—	47.8
UNIVERSITIES (Great Britain)	50	83.4	111	133	118.4
FURTHER EDUCATION	49	54.0	131	243	178.8
Full time	—	—	118.8	—	152.9
Sandwich courses	—	—	13.3	—	15.9
TOTAL	5,438	6,531.0	7,942.0	122	7,696.3
PART-TIME OR EVENING COURSES					
FURTHER EDUCATION	*1,598[e]*	*2,196.9*	*2,302*	*105*	*2,461.6*
Part-time day	*196*	*333.8*	*556*	*167*	*604.7*
Evening courses	*1,352*	*1,863.1*	*1,746*	*94*	*1,856.9*
Adult Education	*137*	*151.6*	*210*	*139*	*203.7*
TOTAL	1,735	2,348.5	2,512	107	2,665.3

SOURCES: *Statistics of Education* and annual reports by the University Grants Committee.

[a] Up to and including 1956–1957 these figures *only* include schools "recognised as efficient."

[b] Bilateral, multilateral, and comprehensive schools.

[c] This figure includes total enrollment in schools classified as "primary and secondary," i.e, for 1961–1962 more than 220,000 pupils under eleven years of age.

[d] Does not include "emergency training" students.

[e] 1957 Report to Parliament.

TABLE A-7 *(Continued)*   SCOTLAND: ENROLLMENT TRENDS
(number of pupils or students, in thousands)

Courses	1951–1952[a]	1961–1962[a]	Variation 1951–1961 1961 INDEX (1951 = 100)
PRIMARY	*578.1*	*609.2*	*105*
Preprimary	4.3	15.4	358
Elementary	561.8	583.4	104
Special courses	12.2	10.4	87
SECONDARY			
General secondary	236.2	287.6	122
TEACHER TRAINING	*3.6*	*6.3*[b]	*175*
FULL-TIME HIGHER EDUCATION	*21.4*	*25.7*	*120*
Universities	15.0	18.5	123
Other higher educational institutes	6.4	7.2	112
TOTAL	839.3	928.8	111
FURTHER EDUCATION	129.8[c]	245.0[d]	189

SOURCES: Unesco statistics.
[a] Public and grant-aided schools only.
[b] 1962–1963.
[c] Includes 3,800 full-time students.
[d] Includes 11,000 full-time students.

TABLE A-7 *(Continued)* NORTHERN IRELAND: ENROLLMENT
TRENDS
(number of pupils or students, in thousands)

Courses	1951–1952	1957–1958	1961–1963	Variation 1951–1961 / 1961 INDEX (1951 = 100)
PRIMARY	*199.3*	*211.3*	*197.8*	*99*
Preprimary	0.7	5.6	9.8	1,400
Primary	197.9	203.8	185.5	94
Special courses	0.7	1.9	2.5	357
SECONDARY	*36.0*	*58.4*	*138.6*	*385*
Secondary schools	31.1	53.0	87.5	281
Technical schools	4.9	5.4	51.1	1,043
TEACHER TRAINING	*1.1*	*1.6*	*1.8*	*164*
HIGHER EDUCATION				
Universities	2.3	3.1	4.3	187
Other schools	—	—	—	—
TOTAL	238.7	274.4	342.0	143
ADULT EDUCATION	—	—	4.0	—
FURTHER EDUCATION	28.1[a]	32.9	—	—

SOURCES: Unesco statistics.

[a] Includes 2,000 full-time students and the majority of others attending evening classes.

TABLE A-8 U.S.S.R.: ENROLLMENT TRENDS
(number of pupils or students, in thousands)

Courses	1927–1928	1940–1941	1952–1953[a]	1962–1963[b]	Variations 1953–1963		1963–1964
					ABSOLUTE VALUE	1963 INDEX (1953 = 100)	
Preschool	107	1,171	1,352	4,171	+ 2,819	309	4,813
Primary and Secondary							
Total	11,589	35,528	32,643	42,445	+ 9,792	130	44,682
Full time							
Classes 1 to 4	9,910	21,375	13,396[a]	19,400	6,004	144	19,600
Classes 5 to 7 (or 5 to 8)	1,332	10,767	14,087	16,200	2,113	115	17,300
Classes 8 to 10 (or 9 to 11)	127	2,368	3,346	2,700[b]	− 646	80	3,400
Special courses	97	274	125	187	+ 62	149	217
Subtotal	11,466	34,784	30,953	38,485	+ 7,532	124	40,478
Schools for young workers and farm workers and schools for adults							
Total	123	744	1,690	3,960	2,270	234	4,204
Classes 8 to 10 (or 9 to 11)	—	—	554	1,876	+ 1,322	338	2,236

Vocational and Technical

Vocational						
Total	243	717	774	1,397	+ 623	180	1,491
Specialized secondary						
Total^c	189	975	1,477	2,668	+ 1,191	180	2,983
Full time	—	787	1,219	1,310	+ 91	107	1,474
Evening courses	—	32	82	489	+ 407	596	536
Correspondence courses	—	156	176	869	+ 683	494	973
Higher Education						
Total	169	812	1,441	2,944	+ 1,503	204	3,261
Full time	—	558	933	1,287	+ 354	138	1,383
Evening courses	—	27	38	374	+ 336	984	439
Correspondence courses	—	227	470	1,283	+ 813	272	1,439
TOTAL	12,297	39,203	37,687	53,625	+15,928	142	57,230
Full time	—	38,017	35,231	46,650	11,419	132	49,639
Evening or correspondence courses	—	1,186	2,456	6,975	+ 4,509	277	7,591

SOURCES: Statistical yearbooks on the national economy of the U.S.S.R.

[a] Enrollment in classes 1 to 4 declined during the 1952–53 school year because of the drop in the birth rate between 1942 and 1946.

[b] The 1962–63 school year reflects the presence of the age group born around 1942 in the terminal secondary cycle.

[c] Courses given in the *tekhnikums*.

TABLE A-9 UNITED STATES: ENROLLMENT TRENDS
(number of pupils or students, in thousands)

Courses	1951–1952*	1961–1962†	*Variations 1952–1962*		1962–1963†	1963–1964†
			ABSOLUTE VALUE	1962 INDEX (1952 = 100)		
Primary	23,835	33,778	+ 9,943	142	34,950	35,400[b]
Kindergartens						
Public	1,272	2,081	+ 809	163	2,156	—
Private	232	375	+ 143	162	404	—
	1,504	2,456	+ 952	163	2,560	—
Elementary (Classes 1 to 8)[a]						
Public	19,409	26,777	+ 7,368	137	27,198	—
Private	2,922	4,544	+ 1,622	155	5,192	—
	22,331	31,321	+ 8,990	140	32,390	—
Secondary (Classes 9 to 12)[a]						
Public	5,882	9,616	+ 3,734	163	10,863	11,300[b]
Primary	656	1,152	+ 496	175	1,287	1,400[b]
	6,538	10,768	+ 4,230	165	12,150	12,700[b]

Higher Education

	A	B	C	D	E	F
Undergraduates	1,931	3,328	—	—	—	—
Graduates	217	397	—	—	—	—
	2,148	3,726[c]	1,578	173	4,500[b]	4,800[b]
Public	—	2,212	—	—	2,900	3,100
Primary	—	1,515	—	—	1,600	1,700
TOTAL	32,521	48,273	15,752	149	51,600	52,900

SOURCES: * *Statistical Summary of Education* (O.E. 10,003—1959).

† *Digest of Educational Statistics* (O.E. 10,024—1963 and 1964).

[a] A substantial proportion of those attending classes 7 and 8 is in fact enrolled in the junior high schools; thus the real numbers in the high schools are higher than those shown under "secondary." For example, in 1961–62, the real enrollment in the public high schools was 13,484,000, of whom only 9,600,000 were in classes 9 to 12.

[b] Estimated.

[c] Does not include 95,000 students in nursing schools not affiliated with higher educational institutions.

TABLE A-10 TRENDS IN BIRTH RATES

Year	Federal Republic of Germany[a]	Belgium	France	Italy	Luxem-bourg	Nether-lands	United States	U.S.S.R.[b]	United Kingdom[c]
1930	—	148,538	748,911	1,085,220	6,377	182,312	2,203,958	6,770,000	769,800
1935	—	128,432	640,527	997,708	4,523	170,425	2,155,105	5,130,000	711,426
1938	—	133,610	612,248	1,037,180	4,486	178,422	2,286,962	6,990,000	735,573
1939	—	130,019	612,395	1,040,213	4,511	180,917	2,265,588	6,090,000	726,618
1940	—	112,497	559,000	1,046,479	3,959	184,846	2,360,399	6,120,000	701,886
1941	—	100,616	520,000	937,546	4,113	181,959	2,513,427	4,750,000	695,721
1942	—	108,603	573,000	926,063	4,620	189,975	2,808,996	3,800,000	771,845
1943	—	123,349	613,300	886,119	4,465	209,379	2,934,860	3,100,000	810,537
1944	—	127,122	629,100	860,128[d]	4,263	219,946	2,794,800	2,800,000	878,319
1945	—	130,526	643,400	823,505	3,857	209,607	2,735,456	4,550,000	795,876
1946	708,659	152,962	840,247	1,021,025[d]	4,364	284,456	3,288,672	5,220,000	955,266
1947	748,975	150,227	866,616	994,674[d]	4,292	267,348	3,699,940	5,060,000	1,025,427
1948	769,111	150,416	867,158	989,041[d]	4,311	247,923	3,535,068	5,010,000	905,182
1950	772,850	145,672	858,124	908,622	4,401	229,369	3,554,149	4,805,000	818,421

1951	758,472	142,314	822,700	860,998	4,482	228,631	3,758,000	4,950,000	796,645
1952	761,944	146,064	820,000	826,105	—	232,596	3,824,000	4,948,000	792,741
1953	778,206	146,125	804,696	842,274	4,565	227,614	3,925,007	4,750,000	804,269
1954	798,479	148,538	810,754	870,689	4,713	227,845	4,040,602	5,040,000	794,769
1955	803,012	149,195	805,917	869,333	4,664	228,878	4,070,960	5,048,000	789,315
1956	838,401	150,210	806,916	873,608	4,833	231,204	4,187,815	5,020,000	825,137
1957	874,365	152,871	816,467	878,906	4,954	233,608	4,279,689	5,110,000	851,466
1958	885,659	155,048	812,215	870,468	4,959	236,543	4,227,571	5,240,000	870,497
1959	930,944	155,237	829,249	901,017	5,037	242,198	4,261,896	5,264,000	878,561
1960	947,124	154,787	819,919	910,192	5,019	238,789	4,257,850	5,341,000	918,286
1961	989,484	156,418	838,633	930,295	5,112	247,009	4,268,326	5,192,000	944,365

SOURCES: Yearbooks of the United Nations and the League of Nations.

[a] Includes the Saar.
[b] U.S.S.R. 1930–1948: Estimates by Dr. Biraben (Institut National d'Études Démographiques, Paris, 1958; 1960–1961: Vestnik statiski 8/1963.
[c] England, Wales, Northern Ireland, and Scotland.
[d] Estimated.

TABLE A-11 COMPARISON OF GENERAL EDUCATION TIMETABLES FOR

	Federal Republic of Germany		Belgium	
Elementary Classes				
Duration[e]	4 yrs. (6 to 10 yrs.)		6 yrs. (6 to 12 yrs.)	
Total timetable	3,290[d]		5,520	
Including mathematics and sciences	700[d]		1,235	
	I[e,f]	II[e,f]	I[e]	II[e]
Secondary Classes ("long" courses)				
Duration[e]	9 yrs. (10 to 19 yrs.)		6 yrs. (12 to 18 yrs.)	
Total timetable	9,675	9,695	7,860	7,600
Including mathematics and sciences[g]	2,030	2,665	1,406	1,938
Including all literary disciplines[i]	4,480	3,290	4,246	2,774
Mother tongue and literature	1,260	1,330	1,140	1,292
Classical languages	2,695	—	1,900	—
Foreign languages	525	1,960	1,216	1,482
Elementary and Secondary Classes				
Duration[e]	13 yrs.		12 yrs.	
Total timetable	13,055	12,980	13,386	13,120
Including mathematics and sciences	2,730	3,365	2,631	2,173

NOTE: There are no official timetables for elementary and secondary schools in the United States and Great Britain.

[a] For The Netherlands, the data represent the commonly accepted timetables.

[b] Timetables applicable in 1959 in the R.S.F.S.R.; the other Republics may have slightly different timetables because of lessons in Russian. The numbers given here are an exact indication of the total "lessons," some of which may last only forty-five minutes. The new reform of August 1964 apparently does not affect the general education timetable.

[c] The number of school weeks per year are as follows: Federal Republic of Germany, 35; Belgium, 38; France, 35 for the elementary classes and 34 for the secondary classes; Italy, 35; Luxembourg, 38; The Netherlands, 35; and the U.S.S.R., from 33 to 36. These timetables, generally speaking, relate to 1960 or 1961.

ELEMENTARY CLASSES AND "LONG" SECONDARY COURSES

France		Italy		Luxembourg		Netherlands[a]		U.S.S.R.[b]
5 yrs. (6 to 11 yrs.)		5 yrs. (6 to 11 yrs.)		6 yrs. (6 to 12 yrs.)		6 yrs. (6 to 12 yrs.)		4 yrs. (7 to 11 yrs.)
4,812		4,200		6,156		5,023		3,708
954		—		1,159		1,094		972
I[e]	II[e]	I[e]	II[e]	I[e]	II[e]	I[e]	II[e]	
7 yrs. (11 to 18 yrs.)		8 yrs. (11 to 19 yrs.)		7 yrs. (12 to 19)	6 yrs. (12 to 18)	6 yrs. (12 to 18 yrs.)		7 yrs. (11 to 18 yrs.)
5,984	6,205	7,735	7,735	8,132	8,360	6,930	6,930	8,894
1,139	1,904	1,015	1,470	1,368	1,596	1,050	1,750	2,755[h]
3,060	2,516	4,060[j]	3,535[j]	4,712	4,712	4,200	3,605	3,156
1,122[j]	1,105	1,646[j]	1,505[j]	—	—	630	630	1,270
1,258[k]	—	1,925	1,225	—	—	3,570	2,975	—
680	1,411	490	805	—	—			726
12 yrs.		13 yrs.		13 yrs.	12 yrs.	12 yrs		11 yrs.
10,796	11,017	11,935	11,935	15,288	14,516	11,953	11,953	12,602
2,093	2,858	—	—	2,527	2,755	2,144	2,844	3,727

[d] State of Lower Saxony.

[e] Column I represents the most literary secondary section, and column II represents the most scientific secondary section.

[f] City-State of Hamburg.

[g] Does not include geography.

[h] These timetables for mathematics and science should be compared with those devoted to theoretical and practical vocational training prior to the 1964 reform: for classes 5, 6, 7, and 8—660 hours; for classes 9, 10, and 11—188 hours.

[i] Does not include history.

[j] Includes philosophy courses.

[k] There are also scientific sections with Latin. The timetable given here refers to the modern sections.

DATE DUE

GAYLORD			PRINTED IN U.S.A.